Walking Sideways

Walking Sideways

THE REMARKABLE WORLD OF CRABS

JUDITH S. WEIS

COMSTOCK PUBLISHING ASSOCIATES

a division of

CORNELL UNIVERSITY PRESS

Ithaca and London

First published 2012 by Cornell University Press
Printed in the United States of America

Library of Congress Cataloging-in-Publication Data

Weis, Judith S., 1941–
 Walking sideways : the remarkable world of crabs / Judith S. Weis.
   p. cm.
 Includes bibliographical references and index.
 ISBN 978-0-8014-5050-1 (cloth : alk. paper)
1. Crabs. I. Title.
 QL444.M33W394 2012
 595.3'86—dc23   2012022194

Cornell University Press strives to use environmentally responsible suppliers and materials to the fullest extent possible in the publishing of its books. Such materials include vegetable-based, low-VOC inks and acid-free papers that are recycled, totally chlorine-free, or partly composed of nonwood fibers. For further information, visit our website at www.cornellpress.cornell.edu.

Cloth printing   10 9 8 7 6 5 4 3 2 1

Contents

List of Vignettes
vii

Preface
ix

Acknowledgments
xiii

CHAPTER ONE
Introducing Crabs
1

CHAPTER TWO
Habitats
23

CHAPTER THREE
Form and Function
44

CHAPTER FOUR
Reproduction and Life Cycle
62

CHAPTER FIVE
Behavior
85

CHAPTER SIX
Ecology
105

CHAPTER SEVEN
Crab Problems and Problem Crabs
129

CHAPTER EIGHT
Crab Fisheries
154

CHAPTER NINE
Eating Crabs
182

CHAPTER TEN
Crabs and Humans
196

Bibliography
215

Index
225

Color plates follow page 128

List of Vignettes

A Little about Lobsters
10

Horseshoe Crab: Not a Crab but a Living Fossil
11

Why Is "Cancer" Both a Crab and a Disease?
18

Essential Fish Habitat
36

Lobster Habitats
37

Horseshoe Crab Blood
47

Feeling Pain
55

Use of Crabs in Neuroscience
56

James Michener on Crab Molting
80

Crabs in Kipling's *Just So Stories*
82

Oppian on Molting
83

Hermit Crabs in Children's Literature
110

Oppian on Hermit Crabs
111

Lobster Migrations
115

Living on a Lobster's Mouthparts
117

Crabs Behaving Badly in Hollywood Movies
145

Lobster Fishery
163

Crab Products Other Than Food
189

Watching Crabs in Art
197

Information about Pet Hermit Crabs
207

Crabs in Astrology and Dreams
209

Crabs in Foreign Myths and Culture
210

Crab Festivals
213

Preface

If we live out our span of life on the earth without ever knowing
a crab intimately, we have missed a good friendship.
WILLIAM BEEBE, 1932

I find crabs fascinating to study and love to watch them. Other people who are not biologists also seem to be interested in crabs for many reasons—they like to go crabbing, they look at them in aquariums or when scuba diving, or they just like to eat them. Some people may be a bit afraid since some crabs can give a nasty pinch. People are curious about the lives of crabs because they seem so alien and different from us. What is life like living inside a shell that you have to shed frequently? What is it like living on the bottom of the ocean? How do you coordinate moving with so many legs? In this book I attempt to provide information about these fascinating creatures that live in such a very different world than we do. I have tried to provide basic biological information at a level understandable by the general public, while including lots of up-to-date scientific information.

As a seven-year-old, summering on Shelter Island, New York, I discovered a fascination with marine life that is still with me. While standing in shallow water one day I came upon a hermit crab walking along in a large whelk shell that was covered with barnacles, seaweed, boat shells, and other forms of clinging sea life. This whole collection of living things walking along in the water seemed like the most amazing thing. My mother, cousin, and friends did not find it nearly as wonderful and exciting as I did, but this formative experience in my early life may have led to my becoming a marine biologist. Despite a crab being the central character in this formative experience, my early career as a marine biologist was not spent studying them, but fish instead. Dr. Evelyn Shaw took me on as an undergraduate for summer research at Woods Hole Oceanographic Institution, where I did my first bit of research (on fish). The following year, the Marine Biological Laboratory's course in marine ecology, taught by such luminaries as Eugene Odum, Howard Sanders, and Laurence Slobodkin, expanded my knowledge of coastal ecology, including fish and crabs. My research work as an undergraduate at Cornell and graduate student at NYU focused on fish. It was only after several years on the faculty at Rutgers that my interests expanded beyond fish to crabs. Spending a summer at the (now-defunct) New York Ocean Sciences Laboratory in Montauk, New York, I made the acquaintance of Jim Hsiang, then a graduate student, who was studying fiddler crabs. He took me along on a collecting trip to a place in Accabonac Harbor called "Louse Point" and showed me the marsh area where he collected them. Watching these crabs wave, dig burrows, and walk around in the air at low tide, I was intrigued. I hesitatingly started to study them, and was insecure because I knew so little. But with the help and encouragement of an old friend, Linda Mantel, who has been a "crab lady" (as she describes herself) for all of her career, I got to know them better. From then on, crabs (especially fiddler crabs) have been an important part of my research program, along with fish, and Louse Point has become an important place for both research and recreation. It has been fascinating to see how crabs and fish are similar and different in the ways they respond to their environment.

The idea for this book was initially generated when I was writing *Do Fish Sleep?* (Rutgers University Press, 2011). That book used a question-and-answer format to cover all aspects of fish biology; as I was developing the questions and answers, in the back of my mind I kept thinking, "I could do this with crabs." This book, though not in a question-and-answer format, covers many of the same topics. Here you will find information about basic biology, the vast diversity of places where crabs live, how they live and adapt to their environment, their amazing behaviors, their incredible migrations, the dangers they face, their ecology, and the ways they can change colors, communicate, and reproduce. Chapters are also devoted to how people can interact with crabs, and how they can catch and eat crabs

(with some famous dishes and specialties). Some space is devoted to issues of the sustainability of crab fisheries and attempts at conservation so
that readers may become better informed about these vital issues. I hope
that the book, written in a nontechnical, readable style, will convey my
enthusiasm about the fascinating lives of crabs and that it will stimulate
readers to learn more and contribute to the conservation of these wonderful creatures.

Acknowledgments

I want to thank my husband, Peddrick (Pete) Weis, who has been a research colleague for decades and a strong supporter throughout the development of this book. Pete also is responsible for taking some of the photographs included here and preparing the photos taken by others, as well as reading and commenting on the first draft. I am grateful to all those who contributed their photos, to Gregory Jensen who informed me about the writings of Oppian (-170 AD) on crabs, and to Ray Toste and Jeff Stephan for their discussions about and insights into crab fisheries of the Pacific Northwest and Alaska.

Many graduate students who worked in my lab have provided stimulation and interesting new information about crab biology. Thank you all for your enthusiasm, good work, and good company. Research associate Dr. Terry Glover provided invaluable insights into animal behavior and statistics.

I want to thank our granddaughters, Emily and Jessica Miner, for not being afraid of crabs or saying "EEEEWWW!!" when we find them on the beach.

I am grateful to the National Science Foundation, National Oceanic and Atmospheric Administration, Environmental Protection Agency, U.S. Geological Survey, New Jersey Sea Grant Program, New Jersey Department of Environmental Protection, and the Meadowlands Environmental Research Institute for supporting our research.

I appreciate all the work and help of Heidi Lovette of Cornell University Press, who was interested in this topic from the beginning and was invaluable to me through the review process. Scott Van Sant contributed many useful suggestions as a reviewer of the manuscript. Many thanks to Susan Specter, also of the Press, who shepherded the book through the publication process.

I also appreciate the hard work of all the environmental groups that are working to protect crabs and their habitats, wherever they are.

Walking Sideways

CHAPTER ONE

Introducing Crabs

Scientists in a research submarine exploring the deep-sea hydrothermal vents south of Easter Island made an amazing discovery in 2005: on the sea floor they found an unusually large crab (about 6 inches long) with its legs and claws all covered with hair. Then they noticed more of the strange crabs, mostly at depths of about 7,200 feet. Many were hiding underneath or behind rocks, and, at first, all the scientists could see were the hairy tips of their arms sticking out.

The crabs were living on recent lava flows where warm water seeps out of the sea floor. Hydrothermal vents often form near mid-ocean ridges, where hot lava rises up, causing the earth's crust to split apart and heated water to gush up from the sea floor. Ever since deep-sea hydrothermal vents were discovered as a new geological feature in the 1970s, marine biologists have been fascinated by the unique animals that live there, thriving in the deep waters that are both extremely dark and low on oxygen. Many new species that are deep-sea vent specialists have since been discovered and described. What made the discovery of these crabs so spectacular was their large size and their unusual hairy form, since most crabs have a hard, shiny outer shell. When the scientists collected some of the crabs to bring them back for identification, they found that they had discovered not only a new species (which they named *Kiwa hirsuta*) that is a distant relative to hermit crabs but an entirely new family since these crabs were so distinct from any other known crabs. Because of its hairy legs, the crab was nicknamed the "Yeti crab," after the shaggy abominable snowman of the Himalayas, the Yeti.

What is it that makes a crab recognizable as a crab? For most people, a crab is generally something with a hard shell and ten legs, with the first pair acting as claws. But this also describes other animals such as lobsters and shrimps. A crab is usually (but not always) wider than it is long, which may have something to do with its habit of walking sideways. It does not have a distinct major tail section, except when seen from below, because this section can be folded up underneath the main body of the animal. Crabs are distinctive creatures and it is remarkable that new groups of animals of this size are still being discovered, but many still are, especially in the deep sea.

The Census of Marine Life, a global network of researchers from over eighty countries, conducted a ten-year study throughout the world to assess the diversity, distribution, and abundance of life in the oceans. They conducted field work in polar regions (Arctic and Antarctic Oceans), continental margins, continental shelves, the deep sea, coral reefs, midocean ridges, seamounts, hydrothermal vents and seeps, whale falls, sunken wood, and near shore. Over 2700 scientists spent over 9000 days at sea on more than 540 expeditions, plus many more days in labs and archives. Using the latest technological advances in remotely operated vehicles (ROVs), autonomous underwater vehicles (AUVs), sonar, and imaging systems, scientists were able to explore previously inaccessible places, including the deepest and darkest areas of the ocean.

The world's first comprehensive Census of Marine Life, released in 2010, included thousands of newly discovered species, mostly from the deep sea. About sixty-five new species of crabs were found, many of which were galatheid crabs (also known as squat lobsters) from deep-sea seeps and hydrothermal vents. An estimated 5000 additional specimens have not yet been named and classified. According to Myriam Sibuet, vice-chair of the Scientific Steering Committee: "The Census enlarged the known world. Life astonished us everywhere we looked. In the deep sea we found luxuriant communities despite extreme conditions. The discoveries of new species and habitats both advanced science and inspired artists with their extraordinary beauty. Some newly discovered marine species have even entered popular culture, like the yeti crab painted on skateboards."

A year earlier, four new species of king crabs (family Lithodidae) were discovered. King crabs are among the largest crabs, so one would think they would be well known by now. But the deep sea is still largely unknown. One of the new species, however, lives in shallow water near the Galapagos Islands, so it is especially surprising that it was not known before. It is clear that many more species of marine animals of all kinds remain to be discovered. Another study of the king crabs from the New Zealand, Australian, and Ross Sea (Antarctic) regions found twenty-three new species, doubling the number of previously known species from that part of the world. Five new species were found exclusively from New Zealand, five from Australia, and four common to both regions. One new species (*Paralomis stevensi*) was discovered in 2006 in the stomach of an Antarctic toothfish.

Almost 2 miles deep in the North Pacific, Brad Stevens, then a biologist with the National Marine Fisheries Service in Alaska, found new crabs while exploring the Patton Seamount in the submersible *Alvin*, some 250 miles south of Kodiak, Alaska. The big surprise was finding a spider crab called *Macroregonia macrocheira*, which has no common name, because it's so rare. It was first described from seamounts north of Hawaii in 1979, so they were surprised to see it near Alaska. It had never been seen that far north. It turned out to be the most abundant crab on Patton Seamount. This spider crab has very thin legs that are about a foot and a half long. Stevens thinks the spider crab lives on the sea bottom throughout the North Pacific but is seldom seen because it lives so deep. He thinks it exists all across the seafloor of the North Pacific and probably has walked, over generations, across the ocean.

In 2008, an expedition to a tiny island in the South Pacific's Republic of Vanuatu found hundreds of new species, including many new species of crabs. Over 150 scientists from twenty countries collected species as part of the survey, studying caves, mountains, reefs, shallows, and forests. Marine biologists from the National Taiwan Ocean University discovered a new species of crab off the southern Taiwanese coast in January 2010. With a bright red shell covered with small white spots, the crab resembles a large strawberry. Scientists said that the new species is similar to a previously discovered species, *Neoliomera pubescens*, which is native to Hawaii, Polynesia, and Mauritius, but it has a broader (1 inch), clam-shaped shell that makes it a distinct new species.

In 2012, four new species of brightly colored freshwater crabs were found on the Philippine Island of Palawan. Approximately 50% of all species living on Palawan are unique to this island and live nowhere else. The crabs are unable to spread elsewhere, as they skip the larval stage in seawater and depend on freshwater at all stages of their development. Although they are newly discovered, they are already under threat from several mining projects.

In 2011, researchers from the Smithsonian catalogued almost as many crab species on tropical coral reef areas measuring just 20.6 square feet as in all of Europe's seas. Instead of the usual collecting techniques, the team used DNA barcoding to quickly identify a total of 525 crustaceans (including

168 crab species) from dead coral chunks taken from seven sites in the tropics, including the Indian, Pacific, and Caribbean oceans. Reflecting the diversity of life found in coral reef ecosystems, over a third of the species were found only once, and 81% were found in only one location. The many recent discoveries of new crabs noted here—typically large and easily identifiable animals—makes it clear that our knowledge of these sideways-walking crustaceans is still actively and productively expanding.

INTRODUCING CRUSTACEANS

To introduce crabs, one must first introduce crustaceans and arthropods. Crustaceans include crabs, lobsters, shrimp, krill, barnacles, and related species, many of which are tiny floating plankton. There are approximately 40,000 crustacean species, most of which are aquatic. They range in size from almost microscopic to weighing over ten pounds. Crustaceans are the only primarily aquatic group in the phylum Arthropoda, which also includes insects, centipedes, and spiders. Like other arthropods, crustaceans have a segmented body, jointed limbs, and an external shell or exoskeleton (or cuticle) made primarily of a tough material called chitin. Most of the larger species strengthen and harden their exoskeleton with calcium carbonate. The exoskeleton covers the entire outside of the animal and even lines the front and rear parts of its digestive system. Because of having this hard exoskeleton, arthropods can grow only periodically, after they have molted or shed the old shell and before a new one has hardened. Like other arthropods, crabs have bodies that are segmented; that is, composed of repeating sections. While this segmentation is obvious in other types of arthropods, in crabs it is visible only from underneath.

Within the class Crustacea is the order Decapoda ("ten feet"). Decapods are a large and diverse order, containing crabs, lobsters, and shrimp. In addition to ten feet, they have two pairs of antennae and a pair of crushing jaws called mandibles. The order Decapoda contains nearly 15,000 species, many of which are crabs. The greatest numbers of marine decapods are found in the tropics, just north of the equator. Within that area, the greatest diversity is in the Western Indo-Pacific, where there are many families not found in other parts of the world. Crabs, like all other plant or animal species, have a scientific name consisting of two parts: a capitalized genus name and a lowercase species name, which are generally Latin words and are in italics. For example, *Callinectes sapidus* is the common blue crab of the Eastern United States. Having a scientific name allows everyone worldwide to know exactly which species is being referred to. Popular names—or common names—will not serve that purpose because many different species may share a common name, for example, "mud crab." Likewise, one species may have more than one common name, such as "green crab" in the United States and "shore crab" in Europe. (Since the crab is not always green, the Europeans have a better name.)

Crustaceans are classified depending on various traits; important ones are how the body is divided and into how many segments. Primitive crustaceans have little differentiation between body segments. Decapods (which include crabs), for example, have a fused head-thorax region and an abdomen. Some other groups have three body regions: a head, a thorax, and an abdomen. A crab's head has appendages for sensing and feeding. The five pairs of appendages on the head are *antennules* (with chemical detectors), *antennae* ("feelers" for touch), *mandibles* (jaws), and two pairs of *maxillae*, which are used in feeding. The head also has eyes, which are on moveable stalks. Its thorax region has eight pairs of appendages: three pairs of maxillipeds, also used in feeding, one pair of legs (the first pair) with claws (*chelae or chelipeds*), and four pairs of walking legs. A firm piece of exoskeleton, called the *carapace*, covers the head-thorax on top and the gills on the sides (Fig. 1.1.). The carapace protects the vital organs inside the body such as the digestive system, heart, reproductive organs, and excretory organs. The abdomen has small appendages called *pleopods* (or swimmerets), and a tail called the *telson*. In lobsters and shrimp, the telson plus the last pair of pleopods (known as *uropods*), forms a tailfan that is easy to see, but it is missing in crabs. There are three subgroups of decapods. One contains lobsters, shrimp, and crayfish, whose abdomen extends out behind; we do not cover this subgroup in this book except for occasional references. The two other subgroups—the focus of this book—are two types of crabs.

The two groups of crabs are the "true crabs" or Brachyura (estimated over 6700 species) and the Anomura (estimated about 2500 species). Unlike in lobsters, whose abdomen (tail) is a large muscular structure behind the rest of the body, the abdomen of true crabs is greatly reduced and tucked underneath their body, so that when viewed from above, all you see is the carapace (see Fig. 1.1). Their body is usually broader than it is long, and they have smaller antennae. Their body is usually rounded or squarish, but some have an unusual shape, such as the crab in Figure 1.1 with long spines sticking

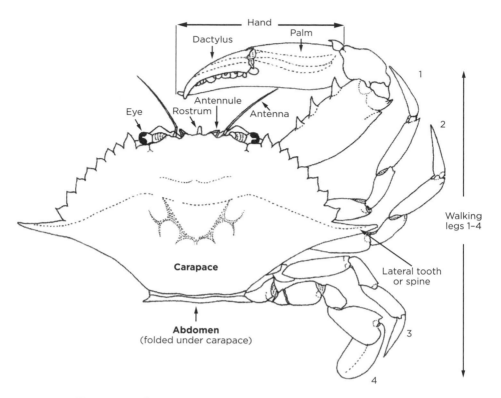

Figure 1.1. Brachyuran (true) crab anatomy, dorsal view. Illustration from UN FAO.

out on the sides. While lobsters and shrimp have five pairs of swimmerets or pleopods on the abdomen (tail) that they use in swimming, crabs, with their smaller abdomens tucked underneath, have very small pleopods that are used only in mating and for egg attachment (not seen in Fig. 1.2). Most crabs are marine, although freshwater and terrestrial species exist as well. The brachyurans are the most highly specialized group of crustaceans.

The anomurans are a large group of marine, freshwater, and terrestrial decapods that exhibit great diversity. While most are called *crabs*, some are called *lobsters*. They include 17 families, over 200 genera, and nearly 2500 species, of which just over half are hermit crabs that live in snail shells. Anomurans have their abdomen not extending straight out (like lobsters) and not tucked totally underneath them (like true crabs). In some it is asymmetrical and curved, soft and unprotected by a hard cuticle (see Fig. 1.3), which is the reason many of them take up residence in empty snail shells and are called "hermit crabs." There are two distinctly different types of

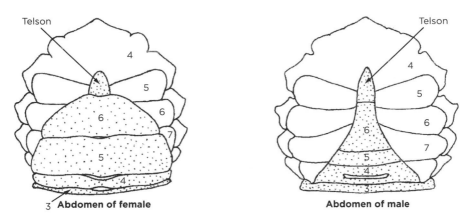

Telson

4

5

6

6

7

5

4

3 **Abdomen of female**

Telson

4

5

6

7

6

5

4

3

Abdomen of male

Figure 1.2. Brachyuran (true) crab anatomy, ventral view. Numbers refer to the segments of the thorax and the abdomen. Illustration from UN FAO.

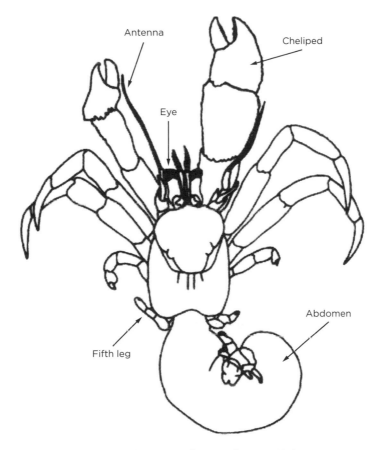

Antenna

Cheliped

Eye

Fifth leg

Abdomen

Figure 1.3. Anomuran (hermit crab) anatomy. Illustration by Joanne Taylor, Museum Victoria.

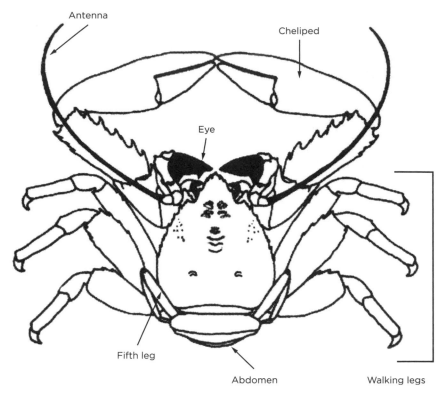

Antenna

Cheliped

Eye

Fifth leg

Abdomen

Walking legs

Figure 1.4. Anomuran (false crab) anatomy. Illustration by Joanne Taylor, Museum Victoria.

anomurans: the hermit crabs that live in snail shells and the "false" crabs, so called because they look superficially similar to true crabs (Brachyura). Both anomuran types have their fifth pair of legs greatly reduced—too small to be used for locomotion—and function in other ways. In false crabs, three pairs of legs are used for walking, and the reduced pair may be hidden inside the gill chamber (under the carapace) and used to keep the gills clean. In hermit crabs, only two pairs of legs (and the claws) are used for walking. The other (small) walking legs are used to hold onto their snail shell from the inside. Among the false crabs are porcelain crabs, king crabs, and mole crabs, all of which can be distinguished from brachyurans by counting the legs—they appear to have six rather than eight walking legs because the last pair is reduced (see Fig. 1.4). Their abdomen is tucked under the body as in brachyurans, but it is not as flat. King crabs have a thick shell but a soft bulbous abdomen, and they burrow backward into the sand. Mole crabs (also known as sand crabs; Fig. 1.5) also burrow backward, using their tail and walking legs to bury themselves in open sandy beaches where the water from break-

Figure 1.5. A handful of mole crabs (*Emerita talpoida*). Photo by S. Bland,
North Carolina Division of Parks and Recreation.

ing waves runs down the beach. Mole crabs have a rounded domed smooth
carapace and large feathery antennae that they raise up to strain food from
this moving water. Porcelain crabs also feed by filtering plankton or detritus
from the water, in this case using their second maxillipeds rather than antennae. Galatheid crabs are anomurans that superficially look more like lobsters and are sometimes called "squat lobsters." Some species of galatheids (red
crabs) swarm in the upper surface of the ocean, while most others are found on
the bottom in the very deep sea. Red crabs can be important food for large fish.

ORIGIN OF DECAPODS

Where did crabs come from? The ancestral crustacean was probably marine
and small, and arose from trilobite-like ancestors near the beginning of the
Cambrian period (542–488 million years ago). Since trilobites have shells,
they are well preserved in the fossil record. The earliest decapods were probably shrimplike and evolved during the Late Devonian period (416–359 million years ago), and over millions of years evolved into modern shrimps and
lobsters. Much later, a group of lobsters evolved into anomurans and then,
perhaps, brachyurans. The earliest clearly crab fossils date from the Jurassic
period (about 199–145 million years ago), although the earlier Carbonifer-
ous fossil, *Imocaris,* known only from its carapace, may be a primitive crab.

A LITTLE ABOUT LOBSTERS

The 400 species of lobsters are decapod crustaceans, belonging to the Astacidea, along with crayfish. These bottom-dwellers are found in all of the world's oceans, as well as in estuaries and even freshwater, where crayfish are common. Like crabs, lobsters have ten appendages—two claws and eight walking legs—with a carapace covering the thorax. The main anatomical difference between lobsters and crabs is that a lobster's tail (abdomen) extends out behind, while a crab's tail is tucked up underneath. A lobster can snap its tail to propel itself quickly backward—a movement that is most often used to escape potential predators. Like crabs, lobsters have compound, stalked eyes, chemosensory antennae, and sensory hairs on various parts of the body to detect touch and motion. The antennae are particularly sensitive, responding to environmental chemical cues regarding food, potential mates, and predators.

The largest lobster ever recorded was an American lobster (*Homarus americanus*) caught off the coast of Nova Scotia, Canada, that weighed 44.4 pounds and was almost 4 feet long. Scientists think it was at least 100 years old. Spiny lobsters have much smaller claws and can grow to 3 feet or more in length. The Norway lobster (*Nephrops norvegicus*) may be the smallest type of lobster, reaching only 10 inches from the eyes to the tail.

The radiation of crabs into many diverse groups took place in the Cretaceous period (145–65 million years ago; the time of the dinosaurs). An early Cretaceous hermit crab fossil was found perfectly preserved within an ammonite (an extinct group of mollusks with a spiral shell resembling a nautilus). As hermit crabs evolved, they developed a dependence on ammonite and gastropod shells for protective covering as their tails became soft and they needed to house their vulnerable abdomens within shells. As the most common mollusks shifted from ammonites to gastropods, hermit crabs coevolved to inhabit these newer shells.

Anomurans apparently evolved first in shallow waters and then moved into deeper waters. The giant king crabs are found in deep waters at temperatures just above freezing; they thrive in some of the coldest waters, living and growing slowly, probably to a very old age. Only in the cold water near the poles can king crabs be found in shallower water. They apparently evolved from hermit crabs similar to the familiar modern shoreline animals.

HORSESHOE CRAB: NOT A CRAB BUT A LIVING FOSSIL

Horseshoe crabs (e.g., *Limulus polyphemus,* the only American species; Fig. 1.6) are not true crabs and not even crustaceans. Instead, they are more closely related to spiders and other arachnids. They are "living fossils," estimated to have evolved over 350 million years ago, long before the time of dinosaurs, and having changed very little in all that time. A horseshoe crab spends most of its time on the bottom of bays and shallow coastal areas, feeding on clams and worms. While its long, pointed tail and sharp spikes along its shell look dangerous, the animal is harmless. The domelike shell protects it, but if the crab is beached upside down, perhaps by a wave, the extent of the upper shell can be a huge problem because its legs flail upward and cannot be used to help it turn over. The tail is the only part the crab can use to get traction in the sand to do so. The horseshoe crabs' large compound eyes on the upper sides of the shell detect light and help them navigate during their migration to and from offshore wintering grounds. A smaller pair of simple eyes, located near the midline of the upper shell, is sensitive to ultraviolet light, thus increasing the spectrum of light they can detect. Neither of these eyes are on stalks as in crustaceans.

In May and June, when the water temperatures rise, horseshoe crabs mate during the very high and low spring tides coinciding with the full and new moons. Females walk out of the water onto sandy bay beaches, with smaller males following and holding on with their claws, which have a special notch to help them hang onto the female. Recent evidence suggests that horseshoe crabs return to the beach where they were born to breed, since they will not breed in the laboratory unless sand from the natal beach is present. Near the high-tide line, the female digs a depression up to 8 inches deep in the sand, where she deposits a few thousand greenish eggs in clumps, and the male releases his sperm to fertilize them. Jane Brockmann of the University of Florida has noted that there are often additional males around the female, trying to get in on the action by releasing their sperm to fertilize some of the eggs. Through genetic studies, she found that these unpaired "satellite males" are actually quite successful at fertilizing eggs. A satellite male's specific location around the female greatly affects his chances of success.

Coinciding with the laying of eggs by horseshoe crabs, hundreds of thousands of shore birds migrate north from South America to summer breeding grounds. Many species, including red knots, stop along the way to feast on the horseshoe crab eggs, which give them the energy they need to complete their long journey to the Arctic. There is concern that bait fisheries for horseshoe crabs (for whelks and eels) are reducing the amount of food for the birds, so the fishery is being regulated in New Jersey and Delaware. (Delaware Bay is an especially important "refueling" area for migrating shore birds.) Eggs that are not eaten by shore birds hatch out in about 2 weeks into larvae that resemble miniature horseshoe crabs without the tail and swim out into the estuary. They will molt five or six times during their first year, but may take a decade to reach maturity after molting sixteen or seventeen times. They molt by splitting the shell along the forward lower edge and crawling out. Empty horseshoe crab shells are commonly found along the beach.

Hermit crab ancestors also gave rise to galatheids (squat lobsters). Although hermit and king crabs look quite different, some details of their anatomy and behavior reveal their relatedness. We can envision how a hermit crab ancestor gave rise to larger free-living crabs by considering coconut crabs, which have soft abdomens and live inside snail shells as juveniles, but as adults are free-living and hard-bodied. Anatomically, the hermit's abdomen is twisted in order to fit into a snail shell. In the evolution of the king crab, the abdomen became shortened and folded underneath the body, but it remains asymmetrical. This ancestry has been supported by recent DNA evidence. Soft-bodied, but shell-free intermediate forms are found only in the shallow waters off Japan, Alaska, and western Canada. Sally Hall, and Sven Thatje from the University of Southampton found that the soft-bodied forms can live at higher temperatures than the hard-bodied forms, but both groups can reproduce only when the temperature is between 34 °F and 59 °F. In order to leave this restricted habitat and spread around the world, the shallow water ancestors of current deep-sea groups had to go down and adapt to life in the cold, deep sea.

Land-dwelling hermit crabs appeared more recently in the fossil record, around the Late Cretaceous period. Most of them apparently evolved from species living at the edge of the sea, but some groups moved onto land only after first colonizing freshwater. Those that came directly from the sea are still found in coastal areas and still have a marine larva, so the adults must return to the coast to deposit the next generation. Those that came to the land from freshwater may be found much farther inland and don't need the

Figure 1.6. Horseshoe crab (*Limulus polyphemus*). Photo by P. Weis.

ocean for reproduction; they can go through larval stages within the eggs and hatch out as miniature adults. Terrestrial hermit crabs moved from the sea onto land, and the large coconut crab (*Birgus latro*) (Plate 1) is believed to have evolved from land hermits that secondarily abandoned the use of shells. Juveniles use snail shells (or broken coconuts or film cans) to protect their soft abdomens, but adults harden their abdomen by depositing chitin.

Brachyuran crabs are the most diverse group of decapod crustaceans, but their relationships to other decapod groups, their origin, and their evolution are still under discussion. Within the last couple of decades, anatomical and molecular studies on living groups and fossils have been used to investigate evolutionary questions about the major groups of Brachyura. Although it is still unclear whether they evolved from Anomurans or lobster-like ancestors, there is no doubt that Brachyura are the most advanced group of decapods, with wide distribution and the ability to leave the original shallow-water coastal environment. By the end of the Cretaceous period, the majority of the "higher" crabs had formed and had become one of the dominant groups in the marine fauna of that time. Brachyuran structure has undergone many modifications in connection with changes of habits and habitats.

CLASSIFICATION OF CRABS

About one-sixth of all crustacean species are crabs. Brachyuran (true) crabs are the largest group of crabs, with about three times as many species as anomuran crabs. There are ninety-three families of Brachyura. Table 1 describes some of the major families.

TABLE 1.
Families of Brachyurans (true crabs)

Family	Characteristics	Examples
Majidae (spider crabs)	Diverse marine family found in both deep and shallow waters. Carapace longer than is broad, forms point at the front. Legs very long in some species, leading to name "spider crab." Exoskeleton bumpy and covered with bristles (Fig. 1.7).	Commercial tanner crab (*Chionoecetes bairdi*; Fig. 8.1) Snow crab (*C. opilio*) Largest crab in the world is Japanese spider crab (*Macrocheira kaempferi*; Fig. 1.14).
Cancridae (cancer or rock crabs)	Predatory crabs, including many species of commercial importance mostly in cooler waters. Oval or hexagonal with teeth (notches) on front of carapace and first antennae folded longitudinally (Plate 2).	Dungeness crab (*Metacarcinus magister* [formerly *Cancer magister*]; Fig. 2.5), important commercial species in Pacific Northwest. Atlantic rock crab (*Cancer irroratus*; Plate 2)
Portunidae (swimming crabs)	Fifth pair of legs flattened into broad paddles for swimming. Have strong, sharp claws; fast, aggressive predators. Many species commercially important.	Blue crab (*Callinectes sapidus*; Plate 3) Blue swimmer crab (*Portunus pelagicus*) (Australia and Pacific) Lady crab (*Ovalipes ocellatus*) Green crab (*Carcinus maenas*; Fig. 1.8)
Xanthidae (mud crabs, pebble crabs, black-fingered crabs)	Oval to hexagonal, broadened in front (Fig. 1.9). Dark-colored fingers on claws. Common in tropical waters. Some poisonous.	Stone crab (*Menippe mercenaria*; Fig. 1.10), U.S. commercial species; only claws harvested. Major predator of oysters.
Calappidae (box or shame-faced crabs)	Rounded, dome-shaped carapace covers legs. Broad, flat claws fold in to make a solid whole with carapace. Claws fold in front of face as if crab is hiding its face in shame.	*Calappa*, large, brightly colored burrowing crab (Plate 4), common in sandy flats. Scissor-like claws used like can opener to rip open hermit crabs.
Grapsidae (marsh or shore crabs)	Square-shaped, flat, with broad fronts and short eyes in front corners of carapace. Among rocks, in estuaries, coasts, and marshes (Fig. 1.11); some semiterrestrial.	Sally Lightfoot (Plate 5), semi-terrestrial, on rocky shores. Marsh crab (*Sesarma reticulatum*), in salt marshes (Fig. 1.11). Sargassum crab (*Planes minutus*), lives in open ocean on floating seaweeds (Plate 16).

(TABLE 1—cont.)

Family	Characteristics	Examples
Gecarcinidae (land crabs)	For living on land, carapace covering gills is enlarged with network of blood vessels that extract oxygen from the air, similar to a lung. Generally live in burrows. Must return to sea to release their larvae.	*Gecarcinus lateralis* (Plate 6) *Cardisoma* spp. (Fig. 2.8) *Ucides* spp. (Fig. 8.3)
Pinnotheridae (pea crabs)	Small and soft-bodied. Commensal or parasitic. Live inside mantle cavity of bivalve mollusks (e.g., oysters, clams) or in tubes of polychaete worms.	*Pinnotheres* spp.; e.g., *Pinnotheres pisum* (Plates 7a, b)
Cryptochiridae (coral gall crabs)	Tiny crabs that live on/in corals. Juvenile takes position in depression of coral, and coral forms a gall or pouch around it, leaving opening to allow water to circulate. Galls inhabited by females only; smaller males free but may join female to mate.	*Hapalocarcinus marsupialis*
Ocypodidae (fiddler crabs and ghost crabs)	Semi-terrestrial, square-shaped. Long eye stalks, with bases close together at front of carapace. On sandy beaches, mudflats, mangrove swamps. Burrowers; many live in colonies.	Fiddler crabs (approx. 100 species), genus *Uca,* live in marshes or mangroves at edge of estuaries, dig burrows, active at low tide (Figs. 2.1, 4.1). Ghost crabs, genus *Ocypode,* on sandy beaches (Fig. 2.3).

Figure 1.7. Spider crab (*Hyas araneus*). Photo from NOAA.

Figure 1.8. Green crab (*Carcinus maenas*). Photo by P. Weis.

Figure 1.9. Mud crab (*Hexapanopeus* sp.). Photo from
South Carolina Department of Natural Resources.

Figure 1.10. Stone crab (*Menippe mercenaria*). Photo from NOAA.

Figure 1.11. Marsh crab (*Sesarma reticulatum*). Photo from
South Carolina Department of Natural Resources.

There are seven families of Anomura, listed and described in Table 2, three of which are hermit crabs that inhabit snail shells.

LARGEST, SMALLEST, AND ODDEST CRABS

The biggest crab in the world is the Japanese spider crab (*Macrocheira kaempferi*; Fig. 1.14), that can have a diameter (carapace width) of 13–14 inches, a leg

---

WHY IS "CANCER" BOTH A CRAB AND A DISEASE?

Dictionary definitions of *cancer*:

1. *Astronomy*: The Crab, a northern zodiacal constellation between Gemini and Leo.
2. *Pathology*: A malignant and invasive growth or tumor, especially one originating in epithelium, tending to recur after excision and to metastasize to other sites.

Carcinus is also a major genus of crabs, and *carcinology* is defined as the branch of zoology that studies crustaceans (also called crustaceology). The prefix *carcino-* refers to the disease as well, as in "carcinoma" or "carcinogen."

This double meaning goes back a long time; in Latin, *cancer* means crab. The image of the crab inspired the use of the word to describe the disease. The physician Galen (129 AD–199 AD) coined the term when he wrote, "Just as a crab's feet extend from every part of the body, so in this disease the veins are distended, forming a similar figure." Even earlier, Hippocrates (ca. 460 BC–ca. 370 BC) described several kinds of cancers, referring to them with the Greek word *carcinos* (crab or crayfish). The name comes from the appearance of the cut surface of a tumor, with "the veins stretched on all sides as the animal the crab has its feet, whence it derives its name."

In German, too, the word *krebs* denotes both crabs and cancer.

---

span of 12 feet, and can weigh over 40 pounds. It is not only the largest crab, but the largest arthropod in the world, although it doesn't weigh as much as a large lobster. The crab is orange, with white spots along the legs. These crabs typically live in the deep Pacific Ocean near Japan and feed on whatever they find on the bottom of the sea, including algae, plants, sea stars, shellfish, and dead animals. They are supposed to live up to 100 years, but it is hard to know. Living so long could account for their very large size. They are known to attach sponges and other animals to their shells to camouflage and protect themselves from predators, such as octopuses. Even though it is one of the largest arthropods, it apparently still needs protection. Some examples in public aquaria include a female crab named Crabzilla, who measures over 12 feet across and resides at the Scheveningen Sea Life center in The Hague, Netherlands, and is a major attraction. She weighs more than 30 pounds, and is one of the largest examples of the species yet captured. "Crab Kong," who weighs 33 pounds and has a claw

TABLE 2.
Families of Anomurans

Family	Characteristics	Examples
Coenobitidae (land hermit crabs)	Terrestrial; tropical and subtropical. Centered in Indian and Pacific Oceans, but also found in Atlantic Ocean and Red Sea.	Coconut crab (*Birgus latro*; Plate 1) Land hermit crabs (*Coenobita* spp.; Plate 8) Several species of *Coenobita* commonly sold as pets.
Paguridae (right-handed marine hermit crabs)	Abdomen spirals to the right; crab holds onto shell from the inside using rear walking legs and left uropod, which hooks around the shell. Right claw larger and flattened to cover opening of shell, functioning as a door. Marine hermit crabs (Fig. 1.12) in coastal and deep waters.	*Pagurus*, common in shallow waters. *Pagurus longicarpus* (Fig. 1.12) *Pagurus dalli* (Plate 24)
Diogenidae (left-handed hermit crabs)	Body coils left, and left claw enlarged instead of the right. Mostly tropical marine hermit crabs; some terrestrial.	*Clibanarius* spp. *Calcinus* spp.
Lithodidae (king crabs)	Often very large (e.g., 1 foot carapace width). Thought to be derived from hermit-crab–like ancestors, which may explain their asymmetry. Support major fisheries in cold-water areas, such as North Pacific.	Red king crab (*Paralithodes camtschaticus*; Fig. 1.13) most common. Blue king crab (*Paralithodes platypus*; Fig. 8.2) Golden king crab (*Lithodes aequispinus*) Scarlet king crab (*Lithodes couesi*)
Galatheidae (squat lobsters)	Body flattened, abdomen typically folded somewhat under, front legs greatly elongated with long claws. Last pair of walking legs hidden within gill chamber under carapace, giving appearance of having only 8 rather than 10 legs. In surface waters and very deep sea, including hydrothermal vents (Plate 9).	Hydrothermal vent crab (*Bythograea thermydron*)
Porcellanidae (porcelain crabs; Plate 10)	Small, with body widths of 0.5 inch or less; more compact and flattened, adaptation for living under rocks. May be symbiotic with sponges or anemones. Large claws, used for territorial struggles. Reduced fifth pair of walking legs used for cleaning gill chamber. Example of "carcinization," where non-crablike form (in this case, relative of squat lobster) evolves into animal that resembles a true crab.	Porcelain anemone crabs (*Neopetrolisthes maculosus*), symbiotic with sea anemones.
Hippidae (sand crabs or mole crabs)	Oval carapace high and domed; longer than is wide. Abdomen with distinct segments tucked up under thorax. Burrow backward into sand on beaches and strain plankton from water during each receding wave.	*Emerita talpoida* (Fig. 1.5) on Atlantic coast beaches.

Figure 1.12. Hermit crab (*Pagurus longicarpus*). Photo by P. Weis.

Figure 1.13. Red king crab (*Paralithodes camtschaticus*), with fishery research biologists Sara Persselin and Brad Stevens. Photo from NOAA (Kodiak Lab).

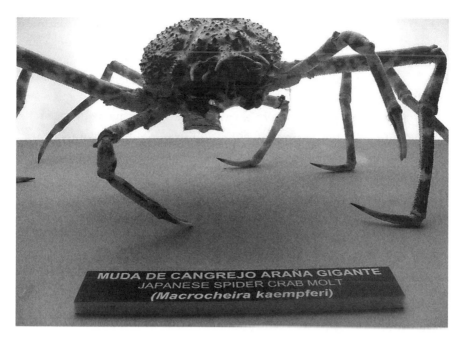

Figure 1.14. Japanese spider crab (*Macrocheira kaempferi*). Photo by Volker Wurst, Wikimedia.

Figure 1.15. Yeti crab (*Kiwa hirsuta*). Photo by A. Fifis, Wikimedia.

span of 10 feet, was caught by fishermen from a small coastal village southwest of Tokyo and was shipped to the United Kingdom for display in an aquarium in Weymouth. Spider crabs seem so enormous because of their astoundingly long legs. The second largest species in the world is the giant Tasmanian king crab, *Pseudocarcinus gigas,* which is not really a king crab at all but a cancer crab. It is plentiful in deeper waters off the eastern coast of Tasmania in the southern waters of Australia on the edge of the continental shelf. It can weigh over 28 pounds and measure 15 inches across the body and have legs with giant pincers around 18 inches long. It is a commercially fished species.

The smallest crabs are probably pea crabs (Pinnotheridae) (Plates 7a and b) that are about ¼ inch in carapace width. They need to be small in order to live inside living clams, oysters, and mussels (see Chapter 6). Coral gall crabs are also tiny, living within coral; as the coral grows and eventually encloses the crab, the crab is protected but imprisoned, and has no room to grow.

Picking the "oddest" crab is more subjective because there are a lot of crabs that could be considered strange (as you will see throughout this book). But one of the oddest is certainly the crab that was discovered during the Census of Marine Life in deep-sea trenches (Fig. 1.15). It is an anomuran related to galatheids. Living next to hydrothermal vents at depths of 7540 feet, the blind white crab, named *Kiwa hirsuta,* was called yeti (or abominable snowman) crab because of its hairy arms, which support colonies of yellow bacteria.

CHAPTER TWO

Habitats

Crabs are found in all kinds of habitats from the shoreline to the deep sea, in marine, estuarine, and freshwater environments, and even on land. Most crabs live in marine and estuarine habitats (which are areas where fresh water and marine water mix, as in river mouths and bays), while only a few specialized ones (e.g., gecarcinids and land hermit crabs) live in fresh water or on land. More species live in shallow water than in the deep sea. Certain groups—namely the grapsids (shore crabs) and ocypodids (fiddler and ghost crabs)—tend to live in shallow and intertidal (shoreline, uncovered at low tide) areas. Grapsids (with broad fronts, short eyes, and almost square-shaped carapace) are found in many types of shore habitats, including marshes, mangroves, and rocky shores. Some of them can leave the water for many hours at a time. Ocypodids tend to be found only on softer substrates (muddy and sandy bottoms) like marshes, mudflats, and beaches.

SALT MARSHES AND MANGROVES

Fiddler crabs are intimately associated with salt marshes and benefit from the habitat and food that the marshes provide. Salt marshes occur along the intertidal shore of estuaries, where the salinity (salt content) ranges from near ocean strength to near fresh water. Salinity and the frequency and extent of flooding of the marsh by the tides determine the types of plants and animals found there. The low marsh zone usually is under water twice daily, while the high marsh floods only during storms and unusually high tides. Animals and plants live in certain zones depending on how well they can withstand the drier conditions of the higher marsh or the wet conditions of the lower marsh. One plant, smooth cordgrass (*Spartina alterniflora*), characterizes the regularly flooded low marsh on the Eastern coast of the United States. Various species of crabs live in salt marshes, where the stems, leaves, and roots of the cordgrass and other marsh plants provide food and shelter from predators. The young of other crab species use the salt marsh as a nursery.

In the United States, the dominant crabs in salt marshes are various species of fiddler crabs (Fig. 2.1), which are active on the marsh surface at low tide and inactive in their burrows when the tide is in, unusual for a marine animal. Other important marsh species are the marsh crabs (*Sesarma reticulatum* [Fig. 1.11] and *Armases cinereum*), which are semiterrestrial grapsid crabs. They may initially be mistaken for fiddlers, but are heavier and chunkier, and their eyestalks are located at the corners of their carapace rather than near the middle of the front. These crabs are active at high tide (as one would expect of a marine animal) and often nocturnal. Smaller mud crabs, *Panopeus* and *Eurypanopeus* species, are abundant in the low tide zone and move up to the edges of East Coast marshes. Blue crabs (*Callinectes sapidus*) (Plate 3) live in marsh creeks and can go up onto the marsh surface with the incoming tide to dine on the rich resources there. Green crabs (*Carcinus maenas*; see Fig. 1.8) can also be found in salt marshes, along with hermit crabs (see Fig. 1.12) of the genus *Pagurus*. Marshes and mudflats in the Indo-Pacific (Indian and tropical Pacific oceans) have additional types of crabs. Sentinel crabs (*Macrophthalmus*; Fig. 2.2), relatives of fiddler crabs, look similar but have symmetrical medium-sized claws. Like fiddlers, they dig burrows in the intertidal area and eat detritus and small worms.

Crabs not only utilize the marshes but also can benefit the marsh plants. Their burrows aid the marsh grasses by allowing more oxygen to get to the root zone. Blue crabs can benefit marsh grasses in an indirect way, as Brian Silliman and Mark Bertness from Brown University discovered: When blue crabs were removed from a Southern salt marsh, one of their major prey—periwinkle snails—flourished, multiplied, and ate up all of the cordgrass. Without the plants to bind sediment and protect wildlife, the salt marsh ecosystem disappeared and became a mud flat. This suggests that the loss of snail predators such as blue crabs may be an important factor contributing to the die-off of salt marshes in the southeastern United States.

In tropical areas, mangrove forests replace salt marshes as tidal wetlands on the edges of estuaries. Mangroves are salt-tolerant trees that grow in the intertidal zone throughout the tropics and subtropics. They are most often

Figure 2.1. Sand fiddler crab (*Uca pugilator*). Photo by P. Weis.

Figure 2.2. Sentinel crabs (*Macrophthalmus* sp.). Photo by Saka Yoji, Wikimedia.

located along sheltered shorelines and can be found high up in estuaries. There are several species of mangrove trees, with the red mangrove (*Rhizophora*) being similar ecologically to the cordgrass because it lives at the lowest area and so is under water for the greatest amount of time. Red mangroves have aerial roots, called stilt or prop roots, which are out in the air at low tide. These roots themselves provide another type of habitat for marsh animals.

Mangrove crabs belonging to many different families (about 275 species) live in this environment, where they play different ecological roles. For example, the land crab *Ucides cordatus* removes a great deal of leaf litter from the marsh. Inga Nordhaus and colleagues from the Zentrum für Marine Tropenokologie in Bremen, Germany, found there were comparable amounts of litter production by mangroves and litter consumption by crabs because of the high crab density and the low frequency of tidal flooding in the mangrove forests. This allows the crabs to feed for a long time without interruption. By processing most of the litter, *Ucides cordatus* and other species help to retain nutrients and energy within the mangrove ecosystem. The semaphore crab, *Heloecius cordiformis,* is a very common purple crab living in muddy estuaries in Australia. It may be so dense under mangroves that the area becomes riddled with burrows; digging all those burrows turns over and aerates the mud in a process called bioturbation. Burrowing semiterrestrial crabs (mostly ocypodids and grapsids) can be called "ecosystem engineers" because they modify the habitat and change the availability and quality of food, shelter, and refuge for other species in the ecosystem. Beneath the surface of the soil, these crabs dig a network of burrows that function like a system of conduits carrying water, dissolved nutrients, and air. There are some swimming crabs in mangroves (portunids, notably *Scylla serrata,* which is commercially important), but most are semiterrestrial or land crabs that dig burrows.

SANDY BEACHES

The sandy beach environment is not an easy place to live. There is no solid material to hold onto, and animals have to deal with crashing waves, changing tides, a beach that changes seasonally, and predators from the sea, the air, and the land. The animals that live in this environment tend to bury in the sand. Mole crabs or sand crabs (anomurans) (see Fig. 1.5) live in the *swash zone* of the beach, which ranges from the lowest to highest reaches of the waves at any given time. Because the zone changes with the tide, the crabs must move up and down the beach. Their legs allow them to swim, crawl, and burrow—which are all done backward. When burrowing backward, the crab's eyestalks stick up above the sand. The first pair of antennae stick up above the sand for respiration, and the second pair, resembling feathers, extend out when the crab feeds on plankton in the water. Along with moving up and down the beach with the tides, they also move down the length of a beach with longshore currents.

Figure 2.3. Ghost crab (*Ocypode* sp.). Photo from U.S. Fish and Wildlife Service.

Higher up on sandy beaches in warmer climates around the world you can find ghost crabs (*Ocypode*; Fig. 2.3), relatives of fiddler crabs. *Ocypode quadrata* has the greatest terrestrial adaptation of any crab on the East Coast of the United States, returning only occasionally to the water to wet its gills. It can also moisten its gills by extracting water from damp sand, using fine hairs near the base of its walking legs to "wick" water up onto the gills by capillary action. Ghost crabs are largely nocturnal, so it is rare to see them until the late afternoon. They feed at night, which reduces predation by visual predators such as shore birds and gulls. If they do leave their burrow during daylight, their ability to change color rapidly (similar to chameleons) to match the sand reduces their chances of being seen. They dig burrows down to 4 feet deep and are found from near the high tide line up to ¼ mile from the ocean.

Additional types of sand dwellers are found in the tropical and subtropical Indo-Pacific. Dotillidae are relatives of Ocypodidae and include about sixty species, including sand bubbler crabs (*Scopimera* and *Dotilla*), which dig burrows in intertidal areas and leave conspicuous round "bubbles" of sand pellets on beaches. Also common in that part of the world are soldier crabs (family Mictyridae; Fig. 2.4), which live on tidal mudflats in sandy estuaries and mangrove areas. Their bodies are spherical rather than flat, and they walk forward instead of sideways. They come out of their burrows when the tide is out to feed on organic material that they extract from the moist

Figure 2.4. Soldier crab (*Myctyris longicarpus*). Photo by LiquidGhoul, Wikimedia.

sand—similar to fiddler crabs. Their name may come from their tendency to form groups of hundreds or thousands of crabs that march together in the same direction down the beach.

BURROWS

Many crabs in marshes, mangroves, and beaches dig and live in burrows. This is particularly true for members of the Ocypodidae (fiddler and ghost crabs), which use burrows for shelter, refuge from predators, mating, and hiding after they molt. The burrow also protects them from temperature extremes; it is cooler than the surface in the summer, and deep enough to be above freezing in winter. Ghost crabs periodically close the opening with sand during the hottest part of the day and stay in the burrow through the colder months.

Burrows, dug with the walking legs, can be simple tunnels or may be branched and complex with many different openings. Ghost crab (see Fig. 2.3) burrows may be Y-shaped with one of the two ascending arms opening on the surface, and the other having a dead end a short distance from the surface of the beach. When threatened, they may push through the sand above the blind end to escape predators. The burrow may slant down at a 45° angle and is constructed with wet sand grains so that it will not collapse. It is interesting to watch some species of ghost crabs build or repair their burrows. They bring up clawfuls of sand and toss them 6–12 inches away from the opening. The crab will later pat down the sand and smooth out the surface with its claws. Other species bring up the sand in the form of little balls and leave them scattered about the entrance. Burrowing activity turns over sediment layers, potentially bringing up nutrients from deeper layers (up to 4 feet) to the surface. Burrows can also supply oxygen or food to the deeper parts of the sediments and make the environment more favorable for small animals and roots of marsh grasses.

Problems may arise in burrows during high tide when the oxygen level in the water may be very low, a condition known as hypoxia. Crabs can reduce their oxygen consumption and still meet their metabolic demands because their respiratory pigment has a high affinity for oxygen, and they are very efficient in using the limited amount available. The walls of their gill chambers have many blood vessels to increase gas exchange, and if it is damp, they can obtain oxygen from the air. Many grapsid crabs actually recycle and reoxygenate the water in the burrow by pumping it over their carapace and back into the gill chamber.

Some crabs that do not make burrows still do bury themselves, such as the mole crab *Emerita* (see Fig. 1.5). Blue crabs, green crabs, lady crabs, and many others bury under the sand to hide from predators, and they may hibernate buried throughout the winter. Land hermit crabs may burrow deeply under dead vegetation prior to molting or during cold weather.

AQUATIC VEGETATION

Some crabs are live in association with submerged aquatic vegetation (SAV) such as eelgrass (*Zostera*) or turtle grass (*Thalassia*) in tropical or subtropical regions. The Dungeness crab (*Metacarcinus magister* [formerly *Cancer magister*]; Fig. 2.5), a species of great commercial importance that reaches about 8 inches across the carapace, inhabits eelgrass beds as well as muddy to sandy bottoms, from the low intertidal zone to depths of about 600 feet. They can

Figure 2.5. Dungeness crab (*Metacarcinus* [formerly *Cancer*] *magister*). Photo © Gregory C. Jensen.

Figure 2.6. Mangrove crab (*Aratus* sp.) on mangrove leaf.
Photo by Ianaré Sévi, Wikimedia.

be found on the U.S. Pacific Coast from the Aleutian Islands in Alaska to south of San Francisco. Submerged aquatic vegetation thrives in shallow water that is clear enough for it to receive adequate sunlight for photosynthesis. In areas where the water is murky or cloudy due to silt or to plankton blooms resulting from excess nutrients, SAV declines, along with the animals that depend on it.

Several species of grapsids climb up and live up in the air in mangrove trees. They show different degrees of adaptation to living in trees, with a few species thriving in the tree canopies and feeding on fresh leaves. Crabs in the genus *Aratus* (Fig. 2.6) are found primarily on the trunks and branches of mangrove trees. The ends of their legs (dactyls) are razor sharp, enabling them to get a good grip. These crabs may enter the water periodically or use the mangrove roots, but most of the time they are up above the water level.

ROCK POOLS AND ROCKY AREAS

Rock crabs, green crabs, and grapsid crabs may live in rock pools, which, like burrows, may be subject to periods of low oxygen. When oxygen is low, they can increase the water flow over their gills to get more oxygen. Green crabs also move into shallow water, raise their body out of the water, and draw air into their gill chamber to aerate the water. Animals in rock pools, like those in intertidal burrows, must deal with changes in salinity and temperature as tides and weather change. They tend to be tolerant of salinity and temperature changes.

OYSTER REEFS

Oyster reefs are found in estuaries and near-shore areas, especially near river mouths where water is less than 30 feet deep. In addition to being commercially valuable, oyster reefs are ecologically important: They provide important habitat for many species, their filter feeding improves water quality, and they stabilize bottom areas and influence water circulation. As generations of oysters settle and grow, reefs become highly complex, with many nooks and crannies that provide habitats for many different species of animals. Crabs that utilize oyster reefs include mud crabs (see Fig. 1.9) and swimming crabs of the genus *Callinectes*. The mud crab, *Panopeus herbstii*, the most common xanthid crab on the East Coast of the United States, grows to be less than 2 inches, but has very thick, strong claws that can crush young oyster shells (spat) to consume the tasty mollusks. Older spat and first-year oysters are preyed upon by blue crabs. Commercially important stone crabs (*Menippe mercenaria*; see Fig. 1.10), both juveniles and adults, also live on oyster reefs.

CORAL REEFS

Coral reefs are colonies of millions of tiny, living animals found in warm, clear, marine waters that contain few nutrients. Coral animals (relatives of anemones) secrete calcium carbonate skeletons around themselves. Sometimes called "rainforests of the sea" the reefs they form are some of the most diverse and beautiful ecosystems on Earth. Decapods are among the most common species in coral reefs, comprising well over two-thirds of all species found there. Although they are often brightly colored, these crabs are not as conspicuous as the reef fish because they are smaller and often hide. Like reef fish, coral reef crabs are popular in the marine aquarium trade. Over one hundred different crab species can be found on coral reefs. Since they use substrates for shelter and feeding, the complex nature of reefs provides them with many suitable sites, shelters, and nutritional sources. The more complex the habitat, the more crab species can be found there. Lawrence Abele, when at the University of Florida, sampled organisms from many different marine habitats, including coral reefs, and noted the environmental conditions and various kinds of substrates in the area. He found that the number of species found in an area was (surprisingly) not greatly affected by temperature range, salinity range, or tidal exposure, but was most affected by the number of substrates available, probably because different species use different structures, thus reducing competition for each type.

Some crabs live in anemones on the reefs. Like the more famous clown fish ("Nemo"), porcelain anemone crabs (*Neopetrolisthes* spp.) live in pairs within the anemone (Plate 10). The stinging cells of the anemone provide protection from predators. The porcelain crab, a filter feeder, captures its food from within the anemone's tentacles.

Reef hermit crabs of the genus *Paguritta* do not live in snail shells like other hermit crabs, but rather inside calcareous worm tubes that are cemented down on reefs or inside holes in the coral itself. Feathered antennae enable the crabs to filter-feed on plankton, an adaptation to this forced stationary lifestyle. When water movements are low, the crab moves its antennae back and forth, and when currents are greater they keep them perpendicular to the current, forming a sieve to trap plankton. These hermits have established a specialized ecological niche for themselves in the complex coral reef ecosystem.

Coral reefs provide shelter and food for many crabs; researchers are finding that some crab species play a key role in protecting the reefs. Tiny crabs that live in South Pacific corals provide regular "housekeeping" services that may be critical to the corals, according to Hannah Stewart and colleagues from the University of California, Santa Barbara. This is one example of symbiosis, an interaction between two different species in which both partners benefit. Trapeziid or guard crabs, such as *Trapezius* sp. (Plate 11), only a half-inch wide, make their home in branching corals and remove sediment that falls onto the coral. When the researchers removed crabs from sections of the branching corals and allowed sediment to accumulate, most of the corals died within a month.

OPEN OCEAN

Most crabs live on or near the shore, or on the bottom in deeper waters. However, the small grapsid crab known as the Sargassum or gulfweed crab (*Planes minutus*; Plate 16) is unusual in that it lives out in the open ocean on floating material (flotsam). The most abundant floating material for centuries was the gulfweed, *Sargassum,* which is abundant in the Sargasso Sea and Gulf Stream of the Atlantic Ocean, so this seaweed gave its name to the crab living on it (though a swimming crab (*Portunus sayi*) is also found associated with gulfweed, and may also be called a "Sargassum crab"). The grapsid crab is also found on other floating material such as driftwood, and on floating species such as sea turtles and jellyfish. While living on sea turtles, the crabs appear to eat some of the attached organisms, and thus provide a cleaning service to the turtle in exchange for the free ride, reminiscent of the symbiosis that has been studied in coral reefs, in which certain fish and shrimp eat the external parasites from other fish, thus obtaining food and ridding the other fish of its parasites, or of the crabs that clean sediment off their coral hosts. Michael Frick from the Smithsonian Institution found that Sargassum crabs living on turtles ate a greater variety of foods than crabs living on inanimate flotsam (such as driftwood) because they could browse on organisms attached to the turtle shell as well as those from the water column. Crabs on inanimate flotsam ate more algae and showed more cannibalism than those on turtles. These days, huge numbers of Sargassum crabs reside in the enormous floating garbage patches, composed mainly of plastic, in the Pacific and the Atlantic oceans, thus providing an example of an animal that derives benefit from the waste of human society.

THE DEEP SEA

Some crabs live at great depths on the ocean floor. King crabs, anomurans that comprise a major fishery in Alaska, have evolved specific adaptations to cope with life in deep water, where food is relatively scarce. Most crabs hatch from eggs as swimming larvae that quickly begin to feed on plankton. Red king crabs (*Paralithodes camtschaticus*; see Fig. 1.13) do this too, but before they become bottom-dwelling crabs, they go through a stage when they do not need to eat at all. Unlike the adults, young red king crabs live in relatively shallow water where they are exposed to seasonally changing temperature and day length. Young crabs are solitary and need coarse substrate, such as boulders, cobble, and shells, or living substrate such as bryozoans (tiny animals similar to coral). Between the ages of two and four, red king crabs tend to form pods of thousands of crabs. Podding generally continues until 4 years of age (at about 2.5 inches), when they join adults and settle with them in waters less than 90 feet for the rest of the year. Golden king crabs (*Lithodes aequispinus*) live much deeper, from 600–1500 feet, and they are not exposed to seasonal changes. As a result, they may not reproduce simultaneously or even in the same season. Eggs of golden king crabs are twice as large as those of red king crabs, and they contain much more yolk, which enables the larvae to live entirely off the yolk until they become bottom-dwelling juveniles many months later. This adaptation allows larvae to survive at depths, even on the bottom, where there is much less plankton available to eat. The scarlet king crab (*Lithodes couesi*) lives even deeper than the golden king crab—below 2000 feet—and its much longer, thinner legs and larger gill chambers are likely adaptations to the low oxygen levels here, near and at the *oxygen minimum* zone. (The distribution of oxygen in the sea typically decreases with depth until an oxygen minimum zone is reached, then increases.)

For both anomuran and brachyuran crabs, gill chambers are larger at greater depths. As David Somerton of the University of Washington and National Marine Fisheries Service showed, enlarged gill chambers or gills are an adaptation for living near the oxygen minimum zones. Thinner legs require less oxygen, hence less energy. Other adaptations to the deep include red coloration, spawning throughout the year, and large eggs. The red coloration of deepwater crustaceans has long been discussed, and the general consensus is that red is protective: because red is the first color to be filtered out of the spectrum as sunlight passes down through the water, a red crab will not be seen at depth, providing camouflage and protection from predators.

The deepest crab in the Gulf of Alaska is the large-clawed spider crab, *Macroregonia macrocheira,* a true crab. Its body is about 4–5 inches across, but the legs reach up to almost 2 feet in length. The claw segment of adult males is over a foot long. They live down to over 11,000 feet in complete darkness, and yet they have eyes. What for? Probably they detect bioluminescence produced by various organisms in the deep sea. We know little about their biology. They apparently can walk long distances across the seafloor. Because there isn't much food down there, they may feed on dead animals that fall from surface waters, such as whales, sea lions, or large fish. They can go for long periods without eating, and when they find a food source, they can live off it for some time, then go on their way searching for more.

Deep-sea red crabs (*Chaceon quinquedens*; Plate 13) (formerly *Geryon quinquedens*), another commercial species, live along the edge of the continental shelf of the Northwest Atlantic Ocean and in the Gulf of Maine and the Gulf of Mexico. They inhabit mud, sand, and hard bottom from about 300 to 5000 feet, at water temperatures around 40°F. Males are believed to need 5–6 years to grow to commercial size, and more than 15 years to reach a maximum size of about 7–8 inches carapace width. Females only reach about 5 inches. Females brood their eggs under their abdominal flap for up to 9 months. After the larvae hatch, they remain in the plankton for varying lengths of time. Larvae settle near the base of the continental slope, and the young crabs move up the slope as they mature. Typical of deep-sea organisms, red crabs are opportunistic feeders, eating a variety of benthic invertebrates (e.g., sponges, hydroids, mollusks, worms, crustaceans, and tunicates) that they find in the sediment or pick off the seabed surface. They can also scavenge on deadfalls (e.g., trawl discards) of fish and squid. There are a few records of predation on red crabs by Atlantic cod and sharks. Their tropical relative, the golden crab (*Chaceon fenneri* [formerly

Geryon fenneri]; Plate 14) is also harvested for food by humans, with commercial fishing starting in the 1980s. It is generally found on deep (about 3000 feet) ocean beds in the tropical and subtropical regions of the Gulf of Mexico and the Atlantic Ocean. This gold or buff-colored crab with a hexagonal carapace the size of a dinner plate eats benthic organisms such as mollusks and worms.

ESSENTIAL FISH HABITAT

Some habitats are protected for commercial species. In the United States, the Sustainable Fisheries Act (Magnuson–Stevens Fishery Conservation and Management Act; commonly referred to as the Magnuson–Stevens Act) aims to stop or reverse the loss of fish (including shellfish) habitats and requires identification of habitats that are essential to managed species and actions to conserve this habitat. The National Marine Fisheries Service (NMFS), regional Fishery Management Councils, and other federal agencies must cooperate to protect, conserve, and enhance "essential fish habitat." Congress defined *essential fish habitat* (EFH) for federally managed species as "those waters and substrate necessary . . . for spawning, breeding, feeding, or growth to maturity." This applies to commercial species of crabs (and other shellfish) as well as fish. Documents have been developed for essential fish habitat for a variety of crabs, including deep-sea red crab, red king crab, blue king crab, golden king crab, tanner crab in Alaska, stone crab in the Gulf of Mexico, and others. Some habitats can be designated Habitat Areas of Particular Concern (HAPC), which allows the most sensitive habitat areas to receive more focused protection measures.

The EFH for deep-sea red crabs (*Chaceon quinquedens*; Plate 13), is along the continental shelf edge and slope of the western Atlantic, mostly between 600 and 5000 feet from Emerald Bank, Nova Scotia, into the Gulf of Maine and along the continental slope of the U.S. East Coast into the Gulf of Mexico. While little is known about larvae and early juveniles, late juveniles and adults are associated primarily with soft bottoms consisting of silt-clay sediments.

The EFH for larvae and early juveniles of king crabs (Fig 1.13) is also unknown, but for late juveniles it is the bottom along the entire continental shelf throughout the Bering Sea and Aleutian Islands (BSAI), where substrates consist of rock, cobble, and gravel, and (for red king crabs) biological structures such as bryozoans, tunicates, and shell. The EFH for adult red king crabs is the bottom along the nearshore, and the inner, middle, and outer shelf throughout the BSAI, where there are substrates of sand, mud, cobble, and gravel. For blue king crab adults, the EFH is bottom habitats along the shelf with substrates of sand and mud adjacent to rockier areas and areas of shell rubble. For golden king crab juveniles, the EFH is bottom habitats along the along the entire continental slope and basins of the BSAI with high-relief living habitats, such as coral, and vertical substrates, such as boulders, vertical walls, ledges, and deepwater pinnacles. The EFH for adult golden king crab is bottom habitats along the outer shelf, entire slope, and basins of the BSAI with the same hi-relief living habitats and vertical substrates as the juveniles. The EFH for late juvenile and adult tanner and snow crabs is the bottom along the entire shelf with substrates consisting mainly of mud.

The EFH for stone crab (see Fig. 1.10) is Gulf of Mexico waters and substrates extending from the U.S.–Mexico border to Sanibel, Florida, from estuarine waters out to depths of 60 feet; and waters and substrates extending from Sanibel to the boundary between the areas covered by the Gulf of Mexico Fishery Management Council and the South Atlantic Fishery Management Council, from estuarine waters out to depths of 90 feet.

There is no EFH for blue crab because as an estuarine species, it is managed by individual states rather than the federal government.

LOBSTER HABITATS

Adult and juvenile American lobsters (*Homarus americanus*) are most abundant on bottoms with shelter in the form of rock crevices, plant life, or soft sediment in which they can dig a burrow or excavate bowl-shaped depressions for cover and protection. These shelters partially protect the lobster from predation and aggression from other lobsters. Lobsters are found from shallow water down to more than 1500 feet deep and occupy a variety of substrates from rocky to silt and clay bottoms.

Caribbean spiny lobsters (e.g., *Panulirus*) are found from shallow water down to 1650 feet. They settle and metamorphose in dense vegetation, especially seaweeds, and juveniles live within it until they are about 0.6–0.8 inches. They then take up refuge in crevices in sponges, soft corals, and holes until they are about 1.5 inches long. At about 2–3 inches, they begin to move from the inshore nursery habitat to coral reefs and other offshore habitats.

HYDROTHERMAL VENTS

In addition to the "typical" cold, dark deep-sea environment, there are sites located along tectonic plate boundaries where sulfur-containing hot water flows up from inside the earth. These hydrothermal vents house a unique community of organisms that thrive there and are found nowhere else. This community is one of very few on the planet that doesn't ultimately depend on the sun and photosynthesis. Rather, bacteria in the water or living symbiotically inside some of the animals found there (such as giant tube worms) use chemosynthesis to derive energy from the sulfur coming out of the hot vents. This powers the whole food chain. The most conspicuous animals at these vents are gigantic tube worms that may be over 10 feet tall. There are also galatheid crabs (anomurans) and several types of brachyuran crabs. The hydrothermal vent crab, *Bythograea thermydron,* is a top predator at vent sites in the Pacific Ocean. This crab is present in such high densities that scientists actually use it as an indicator that they are approaching an active vent field. Vent crabs avoid getting poisoned by the sulfur by having special enzymes that detoxify it. The vent crabs are typically found among dense clusters of tube worms at an average depth of 1.7 miles and can tolerate a temperature gradient from 77°F in the tube worm clumps, to 36°F, the temperature of the water surrounding the vent sites. Because the vent crabs are found at such great depths, they experience about 250 times the atmospheric pressure that we do. While young vent crabs can live for months in the lab at atmospheric pressure, adults must be kept under high pressures similar to those of the deep sea or they will die. Another species of vent crab, *Xenograpsus testudinatus,* lives around sulfur-rich vents in relatively shallow waters off Taiwan, in an acidic environment low in nutrients. They swarm out of their crevices to feed on zooplankton that are killed by the vents' sulfurous plumes. This feeding behavior is one way the crabs are able to survive in the harsh environment of these shallow hydrothermal vents. This environment is hot, toxic, and low in oxygen, but the crabs are tolerant of low oxygen. They can even survive for about 12 hours without any oxygen at all.

As the deep sea is relatively unknown, and only about 1% of it has been explored, it is not surprising that new species—and occasionally new families—are discovered frequently. In 2005, scientists in the submersible *Alvin* spotted a white eyeless crab with long hairy arms and legs living at over 7000 feet of water near a vent in the South Pacific (see Fig. 1.15). It turned out to be not only a new species, but a member of a totally new family of anomurans (see Chapter 1). The Yeti crab is named *Kiwa hirsuta,* after the hairs that cover its body. The hairs house millions of bacteria. Exactly how Yeti crabs fit into hydrothermal-vent ecosystems is still unknown. They were seen eating mussels that were cracked open, but they were also seen holding their hairy claws out over plumes of warm water from hydrothermal vents. Because the hairs support large colonies of bacteria, the scientists speculated that the crabs might be "farming" the bacteria, perhaps as a source of food.

Vents are dark, there are no bioluminescent animals, and adult vent crabs generally lack eyes. However, in the midwater area, many animals can produce bioluminescence and many midwater animals, including larvae of the vent crabs, have eyes to detect it.

COLD SEEPS

Another unusual habitat is found in deep-sea cold seeps, where energy-rich compounds (e g , hydrogen sulfide, methane, and ammonia) seep up to the sea floor from deep reservoirs. Bacteria here, similar to those at the hot vents, use these compounds to derive energy by chemosynthesis and are the base of the food chain. At deep-ocean seeps (and vents), they provide energy to support all of the complex animals that share these unusual environments, independent of the sun and photosynthesis. Some of the bacteria at cold seeps are extremely large and form visible spaghetti-like strings. These bacteria convert sulfate to sulfide, using methane and oil to fuel the reaction. In the Gulf of Mexico, there are places where methane and oil seep together from the sea floor. As oil and gas seep through the sediments, microorganisms convert the oil and methane to carbon dioxide; in the process, they also convert sulfate to hydrogen sulfide. These habitats have their own tube worms, clams, mussels, shrimp, and crabs. Some of the crabs are galatheids, similar to those at hydrothermal vents, and some are tanner crabs, a type of spider crab. Lithodid (king) crabs have been observed feeding in the blackened sediments. Crabs are very diverse in cold seeps, with representatives of four anomuran families and fourteen brachyuran families, many of which are found nowhere else. They tend to be white and congregate in large numbers. A mussel bed at a cold seep was photographed literally crawling with white crabs. Many of the species are not yet named or described. Little is known about the ecology of these places, but crabs that reside there are considered to be largely scavengers or predators. A second species of Yeti crab (*K. puravida*) was discovered in a cold seep 3300 feet deep. The crabs were seen waving their claws back and forth in fluid from the methane seep, apparently "fertilizing" or giving nutrients to their bacteria. This species has a specialized whip-like appendage that scrapes the bacteria from the claws and scoops them into their mouths.

SEA MOUNTS

Sea mounts are high elevations in the deep sea that support unusual deep sea corals, along with a community of organisms that live on these corals, including golden crabs (Plate 14) and galatheid crabs (Plate 9). These corals, unlike shallow-water species, live in cold water and do not have symbiotic algae. Many of the crabs associated with this habitat are relatives of those found at vents and cold seeps. Sea mounts have been highly fished in recent years, and there is great concern about fishing techniques (e.g., trawling) that destroy the corals and thus the habitat of the resident species.

FRESHWATER

Some crabs live in freshwater, either for part of their life or full time in warm, humid parts of the world. About 850 species are freshwater, terrestrial or semiterrestrial; they are found throughout tropical and semitropical regions. Blue crabs and Chinese mitten crabs (Fig. 2.7) can live upstream in freshwater habitats, but must go back down to higher salinity to breed because their larvae can survive only in salt water. Other species spend their entire lives in freshwater. They can be found in slowly flowing rivers, rushing mountain streams and waterfalls, ditches, lakes, ponds, pools, and swamps. In the dry season, they tend to dig burrows or hide beneath rocks, stones, or wood. Freshwater crabs comprise important small-scale fisheries in parts of the tropics and may provide a primary source of protein for local people. They are also an important food for fish and other animals. Recently they have become popular aquarium pets.

Many freshwater crabs belong to the family Parathelphusidae, which is found mainly in Southeast Asia, and, unlike marine crabs, they do not have free-living larval stages, but hatch out as miniature adults. They produce relatively few large eggs, and the hatchlings are retained in the female's ab-

Figure 2.7. Chinese mitten crab (*Eriocheir sinensis*). Photo from
Smithsonian Environmental Research Center.

dominal brood pouch for several weeks after hatching. *Barytelphusa spp.* lives
in ponds that may dry up. It can store water in its gill chamber and recycle it
over the gills. On some tropical islands, freshwater crabs are found in mountain streams, caves, moist rock rubble, water-filled snail shells, and even
water-filled leaf axels of bromeliads. Bromeliads, relatives of the pineapple,
are "air plants" or epiphytes that grow on other plants, usually trees, and can
take their nutrition and moisture from the atmosphere. Bromeliad crabs live,
breed, and even raise their offspring in the tiny puddles of rainwater that accumulate in these aerial plants.

Cave-dwelling crabs (both brachyurans and anomurans) come from
many different families, but show similar adaptations including loss of pigmentation, elongation of legs, and reduction of eyestalks. Their white color
is reminiscent of crabs living in the deep sea. Some are totally eyeless, while
others retain small eyes. Blind crabs retain their eyestalks, probably because
important hormones are made and stored there. Blind cave crabs often live
near small inlets for water that bring in food.

In parts of the tropics, some freshwater crabs have moved onto land and
developed the ability to breathe air as well as water. A reduction in the number of gills is seen in some air-breathing species such as the terrestrial African freshwater crab *Globonautes macropus*. This terrestrial species carries out
aerial respiration by means of a "pseudolung," consisting of a membrane with

lots of blood vessels in the upper part of the gill chamber, although it also has functional gills in the lower part of the gill chamber.

LAND

Crabs in the family Gecarcinidae are true air-breathing land crabs that are stressed if they are submerged in water. They therefore utilize rain and dew to replenish water they lose due to evaporation. They are found in rain forests, mangrove forests, dry plains, and mountain slopes. *Gecarcinus lateralis* (Plate 6) lives in burrows or crevices up to a mile or two inland. It may be an agricultural pest, as it can burrow in lawns and gardens. The borrow serves as a site for reproduction (courting and mating) and protection. Its larger, less colorful relatives, the *Cardisoma* species, (Fig. 2.8), dig deeper burrows that go all the way down to the water table. *Cardisoma guanhumi,* (the blue land crab) which may be 4–5 inches wide, is a scavenger that feeds on fallen coconuts, mangrove leaves, crops, and debris. There is a "fishery" for them in Puerto Rico. Land crabs must migrate back to water for spawning and have larvae that live in the ocean.

Hermit crabs in the family Coenobitidae—which includes the coconut crab (*Birgus latro*; Plate 1) and land hermit crabs (*Coenobita*; Plate 8)—can also climb trees, though they are more frequently found on the ground in tropical and subtropical coasts and islands. Among the Coenobitidae are some species that enter the sea regularly and other species that are fully terrestrial. They perform a useful function in consuming dead organic matter that would otherwise decay. As some scientists and campers have discovered, their diet is wide-ranging as they also can pry open food containers. *Birgus,* found in the Indo-Pacific, will climb palm trees to get the coconuts. Land hermits, like their marine relatives, occupy mollusk shells. Having these shells may have made it easier to adapt to land because the shell not only protects them from predators but also provides a way to carry needed water along with them. The requirement for new shells, however, may limit how far inland they can live because fewer snail shells are available further inland. Coconut crabs do not stay in snail shells as they grow larger, but their abdominal cuticle thickens for protection and reducing water loss. Perhaps one reason they gave up shells was because there were so few large ones available inland. They are a valued food for people in the areas where they live.

Figure 2.8. Land crab (*Cardisoma* sp.). Photo by Hans Hillewaert, Wikimedia.

Given the diversity of crabs, it is not that surprising that they can be found in many different habitats. But considering that they started out as marine animals, it is impressive how they have managed to adapt to living in freshwater, on land, and even up in trees. No other marine group has successfully adapted to so many different habitats.

CHAPTER THREE

Form and Function

While many aspects of crab anatomy and physiology are similar to those of other animals, some may come as a surprise. Interesting, and sometimes odd, examples in crabs include blue blood, taste buds on their toes, and kidneys in their head!

BASIC CRAB ANATOMY

When viewed from above, all you can see is the carapace of a crab, but when viewed from underneath (see Fig. 1.2), we can see its major anatomical features—the boundary between the head and thorax, as well as the segments of the thorax and the attachment of the legs to the thorax. The cephalothorax is generally short and broad, and in some cases extended to the sides. As with other decapods, the first two legs are large claws (called *chelae* or *chelipeds*) for food capture and defense, and the other eight legs are used for walking—usually, but not always, sideways. The attachment of five pairs of appendages within the small space available on the side of a crab makes sideways movement easier than forward movement in which the legs are more likely to get entangled with each other.

The two claws may or may not be symmetrical; in some species, one claw is used for crushing and the other for cutting. The crusher claw is more powerful than the cutter due to its greater mechanical advantage and greater amount of muscle. The legs have six joints: the coxa, ischium, merus, carpus, propodus, and dactyl (see Fig. 1.1). Crabs have two stalked eyes and two rather small pairs of sensory antennae, the first called antennules, and the second called antennae. Gills are used for respiration, and food is processed by a number of jointed mouthparts. Maxillae and maxillipeds manipulate the food, then mandibles grind and crush it so it can be swallowed.

Anomurans also have ten legs, but the last pair is reduced in size and may be hidden under the carapace inside the gill chamber and not visible. They are used for keeping the gills clean. The last two small pairs of walking legs in hermit crabs are used to hold onto their snail shell from the inside (see Fig. 1.3).

DIGESTION

The mouthparts include three pairs of maxillipeds and two pairs of maxillae that hold and manipulate food, and a pair of mandibles that push the food into the esophagus. The gut (digestive system) is basically a tube running from the mouth in the front to the anus at the back. The tube is divided into the foregut, which may be a simple passageway (esophagus) or more complicated with structures for grinding or filtering the food and starting digestion. The foregut generally has small bony structures called ossicles where muscles, which cause the foregut to churn, attach. The stomach that follows has a gastric mill—a structure with plates (teeth) for grinding and breaking down the food particles and mixing them with digestive fluids. The midgut starts where ducts from the midgut gland enter the stomach. Digestion takes place partially in the anterior part of the foregut, partly in the posterior part, and partially within the midgut gland itself, which has several lobes. The food goes into the midgut gland (or hepatopancreas) where chemical digestion continues and nutrients are extracted and assimilated into the body. This gland is responsible for most of the digestive enzymes and assimilation. The midgut that follows it includes various outpocketings—dead-end tubules (diverticula), which increase the amount of surface area for absorbing nutrients, and ceca (blind pouches), which secrete more digestive enzymes. Undigested materials pass into the hindgut, which runs between the lobes of the midgut gland and ends at the anus. It may be short or long, and is lined with chitin.

Animal gut sizes can reflect diet quality because animals that eat low-quality food must eat large amounts to obtain sufficient nutrition. Blaine Griffin and Hallie Mossblack of the University of South Carolina investigated the anatomy of the digestive systems of fifteen different East Coast crab species to see if the morphology would reflect the dietary preferences of species and individuals. The species chosen represented a broad range of dietary "omnivorous" strategies, from almost purely carnivorous to almost purely herbivorous. The researchers examined the stomachs of both males and females and a variety of different sizes of each species, and found that stomach volume can be used to predict the percent herbivory of the crabs, with larger stomachs in more herbivorous species. Stomach size also reflected the relative consumption rates of individual crabs, as observed in experiments.

RESPIRATION

Right under the carapace on both sides of the body, crabs have gill chambers containing gills, which are outgrowths of the bases of the walking legs. Gills are featherlike structures for gas exchange; they have a very thin covering of cuticle so that gases (oxygen and carbon dioxide) can readily move in or out. A structure called the scaphognathite or gill bailer creates a current of water in the gill chamber by beating or flapping, drawing water in from a posterior opening. The water circulates through the chamber and leaves through a more anterior opening. As water flows over the gills, oxygen dissolved in the water enters the blood going through the gills, and carbon dioxide in the blood enters the water. (Periodically, the gill bailer reverses direction, which reverses the flow of water and helps to clean the gills of debris.) The oxygen then attaches to a pigment in the blood and is transported around the body. The blood pigment, called hemocyanin, is a copper-containing molecule that performs the same function as the iron-containing hemoglobin does in humans, but instead of being inside cells (like iron in our red blood cells) it is dissolved in the blood, and instead of being red, it is blue. The circulatory system in crabs is called an "open" one; arteries take blood from the heart and branch out into fine branches that eventually end as thin-walled capillaries. The blood then bathes the internal organs and eventually returns to the heart without being enclosed in veins. The heart, which is a single-chambered muscular sac, is located in the thorax, above the digestive tract. It has several openings through which the returning blood flows. The contractions of the heart pump the blood forward to the head and organs and backward into the abdomen.

The amount of oxygen needed depends on a crab's activity level and the temperature of the water. When the amount of oxygen in the water is low,

HORSESHOE CRAB BLOOD

The blood of horseshoe crabs (see Fig. 1.6)—which are not actually crabs (see "Horseshoe Crab," page 11)—contains blood cells called *amebocytes*, which play a role similar to white blood cells in vertebrates in defending the organism against pathogens (germs). In the 1960s, Dr. Frederik Bang, working at the Marine Biological Laboratory in Woods Hole, Massachusetts, found that when marine bacteria were injected into the blood of horseshoe crabs, massive clotting occurred. It was later shown to be caused by a chemical in the bacteria, called endotoxin, which triggered the amebocytes of the horseshoe crab to clot, and that this process could take place in a test tube. A cell-free product named Limulus amebocyte lysate (LAL) was developed, using amebocytes extracted from horseshoe crab blood. LAL is used by the pharmaceutical and medical device industries to ensure that their products, such as intravenous drugs, vaccines, and medical devices, are free of bacterial contamination. Although LAL cannot discriminate between living and dead bacteria, and cannot differentiate species of bacterial endotoxin, the LAL test can be used to detect toxins from pathogenic Gram-negative bacteria, and to rapidly diagnose conditions such as urinary tract infections and spinal meningitis in humans.

Biomedical companies need many horseshoe crabs to extract the amount of blood needed, but they do not have to kill the crabs to do so. Instead, they catch them, extract about one-third of the crabs' blood, and then release them back into the wild. Most crabs survive this procedure (estimates run around 70–80%), and it is estimated that it takes about 30 days for the crabs to replace the blood that was removed. The LAL test is expensive and subject to seasonal and other factors that may interact with proteins in the crabs' blood. A new test has been developed that involves liquid crystals (the same material used to make some flat-screen computer monitors and televisions), which could eliminate the need to use horseshoe crab blood, with its resultant mortality, for LAL production.

the animal will increase its ventilation to maintain its oxygen requirements. Crabs that live on the bottom are much more likely to encounter low oxygen conditions than animals that swim closer to the surface of the water. However, estuaries frequently have low oxygen. Geoffrey Bell and colleagues at the University of North Carolina investigated responses of blue crabs to very low oxygen levels (hypoxia). While these crabs can tolerate severe hypoxia, their likelihood of survival decreases with longer exposure time, lower level of oxygen, and increasing temperature. Individual differences in survival were related to the crab's size. Crabs from estuaries that were frequently hypoxic survived longer under low oxygen than those from estuaries that did not experience hypoxia. The amount of hemocyanin did not explain these differences, however. The hemocyanin of crabs that were more tolerant to low oxygen had a chemical structure that gave it a higher oxygen affinity, suggesting that the "quality" or chemical structure of the hemocyanin is more important than its quantity.

Crabs that live in oxygen minimum zones or at hydrothermal vents in the deep ocean, where hot sulfur-rich water supports a unique community of marine life, are almost always in hypoxic water. These species tend to have enlarged scaphognathites, which send more water flowing over their gills with each beat. This is probably more efficient than continued rapid beating. Unlike some other vent-dwelling species, these crabs do not have greatly enlarged gills, probably because of space limitations within the gill chamber that is, after all, enclosed inside the carapace. The gills of some vent crabs also have a greater surface area, further increasing their efficiency.

Crabs that spend time in the air (which has 30 times as much oxygen as water) have less gill tissue and a thicker gill surface. Air-breathing species tend to have higher oxygen consumption than aquatic ones. Land crabs take up water from damp soil and store it in the gill chamber, which is enlarged and may have complicated foldings that increase its surface area, along with lots of blood vessels to extract oxygen from the air. The wall of the gill chamber has evolved into an accessory structure for gas exchange in both brachyuran and anomuran land crabs. Land hermit crabs have a less complex chamber than land brachyurans and utilize their gills to a greater degree than their large relative, the coconut crab, which relies almost totally on its elaborate air-breathing chamber. The coconut crab can survive in air with its gills removed but will actually drown if submerged in water. Its lungs are not particularly efficient, but they don't need to be because oxygen is never in short supply in the air.

METABOLIC RATE AND BIOLOGICAL RHYTHMS

The metabolic rate of crabs (and other invertebrates) depends on the temperature of the water. Unlike mammals and birds, whose internal body temperature remains constant, the body temperature of these "cold-blooded" animals goes up and down with the water temperature. So when the water is cold, a crab's metabolism will be low and the crab will be inactive. However, not all crabs are the same: the metabolism (and activity level) of a "cold-water" crab, in its native, cold, water temperature, will be higher than the metabolism and activity level of a "warm-water" one (e.g., a tropical crab) were it to be put in water of the same cold temperature. This shows how crabs can adapt to temperature.

Returning to Massachusetts from a Florida field trip, biologist John Palmer put a large land crab in a plastic bag into his briefcase and carried a box containing another 150 land crabs aboard the plane. When people seated near him asked what was making the scratching noises they heard, he told them he studied biological clocks in crabs and other aquatic life forms. These crabs spend the day nearly motionless, and their activity cycle started at 6 PM, he explained. When the plane landed at 7 PM, he opened his case to replace some papers. The crab, now wide awake (and undoubtedly angry), burst out, its huge claws open, briefly terrorizing the passengers.

Crabs tend to show rhythms in their metabolic rate, corresponding to day/night cycles or, for those that live in shallow water, tidal cycles. These *circadian rhythms* have been studied extensively and are an expression of a "biological clock" that is internal, but that is set by environmental changes such as the tides or light/dark cycle. The rhythms persist for a time when the animal is kept in constant conditions in the laboratory, showing that there is an internal clock. Rhythms can also be seen in pigmentation changes, activity level, reproductive activity, and even egg hatching. Biological rhythms tied in with the lunar cycle are common. In the sea, the moon's gravitational pull on earth is the principal cause of the tides, which are highest and lowest during the new and full moons. Many crab species synchronize spawning to this time.

Crabs spend some part of the day or night in an inactive state that can be interpreted as sleep. Some species are diurnal (active during the day) and some are nocturnal. Many crabs in temperate climates spend much of the cold winter hunkered down in the sediments, probably sleeping. Pet hermit crabs can be observed sleeping. A sleeping hermit crab is very relaxed, its eyes and antennae are pointed down, and they are usually part way out of their shell. A sleeping crab will often not move or withdraw when you walk by the tank and may stay in that one spot for hours.

EXCRETION OF WASTES

Nitrogen compounds, including proteins and nucleic acids, are involved in all aspects of an animal's metabolism. These nitrogen-containing molecules become wastes after they are metabolized. Crabs can get rid of wastes by diffusion across the gills, but they also have specialized excretory organs to eliminate nitrogen-containing wastes (or urine, which is mostly ammonia). The paired excretory organs (similar to our kidneys), called "green glands" or antennal glands, are located in the head near the antennae, unlike most other animals, whose excretory organs are located farther back in the body. These glands may also be involved with the balance of salt and water. There is a glandular portion that secretes urine and regulates salts, and a large bladder in which urine is stored before it is released through ducts to the exterior. The opening of the duct, which is at the base of the antenna, is covered by a moveable cover.

SALT AND WATER BALANCE

Salt and water balance, or *osmoregulation*, has long been studied in crabs. Some species tolerate only small variations in salinity, and the salt level in their blood is in equilibrium with the surrounding sea water. Others have broader tolerance and can function well in a wide range of salinities. In general, adult crabs can tolerate greater salinity fluctuations than younger stages of crabs. Some species are *osmoconformers*, meaning their internal salinity will match that of the water in which they live, while *osmoregulators* can maintain their internal salt concentration regardless of the salinity of the water.

During its life, the blue crab (*Callinectes sapidus*; see Plate 3) moves from the ocean to an almost freshwater environment and will regulate the concentrations of ions in its blood (called hemolymph). Ions in the hemolymph will remain relatively constant over this vast change in environmental salinity. This ability indicates this crab is an osmoregulator. Not only does it tolerate a wide range of salinities, but it can tolerate a rapid transfer from very salty water to freshwater—which would kill most organisms. The gills are the primary organ used to osmoregulate; during acclimation to various salinities, the crab changes the activity of the enzyme sodium-potassium adenosine triphosphatase (Na^+,K^+-ATPase) in the gills.

Osmoregulation involves reducing the animal's permeability to water and actively moving ions in or out—which requires energy. When a crab is in water of low salinity or freshwater, water will tend to enter the animal (a process known as *osmosis*). Freshwater species must reabsorb the salt and eliminate this excess water. To do this, they reduce their permeability to water, specialized cells in the gills take up salts, and the green glands increase the amount of urine excreted to get rid of the excess water. In high salinity, there is the opposite problem—water will tend to leave the animal. To compensate for water loss, the animals take in water and produce very little urine. The green glands function in volume regulation and regulating the concentrations of salts by controlling their concentration in urine; large amounts can be reabsorbed to conserve sodium ions.

Many aquatic organisms can take up water through their skin. Since crabs are covered with an exoskeleton rather than skin, osmotic exchanges take place mainly through the gills. Gills, especially the posterior ones, play a major role. Ion-transporting cells are clustered into osmoregulatory patches on the posterior gills. When Donald Lovett and colleagues took crabs that had been living in seawater and placed them in low salinity, the size of the osmoregulatory patches and the activity of the enzyme Na^+,K^+-ATPase increased after 24 hours and continued to increase gradually for 6 days following transfer, showing the importance of this patch and of the enzyme for osmoregulation at low salinity. Crabs also control gill transport processes by hormones and their digestive system. The gut, particularly the foregut, plays a role in the movements of ions and water. Ceca (blind pouches) of the gut may play a role in uptake of water.

Land crabs (gecarcinids) can tolerate fresh to salty water, and can tolerate drying out; they produce urine comparable to that of marine crabs. Their major challenge is to obtain and conserve enough water, since they are apparently able to conserve salts. Some species (e.g., *Cardisoma*; see Fig. 2.8) can access water at the bottom of their deep burrows, while others (e.g., *Gecarcinus*; see Plate 6) actively drink water by dipping their chelae into rain and dew. Semiterrestrial and terrestrial crabs are able to minimize salt loss by reprocessing their urine; that is, passing their urine (which contains as much salt as their blood) over their gills, which have powerful ion pumps that reclaim most of the salts before the "final excretory product," by now as dilute as tap water, is discarded. (Since "final excretory product" is a long and cumbersome term, Tom Wolcott has used his sense of humor in assigning the initial *P* as the abbreviation in the scientific literature.) The urine (*P*) reaches the gills by trickling down into the gill chamber from the pores of the green gland—a good reason to have it in the head rather than farther back in the body. All terrestrial crabs use this same method to get around their green gland's inability to produce dilute urine.

Some crabs that are not good osmoregulators have developed behaviors to help them cope with salinity changes. *Cancer edwardsii* juveniles, for example, live in estuaries that are occasionally subject to inflows of large amounts of freshwater after rainfall, which greatly reduces the salinity. This species manages to survive the low salinity by burying itself in the sediments where there is higher salinity in the pore water. Luis Pardo and Chilean colleagues exposed crabs in the laboratory to varying salinities for different periods of time and videotaped them; burying behavior was found to play a key role in allowing the crabs to survive in estuarine areas where sudden and unexpected low salinity events occur.

THE FIVE SENSES

Vision

Crabs and many other crustaceans have compound eyes on stalks that are very different from the eyes of vertebrates. Being on stalks, the eyes can be withdrawn into sockets for protection and can be moved in all directions. Some shallow-water and terrestrial crabs appear to have color vision, while others do not. Compound eyes are composed of hundreds or thousands of small hexagonal units called *ommatidia*, each of which focuses the light that it receives on its rhabdom, the equivalent of the retina (Fig. 3.1). What the crab sees is not a single image, but a mosaic of repeated images, each of which is somewhat blurry. The outer surface of the eye is covered with a cornea, a transparent part of the body's cuticle. The crystalline cone acts as a lens and links the cornea to the light receptors in the rhabdom below. The rhabdom is made up of thousands of tightly packed tubules (called microvilli) that together make up the light-absorbing structure. The visual pigment rhodopsin is present in the membranes of the microvilli. Retinal cells contact nerve fibers that form the optic nerve to connect to the brain.

The number of ommatidia in a compound eye varies up to several thousand. There is an optimal number, however, because the more ommatidia there are, the finer the detail that can be resolved, but also the less light that can come into each one. The eye may have each unit screened from all the others with each rhabdom receiving light from only its own ommatidium, or each unit may not be screened from the others, so that light from several different ommatidia can be focused on each rhabdom, increasing the brightness of the image. Black pigment on the outside of each of the ommatidia can move up and down to screen or not screen them from one another. In bright light, dark pigment granules screen the crystalline cone and rhabdom, reducing the

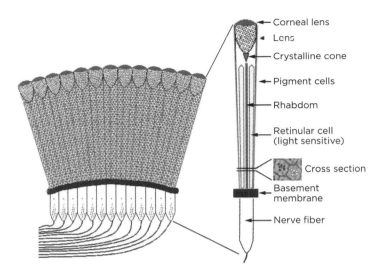

Figure 3.1. Compound eye. Diagram from blackspvbiology, Wikimedia.

amount of light that reaches the rhabdom. In dim light, the granules concentrate, leaving the crystalline cone and rhabdom exposed to more light, enhancing the light-gathering ability of the eye. Movement of these pigments helps the eye adapt to brighter or dimmer conditions. An increase in eye size increases sensitivity, so that animals in deeper waters tend to have proportionately larger eyes, as is also seen in deepwater fish. Also, as in fish, the visual pigments and sensitivity tend to match the color of the water, with estuarine animals being most sensitive in the green range and oceanic species being more sensitive in the blue range. Unlike fish, however, deep-sea crabs have not evolved bioluminescence to increase the amount of light in that dark environment.

Hearing

Some crabs can communicate using sound. Since crabs can produce sound, it makes sense that they would have a way to hear it. Crabs, however, do not have a structure you would call an ear. When we hear, our ears detect sound waves, which are changes in air pressure. Crabs do a similar thing, but they pick up changes in water pressure using microscopic hairs all over their shell. Several different types of hairs are connected to nerves that connect them to the central nervous system. The hairs concentrated on the legs respond to vibrations or changes in water pressure and function in hearing.

It has been shown that hearing plays an important role in behavior of larval crabs. Coral reefs are noisy places, with shrimp snapping and fish grunting and chirping. But it wasn't known whether larvae of various organisms respond to these sounds. Stephen Simpson of the University of Bristol found that larvae of fish and corals are attracted to the noise of the reef, which for them is an attractive place to settle. It was a different story with crustaceans. When pairs of traps were set at a distance from the reef, one trap with reef noise pumped in and the other silent, most crustacean larvae avoided the noisy trap, probably to steer clear of predators or habitat unsuitable for them. Only the larvae of crab species that normally settle on reefs were more abundant in the noisy trap. The types of crab larvae caught in the quiet trap lived as adults primarily in the open water or in bottom sediment, rather than in reefs.

Smell

Crabs are capable of detecting minute amounts of chemicals in the water, using an acute sense of olfaction, or smell. Tiny structures called *sensilla* on the outside of the shell provide information about chemicals in the environment—a process known as *chemoreception*. Though located in many places, the sensilla are most concentrated on the first antennae (antennules), the dactyls (last segment) of the walking legs, and the mouthparts. Having smell sensation in the dactyls lets crabs detect food hidden in the bottom sediments (e.g., sand or mud). The antennules are very sensitive to odors of chemicals in the water. The sensilla on setae (hair like processes) projecting out from the surface of the exoskeleton respond to a wide array of substances in the water. They are particularly receptive to extracts of food organisms (feeding stimuli) and sex pheromones at extremely low concentrations—less than a picogram per liter—that's one trillionth of a gram, or one part per quadrillion! Flicking movements of the antennules allow the odor to have better access to the receptor; the muscles of crab antennules have the fastest twitch times of all crustacean muscles.

Terrestrial crabs have similar systems, using air rather than water as the medium for the chemicals (although, interestingly, the larvae of land crabs can detect molecules in solution, whereas adults can only do so in air). This sense of smell allows them to detect hidden food. How do land crabs do this? Markus Stensmyr of Sweden and colleagues found that adult land hermits have evolved an olfactory sense that is very different from that of marine crustaceans but resembles that of insects in many ways—anatomically, physiologically, and behaviorally—though it is much less sensitive.

Taste

Chemical receptors for odors and for taste are similar, but the sensilla on the antennules are considered organs of smell because they detect stimuli from a distance away, while those on the mouthparts and dactyls of the legs are considered taste receptors because they detect stimuli that are close or in direct contact. Having sensilla on the dactyls is like having taste buds on your toes. Dactyl chemoreception is the primary sense involved in food detection. Thomas Trott, Rainier Vogt, and Jelle Atema of the Marine Biological Laboratory in Woods Hole, Massachusetts, studied responses of chemoreceptor cells on the dactyls of fiddler crabs to various chemicals. They found that the cells responded to compounds that occur naturally in salt marshes, such as algal and animal constituents, exudates, and decomposition products; these materials would be found in the sediments that the crabs process to get their food.

Touch

A mechanoreceptor is a sensory receptor that responds to mechanical pressure or distortion. Within the flexible parts of the crab cuticle are mechanoreceptors consisting of nerve cells that are sensitive to bending of the cuticle. These organs consist of modified sensory hairs (setae) that project above the

---

FEELING PAIN

Crabs not only have a sense of touch, but research from 2009 suggests that, contrary to previous belief, they can feel and remember pain. Robert Elwood and Mirjam Appel from the School of Biological Sciences at Queen's University, Belfast, studied reactions of hermit crabs to small electric shocks. Wires were attached to shells to deliver small shocks to the crabs' abdomen. Only crabs that received shocks moved out of their shells, indicating that the experience was unpleasant for them. The main aim of the study, however, was to then deliver a shock just under the level that would cause crabs to leave their shell to see what happened when a new shell was offered. Indeed, after receiving this lower-intensity shock, crabs were more likely to abandon their old shell and trade it in for a new one. Crabs that had been given the first shock but had remained in their shell appeared to remember that unpleasant experience because they quickly moved toward the new shell when offered.

surface of the exoskeleton. The antennae are also sensitive to mechanical stimuli of various kinds—touch and vibrations—that can provide information about water movements. Crabs also have mechanoreceptors within their muscles that allow them to be aware of the position of the muscle and movements of their body. Inside the muscles, they have tension receptors that monitor the degree of contraction of the leg muscles.

CENTRAL NERVOUS SYSTEM

The basic plan of the nervous system of crustaceans reflects the segmentation of their bodies. While primitive crustaceans probably had a ganglion (group of nerve cells) in each segment of their body, this plan is modified in crabs. There is not a separate ganglion in each segment; rather the ganglia

---

USE OF CRABS IN NEUROSCIENCE

Crabs can be used as "model organisms" in biomedicine, especially in neuroscience, which involves studying the functioning of neurons (nerve cells) and their networks. Neuroscientists are interested in understanding how the structure and function of individual neurons control their connections and networks, and the crustacean stomatogastric nervous system is ideal for studying this. This system includes the stomatogastric ganglion (STG)—a group of about 30 large neurons sitting on top of the stomach, which are easy to record and continue to produce rhythmic motor patterns when removed from the animal and so can be studied externally. Studies of this system (commonly using the Jonah crab [*Cancer borealis*]) have led to a better understanding of how rhythmic motor patterns (which are found in a wide variety of animals) are generated. The crabs' nervous system is not only excellent for studying the neural basis of rhythmic behavior but also ideal for studying *neuromodulation*—a process in which chemicals called neurotransmitters regulate populations of neurons and change their excitability. The STG has few neurons but many neurotransmitters, including serotonin and dopamine, which are present in humans as well. Neuromodulation allows nerve cells to react in diverse ways and allows neural networks to behave differently in different situations. Understanding the roles of the various neurotransmitters is important for understanding how the nervous system works. Gaining a broader understanding will allow scientists to develop better insights into, and possibly treatments for, depression and other serotonin- and dopamine-related conditions.

have fused so that there are relatively few, large ganglia. In crabs, ganglia have fused into a single mass, the *thoracic ganglion*, from which nerves radiate out into the appendages. The thoracic ganglion connects to the brain (the supraesophageal ganglion) by two large nerves, which have slight swellings indicating the position of the stomatogastric ganglion, which supplies nerves to the foregut. Unlike in vertebrates, the nerve cord and ganglia are located ventrally, underneath the body, rather than dorsally (on the top).

COLORS AND COLOR CHANGE

The body color of crabs is produced by pigments in the exoskeleton or the epidermis just below it. In addition to producing colors, these pigments may also protect against heat and intense radiation. The upper (dorsal) side is richer in pigments than the underside, which is often white. Different types of pigments produce different colors: carotenoids (such as carotene) produce the bright red, orange, and yellow colors; carotiproteins make blue; melanins produce dark brown or black color, both in the body and in the compound eyes; and guanines produce white. Melanin, like sunscreen for humans, can protect the crab against the harmful effects of ultraviolet (UV) radiation.

Pigments are contained in cells called *chromatophores*. Each cell has a central area and many radiating, often highly branched, extensions. Different cells generally contain different types of pigments; for example, melanophores have black/brown pigments, leucophores white, erythrophores red, and xanthophores yellow. Pigment movements have been studied in crustaceans since the nineteenth century, with fiddler crabs being the most often studied. Pigment granules move within the fixed branched cells so that the pigment can disperse over a larger area or can be concentrated in a very small area (Fig. 3.2). Chromatophores respond to environmental factors. Generally, when there is more illumination, pigments—both dark and light ones—disperse more. Crabs may also have a diurnal rhythm in which they darken during the day and become pale at night, or they may change color in response to temperature, becoming lighter in warm temperatures and darker in the cold. Fiddler crabs concentrate their black pigment and disperse the white as the temperature rises, thus getting paler and decreasing absorbance, to regulate their temperature, similar to a person wearing light-colored clothing on a hot sunny day. The response to temperature occurs very quickly, suggesting that this color change is a direct response of the chromatophores to the temperature, rather than being mediated through hormones, which usually control color change.

Figure 3.2. Chromatophores (melanophores) on crab larva. Photo by Linda L. Stehlik.

The two other general ways in which crabs can change color are physiological and morphological. The movements of the pigments are controlled by hormones that make the crab lighter or darker. These hormones are produced in the eyestalks in a structure called the X-organ. If you remove their eyestalks, crabs will get paler. These relatively rapid color changes due to hormones are called "physiological" color change. The other way to change color takes a longer time—by changing the number, types, and distribution of chromatophores. This slower process is referred to as "morphological" color change.

Both types of color change allow the animal to adapt to or blend in with its environment. For example, animals get darker when maintained on a dark background. The ability to blend in with the environment is seen clearly in the kelp crab (*Pugettia producta*), which can be found in dense kelp beds and tide pools covered in sea grass or algae. This spider crab native to the Pacific Northwest has a unique, elongated carapace, resembling an upside-down shovel with the handle end in the front (Plate 15). Its color depends on the type of algae it consumes. In the low rocky intertidal zone, it eats kelp, sea lettuce, and rockweed, enabling it to be dark brown, olive green, or a mixture of the two, to blend in with the environment (cryptic coloration). This adaptation provides a natural camouflage. Another example is the colorful Sargassum crab (*Planes minutus*; Plate 16), associated with gulfweed (*Sargassum*). Its predominant color is brown, but it ranges from yellow to red, matching the color of the seaweed on which it lives. The brown may be broken up by white patches of various shapes and sizes, which appear to be an imitation of the white tubes of worms that also attach to the gulfweed.

Color pattern can have other functions beyond camouflage. Pigment can have a reproductive function; in some crabs the male becomes more brightly colored during the breeding season to attract females. Many species show variations in coloration over their range of distribution. For example, Japanese freshwater crab (*Geothelphusa dehaani*) may be dark brown, blue, or red. Dark brown crabs are found in the upper reaches of rivers, and blue crabs in the lower reaches. These color variants are genetically different from each other.

Coloration differences are also seen among individuals of the same species at the same location. In blue crabs (*Callinectes sapidus*), for example, females have red on the tips of their claws (see Plate 3), while males do not. Some studies suggest that male blue crabs choose mates partly based on the color of the female's red claws, indicating that they are able to see in color.

In some cases, colors may be a response to predators. Jan Hemmi and colleagues at the Australian National University looked at variations among fiddler crabs (*Uca vomeris*) from three different areas: one group was dull, another was colorful, and a third group had both dull and colorful individuals. They found differences in the numbers of crab-eating birds at the three locations, with few birds living where the crabs were colorful. They set up an experiment to test whether the crabs changed their color in response to the threat of being eaten. They set up a wooden screen between pairs of very colorful crabs living close together. One crab of each pair was subjected every couple of minutes to a fake bird (actually a small foam ball suspended on wire), while the control was left to go about its life normally. While the control crab remained colorful, the crab subjected to the "predator" changed its color to a duller, inconspicuous muddy shade.

There also may be differences between the colors of juveniles and adults. Alvaro Palma and Robert Steneck of the University of Maine found that newly settled rock crabs (*Cancer irroratus*) had a variety of colors. These multicolored crabs lived mainly in multicolored habitats where the color helps to make them inconspicuous to predators, another example of cryptic coloration. Experiments showed there were fewer of these multicolored types in single-colored habitats with predators or in multicolored habitats from which predators were removed. On the U.S. West Coast, red rock crabs (*Cancer productus*) are red as adults. However, as juveniles, they have a wide variety of colors and patterns. Green crabs (*Carcinus maenas*; Fig. 1.8) may not be green at all (perhaps why they are called "shore crabs" in England), but may be orange-red or brown (Plate 17 shows a brown-phase male). Orange and brown coloration is seen only in larger crabs that are in a prolonged intermolt period; they have more attached organisms on their shell and a thicker, stronger carapace. In contrast, green-colored crabs occur at all sizes, carry fewer attached organisms, and have a thinner carapace. The green ones appear to be actively molting forms. There are physiological differences between the two color variants. For example, orange crabs are less tolerant of low salinity. D. G. Reid and J. C. Aldrich of Trinity College in Ireland found that orange crabs also had less tolerance for low oxygen than green crabs; orange crabs in water with declining oxygen tried to move out of the water and had a higher death rate than green crabs when exposed to low oxygen.

Color can also change in response to the molt cycle, salinity, and exercise. The color is frequently brighter in the new shell shortly after a molt. Salinity can affect coloration of red king crab larvae. At lower salinity, red pigment concentrates in erythrophores, causing a reduction in red coloration. Crabs subjected to strenuous exercise may show a blanching and/or reddening of the body and legs, due to white and red pigment dispersing and black pigment concentrating. The pigment movements were induced by hormones present in the blood of exercising crabs. Blood removed from an exercised crab and injected into other crabs will change the color of the injected crab to match the exercised crab—proving that something in the blood (hormones) is involved in the process.

Diet can also alter the coloration of a crab. In addition to the kelp crab discussed above, this has been noticed mostly in pet hermit crabs The strawberry hermit crab (*Coenobita perlatus*) is one of the most colorful species of land hermit crab. The crab is generally a reddish orange color, but the intensity of the color depends on the crab's diet. Strawberry crabs that are fed adequate amounts of food containing carotene will retain their bright red color after they molt (crabs and most other animals cannot make carotene). If the crabs do not get enough carotene, they will become lighter after they molt.

CHAPTER FOUR

Reproduction and Life Cycle

Just about all crabs have distinct male and female forms, and some species show major differences between the sexes. You can tell a crab's sex by turning it upside down and looking at the abdomen. A mature male's is narrow and a mature female's is quite wide (see Fig. 1.2). Some species have additional differences, such as the enlarged claw of male fiddler crabs or the red tips on the claws of female blue crabs. The age and size at which crabs become sexually mature vary among species and geographic location. Some groups of crabs undergo a pubertal molt in which there is a major change in appearance, such as an increase in male claw size or a widening of the female abdomen. Hormones play an important role in sexual development. Development of testes in males is controlled by an androgenic hormone. There does not appear to be a female hormone; rather, femaleness is a default condition in the absence of the androgenic hormone. Genetics is only one factor responsible for the development of males and females, and a few types of crabs can change sex as they mature. Environmental factors such as day length, temperature, food availability, social conditions, and parasites can also play a role. For many crabs, reproduction is a seasonal event. Some, mainly tropical, crabs, however, may produce broods all year round, taking more sperm from storage following a single mating. Deep-sea crabs live in a nearly seasonless environment and may not have a particular reproductive season.

ANATOMY OF THE REPRODUCTIVE SYSTEM

Internally, the female's ovaries, which make eggs, connect to each other behind the foregut and may appear roughly H-shaped. From the ovaries, paired oviducts run forward and downward and then, in brachyurans, widen to form an oval-shaped seminal receptacle, which stores sperm from the male. The seminal receptacles, which can be very large, especially when full of sperm, lead to an opening on the sixth thoracic segment, from which fertilized eggs can be released. When ripe eggs are released from the ovaries and move down the oviduct, they may be fertilized in the oviduct or seminal receptacle.

In the male crab, testes, which make sperm, are a pair of slim glands that lead to the thinner, coiled vas deferens, where sperm are gathered in bundles called *spermatophores,* which are capsules that protect the fragile sperm against microorganisms and desiccation during transfer to the female. The spermatophores must pass through a long portion of the vas deferens before reaching the first pair of abdominal appendages (pleopods or swimmerets), which are elongated and grooved to aid in copulation. During mating, these appendages are inserted into pores in the female, and transferred sperm reach the seminal receptacle of the female where they are stored.

ATTRACTING A MATE

Crabs must communicate with each other—through chemical, visual, or auditory signals—to find a mate.

Pheromones—Sex Attractants

Many animals use chemical signals, called pheromones, to communicate with others of the same species. Many of these pheromones are sex attractants. Female blue crabs become sexually mature immediately following a pubertal molt, and they mate only once in their life. When approaching this pubertal molt, their urine contains a pheromone that attracts males when released into the water. Male blue crabs have a courtship display in which they elevate their body by standing high on their legs, open their chelae, and paddle their swimming legs. If a male can reach a female, he grabs her and guards her. If the female is not accessible because she is hiding in a refuge, the male creates a water flow toward the female by moving his swimming paddles (a behavior known as "courtship paddling"), sending his pheromone to lure her out from the refuge. Males may have to compete with each other; the winner protects the female until she molts. He carries her underneath him with his walking legs ("cradle carrying") and guards her for several days until she molts. He may move with her to eelgrass habitat where there is more protection. When she molts, he protects her by standing high up on his legs making a cage around her. During this molt, her abdomen changes from V-shaped to semicircular. When her new shell is still soft, they mate; she turns over on her back and unfolds her abdomen, exposing her genital pores. Copulation may last many hours, after which the male will continue to guard her for a few days (dorsal side up) until her new shell hardens.

These two characteristics—the release of pheromones by females and the timing of mating immediately after the female molts—are common traits found in many other marine crabs. In other portunids, king crabs, and Dungeness crabs, mating occurs between hard-shelled males and newly molted, soft-shelled females. Male Dungeness crabs find females by pheromones and then initiate a protective premating embrace (known as "grasping") that lasts for several days prior to mating. In this embrace, the female is tucked underneath the male, oriented such that their abdomens touch and their heads face each other. After mating, the male may remain with the soft-shelled female for 2 days to ensure her protection.

Pheromones have been chemically analyzed, and in some crabs that mate after the female molts, molting hormones (called *ecdysones*) themselves serve as the sex pheromones, doing double-duty. Some semiterrestrial crabs also utilize pheromones; for example, in small shore crabs (*Pachygrapsus* spp.), the sex pheromone is also a molting hormone. In helmet crabs (*Telmessus cheiragonus*), a test method has been developed to detect female sex pheromones based on the grasping behavior of males. This behavior is induced by urine from pre- and post-molt females, but not by other substances. The response was reduced when the outer branch of the males' antennules were removed, suggesting that this is the organ that detects the females' sex pheromones.

Visual or Acoustic Signals

Many terrestrial and semiterrestrial crabs use visual or sound signals, or both, rather than chemical ones. Fiddler crab (and other ocypodid) males wave their large claw to attract wandering females for mating. This oversized claw, seen only in mature males, can be up to 50% of the crab's weight. They wave it around in territorial and courtship displays; this waving motion is probably the reason they are called "fiddlers." Males of different species have specific patterns of waving to attract females (Fig. 4.1). When a female approaches a male's burrow, he makes additional movements of his claws and walking legs. In some species, a receptive female will follow the male down into his burrow

Figure 4.1. Waving fiddler crab (*Uca terpsichores*) by hooded burrow. Photo by Taewon Kim
(Kim TW, Christy JH, Choe JC, 2007. A Preference for a Sexual Signal Keeps Females
Safe. PLoS ONE 2(5): e422. doi:10.1371/journal.pone.0000422).

to mate, while other species mate on the surface; some species can mate in either location, depending on crab size and population density. Tropical fiddler
crabs seem to court throughout the year, while temperate species are dormant
in the winter and so have a much shorter opportunity for mating. Semaphore
crabs (*Heloecius cordiformis*) of Australia wave both of their claws, which gives
them their common name. The waving, similar to that of fiddler crabs, is both
to repel other males and entice female crabs to enter the male's burrow.

Some fiddler species also build a special type of burrow for mating. Males
carry excavated mud or sand to the burrow entrance and build a tubular structure termed a *chimney*, a small heap called a *pillar*, or an arched hood at the
side of the burrow (see Fig. 4.1). The male's burrow appears to play a major
role in a female's choice of a male for mating. John Christy of the Smithsonian
Institution found that females of *Uca beebei* were attracted to the burrows of
courting males more often when the burrows had pillars than when they did
not. Courting males of *U. musica* sometimes build hoods at the entrances of
their burrows; females of this species show a preference for hood builders.

Location, rather than appearance, of the burrows of male sand fiddlers
(*U. pugilator*; see Fig. 2.1) is important for attracting females because

burrows built in the sand may collapse when flooded by water. Females prefer to mate with males that have deeper, more stable burrows at higher locations. Christy found that males court from and defend higher burrows above the tide line, in which females will come to mate, release eggs, and reside for about 2 weeks while incubating their eggs. Larger males courting from burrows higher on the beach mated more often than smaller males with burrows lower down on the beach. Two separate but related factors seem to affect female preference: the size of the male and the location of his burrow.

Male ocypodids may supplement their waving with sounds produced by rubbing their legs together, thumping on the ground with their large claw, or drumming on the ground with their legs. These acoustic signals, performed by ghost and fiddler crabs, occur only during the mating season and enable courtship to take place at night. Male land crabs (*Gecarcinus*; see Plate 6) also make sounds to attract females, rapping their claws against the ground.

MATING AND SPERM STORAGE

The vast majority of brachyuran crabs have internal fertilization and mate belly to belly (as in the green crabs shown in Plate 17). The actual mating process may last for several days. The mangrove crab (*Aratus pisonii*), mates while balancing on a tree trunk, demonstrating a considerable amount of balance and dexterity. While most aquatic species mate right after the female molts and still has a soft shell, some aquatic crabs and most ocypodids, grapsids, and gecarcinids (the terrestrial and semiterrestrial families) mate when the female has a hard shell; a soft-shelled female on land would be very vulnerable to drying out or to injury. Snow crab (*Chionoecetes opilio*) females can copulate in either a soft- or hard-shelled condition. In all cases males produce a spermatophore. The elongated appendages (their first swimmerets, or pleopods) of the males place the spermatophore into a pair of depressions (genital pores) on the female that lead to the oviducts and seminal receptacle.

Females can store the spermatophore for some time before using the sperm to fertilize the eggs. A blue crab female (Plate 3), for example, stores the sperm for many months. Once her shell has hardened and the male releases her, she will migrate, sometimes a considerable distance, to higher salinity waters in the lower part of an estuary or at the mouth of a bay. Sperm can live in the female's reproductive tract for over a year and can be used to fertilize two or more broods. Males may mate several times, but they generally have less reproductive success at each mating because of decreasing sperm count. Males show little ability to regenerate sperm, so reserves are limited.

Sperm storage in females is thought to provide resilience to a population, especially when males may be scarce and females can rely on stored sperm for fertilization. This can happen when males are targeted in a fishery, such as the tanner crab (*Chionoecetes bairdi*; Fig. 8.1) in Alaska. As a conservation measure, many fisheries focus on males. Joel Webb of Alaska Fish and Game examined females that extruded eggs in the lab in the absence of males, and found that in almost half the females, stored sperm reserves were not adequate for full fertilization of a second egg clutch. Repeated mating, therefore, is important to maintain reproductive potential in this species. In contrast, female spider crabs (*Maja squinado*) held in aquaria without males produced broods successfully up to five times after a single mating.

Courtship behaviors of hermit crabs involve actions such as stroking, jerking, and shell-rocking. With their abdomens inside snail shells, both sexes must partially emerge to transfer the spermatophore from the male to the female. The size and shape of the snail shell can affect the crabs' ability to do this; some shell types make it difficult. Many anomurans, including hermit and king crabs, have external fertilization, where egg and sperm meet outside rather than inside the female's body, and females lack a sperm storage organ. Instead, female hermit crabs lay thousands of eggs (a process called *spawning*) and deposit them along the side of their abdomen, where the eggs develop protected inside the snail shell. In some hermits, the male guards the female prior to mating, grasping the edges of her snail shell. After mating, female coconut crabs and king crabs glue the eggs to the underside of their abdomen, similar to hermit crabs, and carry the fertilized eggs underneath them.

Marianna Terossi and colleagues compared reproduction of the hermit crab *Pagurus exilis* at the extremes of its geographic distribution (Brazil and Argentina) to see how geography affected aspects of reproduction. Reproduction in Brazil occurs year-round, while in colder Argentina it occurs only in spring and summer. Egg-bearing females were larger in Brazil than in Argentina and carried more eggs, but Argentina eggs were larger than the Brazilian. These differences may reflect adaptations to the local environment; production of fewer, larger eggs is a trend often seen in cold-water regions.

Adult female red king crabs (Fig. 1.13) first must molt in order to reproduce. A king crab male approaches a female that is close to molting and grasps

Figure 4.2. Female red king crab (*Paralithodes camtschaticus*) with egg mass (or "sponge") attached to the underside of her abdomen. Photo from NOAA.

her in a face-to-face position; they may stay together this way for several days until the female molts. The male may assist her in shedding the shell, then help her turn over so their ventral surfaces are close together. Spermatophores emerge from the male, and eggs from the female (43,000–500,000 of them), and the fertilization takes place externally on her abdomen, where the fertilized eggs will attach. The female holds the developing embryos underneath her tail flap for 11 months before they hatch (Fig. 4.2). Prolonged development times like this—almost a year—are common in cold-water species.

Mole crab (Fig. 1.5) males are much smaller than females. Two or three gather around a female before she lays eggs and may cling to her. They deposit ribbons of sperm in mucus on her underside, which will fertilize the eggs externally as she lays them. Some species of mole crabs change sex from male to female, so that there are two kinds of females in the population—primary females that were female all along and secondary females that started out as males. The sex reversal in secondary females occurs when they are about the same size as primary females who become sexually mature. This sex change increases the number of egg-laying females in the population, which may contribute to population growth. Sex change and hermaphroditism are common in some animals but are relatively rare in crabs.

EGG LAYING, DEVELOPMENT, AND HATCHING

The process of releasing eggs through the oviduct onto the abdomen is called spawning. Most female crabs keep their eggs underneath the abdomen, where they adhere to the small pleopods. The time between mating and egg-laying can vary from as little as 1 month to 2 years, depending on the species and on environmental conditions. Some species can release several different broods during a single molt cycle. Females of different species have different techniques for extruding eggs and attaching them to their swimmerets (pleopods). Some species partially bury themselves in the sand or mud, others elevate their body and lower their abdomen, "catching" the eggs as they are shed. Other species extend their abdomen backward and shed the eggs onto the substrate, then pick them up and attach them to the pleopods. While they develop, eggs are guarded, aerated, and protected until they hatch. Females carrying eggs are said to be "ovigerous" or "in berry," since the eggs resemble tiny berries; the egg mass is called a *sponge*. The eggs go through embryonic development while attached on the "berried" female (see Fig. 4.2). No additional eggs can be laid until the previous batch has hatched.

After mating, female blue crabs (Plate 3) spend the winter burrowed in the mud and release their eggs (i.e., spawn) the following summer. They extrude about two million fertilized eggs as a yellowish sponge, which remains attached to their abdomens, secured with a cement-like material, until the larvae hatch. As the embryos develop, the color of the egg mass darkens to orange, then brown, and finally black. Eggs hatch, and larvae are generally released over a period of minutes or a few hours, a relatively short time period that can be synchronized by the female vigorously pumping her abdomen in response to pheromones released from the hatching eggs. In this way, all larvae are released together. In Dungeness crabs, females also store sperm in a seminal receptacle until the fall when their eggs are fertilized and spawned. When the fertilized eggs are extruded, the sponge remains attached to the female. The eggs are initially white, but as they develop they turn pink, then red. A large female may carry in excess of 2.5 million eggs. Females carrying eggs usually bury themselves in sandy beaches during the fall.

The number of eggs (i.e., *fecundity*) increases as a female grows, so the largest females contribute the greatest number to the next generation. But there are differences, even among closely related species. Studying deep-sea lithodid crabs, S. A. Morley and colleagues from the British Arctic survey found that depth played a major role in reproductive biology. The highest fecundity and smallest egg size was found in *Paralomis spinosissima,* a shallow-water species, while the lowest relative fecundity and largest eggs were found in the deeper species *Neolithodes diomedeae.* These different reproductive "strategies" are an adaptation of reproductive traits to temperature and food availability.

Crab eggs are filled with yolk, and as development proceeds the outer-most portion of the egg divides into many cells, so there is a single layer of flattened cells surrounding a solid mass of yolk. Then, some of the cells migrate into the yolky interior (a process called *gastrulation*) where they give rise to different tissues of the embryo. The developing embryo is surrounded by two outer membranes, which rupture when the embryo is ready to hatch out and become a larva. The larva is very small, and floats in the ocean along with many other small organisms that are collectively referred to as *plankton.* Plankton includes microscopic photosynthetic organisms (the *phytoplankton*) and somewhat larger animals such as crab larvae (the *zooplankton*), which feed on the phytoplankton. In the zooplankton are larvae of most marine invertebrates that live as adults on the bottom, as well as many types of crustaceans and other animals that remain planktonic for their entire lives.

In intertidal crabs, females' reproductive cycles are timed with tides so that they release young at the best time for larval dispersal and survival. Larval release in many species is a one-time event; that is, each female sheds all her larvae within a few hours. Usually controlled by an internal biological clock, hatching is synchronized to occur at a specific time, often at night, co-inciding with ebbing high spring tides (particularly high tides caused by the pull of the sun and moon together) that sweep the larvae rapidly out of the estuary to the ocean. Larval release near the time of high tide and at night is common among crabs living in tidal areas. This timing moves the larvae away from areas where predation and the likelihood of stranding and exposure to low-salinity waters are high, and reduces the probability of predation on the females. In the case of mole crabs living in the surf zone, larger waves cause more rapid flushing of the water. Larvae released during large-wave events have a shorter residence time in the riskier surf zone.

M. C. DeVries and Richard Forward of Duke University brought a group of gravid mud crabs, *Neopanope* (*Dyspanopeus*) *sayi* (a subtidal species) and *Sesarma* (*Armases*) *cinereum* (an intertidal species), into the laboratory, kept them under constant low light for 5 days, and found that the release rhythm persisted, implying that the rhythm is an internal biological clock. Ovigerous striped hermit crabs (*Clibanarius vittatus*) were examined by Tracy Ziegler and Richard Forward of Duke University in the laboratory in constant conditions. They found that release of larvae was synchronous, occurring near the time of expected sunset. Crabs released larvae in bursts at sunset over several consecutive nights. When crabs with early-stage embryos were kept under a shifted light-dark cycle (advanced 12 hours so it was dark when it was light outside) before being placed under constant conditions, they advanced their larval release by 12 hours, showing that the rhythm was altered by the light-dark cycle.

In deeper water species, timing may be also affected by environmental cues. In his study of Alaskan tanner crabs, Bradley Stevens of the National Marine Fisheries Service found that most hatching coincided with the strongest tides. Individual crabs in the laboratory released larvae over a period of about 9 days, with most of the larvae hatching in the evening, suggesting that larval hatching is timed to take advantage of both tidal current patterns and times of reduced light, just as in shallower water species.

While many other species synchronize the hatching of their broods, deep sea scarlet and golden king crabs (*Lithodes couesi* and *L. aequispinus*) show extended hatching, taking place over many days or weeks. This may be an adaptation to the uncertainty and generally low level of food availability in the deep sea. After a batch of golden or scarlet king crab eggs hatch, females mate again, so that they are seldom without eggs. Many aspects of reproductive biology and early life stages of deep-sea lithodid crabs reflect adaptations to the cold environment. These include reduced egg numbers, increased egg size, and hatching of large and advanced larvae. Shortened larval development saves energy, and the larvae are resistant to starvation. The golden king crab, for example, skips some larval stages to save energy.

LARVAL DEVELOPMENT

Crab offspring hatch out into the water as tiny *zoeae*—free-swimming planktonic larvae that have a dorsal spine and a pair of large compound eyes (Fig. 4.3). The spines may help prevent them from sinking and also deter predation by small fish—they make the zoea effectively larger, and the sharp spine is an additional deterrent. When spines were experimentally cut off some zoeae, they were more likely to be eaten than intact larvae. Their thoracic appendages with numerous bristles are used for swimming.

The ability of planktonic larvae to float and harness water currents is a way for animals to increase dispersal. The amount of dispersal depends on the currents and how long the larvae remain in the plankton, which varies among species from weeks to over a year. Having dispersing larvae enables a species to settle in new areas, reduces the risk of population extinction

Figure 4.3. Zoea larvae of fiddler crab (*Uca* sp.). Photo from NOAA.

from unpredictable events in the home area (such as an oil spill), and reduces competition for space. Disadvantages of planktonic larvae include a very high risk of getting eaten, the possibility of getting moved into unfavorable areas, and uncertainty about food availability. Overall, the advantages of planktonic larvae apparently outweigh the disadvantages because this is the most common mode of life, not only for crabs, but for most benthic marine invertebrates. The major risk is the threat of predation. Larvae are small and numerous (female crabs may hatch thousands to millions), and many animals feed on them. They are an essential part of the food web, playing a significant role in maintaining healthy finfish stocks. The situation is particularly dangerous in estuaries, which are nursery grounds for many fish. Strategies to cope with the risk of predators include defense and avoidance. Larvae that remain in estuaries tend to be larger than those that develop in the open ocean, and they have larger spines and other protective structures that make them more difficult to eat. Larvae also sink to darker, deeper waters during the day to protect themselves because most fish need light to hunt, and they come up to shallower water at night to feed. This diurnal vertical migration is the main predator-avoidance strategy for larvae of all kinds of animals in the open ocean. On a larger scale, most larvae of estuarine invertebrates leave the estuary altogether and develop in the open ocean, which has fewer fish and other predators.

Since all larval stages must live in the water, female land crabs must undergo lengthy migrations from inland sites that may be miles away to release their larvae. A female *Gecarcinus* (Plate 6) stands high on her claws at the water's edge and, as a wave covers her, moves up and down so that the larvae are washed off; she then scoots back up the beach, clearly not liking to be wet. Other terrestrial species seem to be even less willing to get wet in the process of releasing larvae. Some land hermit crabs stand at the edge of the water and "shoot" or "spray" their eggs into the water to avoid immersing themselves, while others place the eggs on rocks at the edge of the water at low tide so they can be washed away when the tide rises. They know when the tide will be low and migrate down to the beach at the right time. Tree-dwelling grapsid crabs, such as some species of *Sesarma*, move to the edge of the mangroves, cling to aerial roots, and vibrate their abdomens to release their larvae into the water from above.

The terrestrial Caribbean hermit crab (*Coenobita clypeatus*; Plate 8) in some parts of Curaçao cannot get to the ocean because of high cliffs. In this situation, P. A. DeWilde found an amazing behavior: The females pick off clumps of larvae from their abdomen with their fifth walking legs (the little ones inside the shell), pass them forward to the claws, and toss them off the cliffs into the water down below. In the lab, these crabs were seen to throw their clumps of larvae a considerable distance.

The duration of embryonic and larval life varies from a few weeks to over a year. Egg development may take many months in the deep, cold water. In Alaska, larval development of Dungeness crabs takes up to 1 year. For the snow crab (*Chionoecetes opilio*) in the Gulf of St. Lawrence where the water temperature is around the freezing point, embryo development takes a full 2 years. Golden king crabs incubate their egg clutches for about a year, and then wait almost 2 years to produce another.

For terrestrial crabs, larval life is generally short, about a month in *Gecarcinus*. Freshwater crab embryos generally hatch directly into crablike form, bypassing planktonic larval stages altogether, with the female carrying around the miniature adults for several days after they hatch. This life history limits their dispersal ability. Bromeliad crabs (*Metapaulius depressus*; Fig. 4.4) of Jamaica are unusual in that they live their entire lives in small pools of water in bromeliad plants up in a tree and they have zoeal stages; they are unique in that they provide care for their young. They have relatively few (less than 100) large eggs that hatch into zoea larvae within the water reservoir in the plant and pass through a shortened development (9–10 days). The young crabs remain in the plant "nurseries," where the mother crabs continue to feed and tend to them for several months. Rudolph Diesel of the University of Bielefeld, Germany, found that the mother crabs remove leaf litter and other debris, circulate the water to add oxygen, and bring empty snail shells to the water to buffer the pH and add calcium. The removal of debris (except for snail shells) improves water chemistry in the nurseries, increasing the oxygen levels, while the snail shells raise the pH of the water, preventing it from becoming too acidic for the larvae. Females also defend their young against predators, mainly damselfly nymphs and spiders, and feed them prey (snails and millipedes) that they catch on the bromeliad, rip into pieces, and carry into the nurseries to feed the young. This unique caregiving behavior means that unlike the typical female crab, who lays huge numbers of eggs and never sees them again as the larvae fend for themselves, bromeliad crabs can succeed by raising just a few babies.

Meanwhile, back in the ocean, zoea larvae have no mother to care for them and need to find their own food; in most cases they are carnivorous, eating smaller zooplankton, which provides them with needed protein, although some species eat phytoplankton. Dietary requirements vary for different stages and different environments. Species that eat plankton (referred to as *planktotrophic*

Figure 4.4. Bromeliad crab (*Metapaulius depressus*) on bromeliad leaf. Photo by S. Blair Hedges.

larvae) depend on the seasonal supply of plankton in the surface water during the spring blooms to survive. Some anomurans such as golden king crabs and some hermit crabs provide enough yolk in their eggs that the larvae don't have to eat, but live off this yolk, losing weight as they develop. This is called *lecithotrophic* development (*lecith-* refers to yolk, *trophic* to feeding). Such organisms can be raised without eating anything during their entire larval life. Crabs with lecithotrophic larvae generally produce larger and fewer eggs with greater amounts of nutrition provided to sustain the larvae. Some of these larvae may live at or near the bottom and, since they are not dependent on spring blooms for food, can be produced any season of the year. The golden king crab releases its larvae in waters deeper than where adults live, which suggests that adults would eat the larvae. Larval life in the cold deep water is hard enough without needing to find food, which is not abundant. When these larvae run out of yolk, however, they need to metamorphose quickly to avoid starvation. If they metamorphose far from a suitable settlement site, they will die. When scientists raised blue king crab zoea, they found zoea did need food, but the next larval stage (called *glaucothoe*) did not need to eat. In contrast, the lithodid crab *Paralomis spinosissima*, which lives in deep water off South Georgia in the southern Atlantic Ocean, appears to have lecithotrophic development throughout its entire 14-month larval period, as shown by Sven Thatje and Nélia C. Mestre of the University of Southampton, England. Deep-sea crabs have very slow development, slow growth, and long lives.

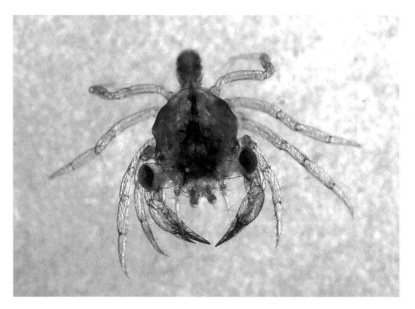

Figure 4.5. Megalopa larva. Photo from NOAA.

Zoea larvae go through several molts (the number depends on the species), and as they grow they develop more spines and appendages; specialists can identify not only which species a zoea is but also which stage. Zoeae metamorphose into a megalopa stage (or glaucothoe stage in anomurans). The megalopa larva has large, stalked eyes and looks like a miniature adult crab except that the abdomen retains its appendages and is not tucked up underneath but extends out behind (Fig. 4.5). After one more molt, the abdomen of brachyurans gets tucked underneath, and the crab, now having completed its planktonic larval life, becomes a juvenile and settles out from the plankton to live on the bottom. The thoracic appendages now are adapted for walking rather than swimming. Even though it is still tiny, it is recognizable as a crab. The glaucothoe of the hermit crab *Pagurus* is initially free-swimming, but then takes over a tiny snail shell before its next molt. The percentage of larvae that survive to become juveniles is generally tiny because most of them become food for bigger animals. It is estimated that of the two million eggs produced by a blue crab, only two will survive to reproduce, thus maintaining a constant sized population.

Scientists have long wondered how the tiny larvae of species that live in estuaries as adults can return from the ocean to the estuaries: How do the larvae return up the estuary and prevent themselves from being swept back out to the ocean when the tide goes out? Larvae undergo vertical migrations to deeper water where they can get more flow up the estuary during incoming tides. While blue crab zoeae tend to swim near the surface, sweeping them seaward to the oceans, the returning megalopae go deeper and get transported back upstream on incoming flood tides for return into the estuary. This may explain why freshwater species generally bypass the larval stage altogether, since the perpetual downstream river currents would make it impossible for larvae to return upstream. Eggs of freshwater crabs are larger and fewer than those of marine crabs, and they undergo larval development within the egg. When the eggs hatch, tiny crabs emerge rather than larvae. The tiny crabs may cling to the mother for several days.

SETTLEMENT, METAMORPHOSIS, AND EARLY CRAB STAGES

Return of larvae into the adult population—a process called *recruitment*—is essential for a population to continue. Larvae need to settle out and metamorphose in an appropriate location where they can find food and shelter from predators. In some species, larvae are attracted to adults of the same species, which ensures that they are in a good habitat (provided the adults are not cannibalistic). Semiterrestrial species such as fiddler crab larvae settle in marshes, the habitat of adults. Julie Anderson and Charles Epifanio of the University of Delaware exposed megalopae of the Asian shore crab (*Hemigrapsus sanguineus*; Fig. 4.6) in the lab to different stimuli and found that metamorphosis is promoted by cues from various sources including adult shore crabs, biofilm (i.e., slime) covering rocks in natural habitat for this species, and rocks from the natural habitat, even without attached biofilm. This crab's response to various cues, particularly rocks in the absence of adults, helps this species colonize new habitats and helps explain the rapid spread of this invasive species (see Chapter 7).

Initial growth of juveniles is very rapid, with individuals molting around five or six times in the first month. After blue crab megalopae settle and metamorphose into the first crab stage, they start moving up the estuary into less saline water. They grow within shallow coves with fringing marshes, sea grasses, and abundant food, foraging in shallow water where there are fewer predators, and they often move to coarse woody debris to obtain refuge during molting. They spend over a year developing from egg to mature adult.

Figure 4.6. Asian shore crab (Hemigrapsus sanguineus). Photo from U.S. Geological Survey.

After zoeal and megalopal stages in the ocean, juvenile land crabs must carry out in reverse the adult migration to the ocean. These very small crabs must find their way out of the ocean, across the beach or rocks, and migrate uphill, often hiding under rocks or in detritus. Megalopae of coconut crabs leave the sea carrying snail shells for protection. They also prefer a humid environment, so high humidity and the availability of shells and shelters stimulate them to emigrate from the sea.

GROWTH AND MOLTING

To grow, crabs and other crustaceans must shed their outer shell (exoskeleton or *cuticle*), in a process called *molting* or *ecdysis*. (Shed shells often wash up on beaches, making casual observers think that lots of crabs have died, but if you look inside, there's "nobody home," and it is an empty shed shell, or *exuvium*.) The exoskeleton is made of *chitin*, a long-chain molecule of nitrogen-containing carbohydrate material and proteins, which is further hardened by calcium salts. The cuticle has three layers: the outermost layer made of protein, lipids, and calcium, and the middle and inner layers made mostly of chitin. The cuticle not only covers the whole outside of the animal, it also lines the front and back parts of the gut, so shedding it is a difficult and complicated process. The molt cycle consists of *premolt* (preparing for the molt), molting itself (*ecdysis*), *postmolt* (recovering from the molt), and *intermolt* (when none of these processes are happening and the crab can go about the rest of its life). When crabs are preparing to molt (premolt stage), they reabsorb calcium into the body and store it internally, then dissolve the inner layer of shell, making it thinner and weaker. Meanwhile, they lay down the soft, thin beginnings of a new shell underneath the old one. This new one is complete in all details. At molting, the softened, old shell cracks along a weak seam on the animal's back (Plate 21). The crab must now extricate itself from the old shell, taking along all of its mouthparts, gills, legs, eyestalks, and other body parts (including the lining of the foregut and hindgut). Imagine yourself in a suit of armor that cracks down the back, from which you have to get out without using your hands to pull—quite a daunting challenge. Some crabs have large claws with narrow bases; it would seem impossible to extract this large structure—even soft—through a narrow opening. They accomplish this by breaking down much of the claw tissue before molting. Crabs go through this difficult process twenty or more times in their lives. Some individuals do get stuck during molting and die. Upon molting successfully, the emerged crab has a very soft, bendable paper-thin shell that it expands rapidly by taking in a lot of water, making room for future growth before the new shell hardens. Hardening, which may take several days, takes place through "tanning" of the new chitin, redepositing the stored calcium salts and absorbing even more from the surrounding seawater. The calcium salts fill in the spaces between the chitin fibers and harden the shell. A newly molted crab is soft, immobile, and helpless, so most crabs take refuge in a burrow or under a rock before they molt. Crabs generally remain secluded without eating or moving until the new shell has hardened because many marine animals (and people) like to eat soft-shell crabs. Even otherwise peaceful fiddler crabs may make a meal out of an unfortunate tank-mate that molts in a tank without a hiding place.

Having to molt to grow seems inefficient from our human-centered point of view. A crab must spend much of its time and energy preparing for a molt, molting, and recovering from a molt. While soft, crabs are especially vulnerable and are easy prey unless they stay well hidden. This growth pattern

JAMES MICHENER ON CRAB MOLTING

The blue crab was the subject of a story titled "Jimmy the Crab" by James Michener within his novel *Chesapeake*. Jimmy had to go through his molt during a hurricane and experienced problems when large amounts of fresh water moved farther down the bay, causing the salinity to become very low. Michener describes molting very effectively:

> Swimming easily to the bottom of the bay, he found a sandy area, a place he would never have considered for a moult in normal times, and there began his gyrations. First he had to break the seal along the edge of his present shell, and he did this by contracting and expanding his body, forcing water through his system and building up a considerable hydraulic pressure that slowly forced the shell apart. . . . Now he began the slow and almost agonizing business of withdrawing his boneless legs from their protective coverings and manipulating them so that they protruded from the slight opening. With wrenching movements he dislodged the main portion of his body, thrusting it toward the opening, which now widened under pressure from the legs. He had no skeleton, of course, so that he could contort and compress his body into whatever shape was most effective, but he did continue to generate hydraulic pressures through various parts of his body so that the shell was forced apart. Three hours and twenty minutes after he started this bizarre procedure, he swam free of the old shell and was now adrift in the deep waters of the bay, totally without protection . . . no covering thicker than the sheerest tissue paper, no capacity for self-defense. . . . And yet, even at his most defenseless moment his new armor was beginning to form. Eighty minutes after the moult he would have a paper-thin covering. After three hours he would have the beginning of a solid shell. And in five hours he would be a hard-shelled crab once more, and would remain that way until his next moult.

nevertheless works well, given that it is the way of life not only for crabs but for all arthropods, which, since they include insects, are the most successful and abundant animal phylum on the planet.

It is possible to tell if a blue crab is getting ready to molt by examining the next-to-last segment of the swimming leg. Here you can see whether the cuticle is beginning to separate from the tissue beneath by changes in color. "White sign" crabs, with a white color around the edge (the first faint outline of the new exoskeleton forming underneath) will molt in about 2 weeks, "pink signs" will molt within 1 week, and "red signs" will molt in a day or two. This is extremely useful information for crabbers in Chesapeake Bay who can keep the crabs until they molt and then market the desirable soft-shell crabs for a lot more money.

Molting also helps crabs to live successfully in a contaminated environment. Lauren Bergey, a graduate student who worked in my laboratory, measured the levels of metal contaminants in the shell and inner tissues of fiddler crabs during intermolt stages and immediately after they had molted. She found that crabs, particularly ones from a highly polluted area, moved toxic metals such as lead and mercury from their soft tissues into their exoskeleton shortly before shedding it. This allowed the crabs to naturally rid themselves of lots of contaminants. We need to determine whether crabs in the wild benefit from this process, given the possibility that they might eat the shed exoskeleton and recover all the contaminants again.

Terrestrial crabs have different strategies for collecting the water that is needed to stretch out the new cuticle after molt. They can use the water at the bottom of their deep burrows (e.g., *Cardisoma*; Fig. 2.8), seal themselves in a damp burrow (e.g., coconut crabs; Plate 1), or accumulate water from damp sand during premolt and store it internally in structures called *pericardial sacs* (e.g., *Gecarcinus*; Plate 6), which are pouchlike organs at the back of the gill chamber that are enlarged in land crabs. In this process, water can be collected when available, stored, and eventually used to stretch the new shell when needed.

After molting, a crab's size can increase by over 20%, and this increment may or may not decrease over time as the animal grows. The increment will be less if there is an inadequate food supply. Some species consume the old shell after shedding it and regain whatever nutrients (and contaminants) are left in it. The length of the various stages of the molt cycle and the frequency of molting depends on the species and size of the individual. Small individuals that grow rapidly go through molt cycles frequently, spending most of their lives either preparing for a molt, molting, or recovering from a molt. Larger individuals grow and molt more slowly; some molt only once a year or even less often. The intermolt period varies greatly and is influenced by environmental factors such as food supply, temperature, and parasites. Females incubating embryos do not molt. Some groups, such as cancer crabs, apparently can go on molting and growing indefinitely, while others, such as swimming crabs and spider crabs, have a "terminal ecdysis" when they

CRABS IN KIPLING'S *JUST SO STORIES*

Kipling's "The Crab That Played with the Sea" is one of his *Just So Stories*. The giant crab in this story, Pau Amma, goes to the bottom of the sea and causes turbulence and flooding. A magician punishes him for this disturbance, causing him to lose his shell and become vulnerable, but a compromise is reached so that he becomes smaller in size and in exchange is given "a scissors." At the end of the story, Kipling explains crab behavior:

> You can see when you go to the beach, how all Pau Amma's babies make little Pusat Taseks [the heart of the sea] for themselves under every stone and bunch of weed on the sands; you can see them waving their little scissors; and in some parts of the world they truly live on the dry land and run up the palm trees and eat cocoa-nuts, exactly as the girl-daughter promised. But once a year all Pau Ammas must shake off their hard armour and be soft—to remind them of what the Eldest Magician could do. And so it isn't fair to kill or hunt Pau Amma's babies just because old Pau Amma was stupidly rude a very long time ago.

reach a final maximum size and never molt again. One advantage of molting is that a new, clean and uninjured shell can replace an old, battered and cracked one.

Hormones control the molt cycle. Molt-inhibiting hormones are produced in the eyestalks in a structure called the *X-organ*, which is located near the sinus gland. Molt-promoting hormones (*ecdysteroids*) are produced in another gland called the Y-organ, located in the front of the head. (In species with a terminal molt, the Y-organ degenerates after this final molt.) The balance between these opposing hormones determines the stages of the molt cycle. Environmental conditions affect the balance of the hormones; darkness, solitude, moisture, and warmth (factors found in the bottom of a burrow) promote molting. Until the 1950s it was thought that the sinus gland produced the molt-inhibiting hormones, but this was discovered to be only the storage place, whereas the X-organ, made up of nerve cells, actually produces the hormones. This discovery was one of the first cases found of *neurosecretion*, in which nerve cells produce hormones. Since then, neurosecretion has been found to be a com-

OPPIAN ON MOLTING

Crabs were known to the ancient Greeks. In ca. 170 AD, the poet Oppian described in *Halieutica* molting and the lack of activity while crab's new shell is still soft:

All those whose body is set beneath a shell put off the old shell and another springs up from the nether flesh. The Pagurus, when they feel the violence of the rending shell, rush everywhere in their desire for food, that the separation of the slough may be easier when they have sated themselves. But when the sheath is rent and slips off, then at first they lie idly stretched upon the sands, mindful neither of food nor of aught else, thinking to be numbered with the dead and to breathe warm breath no more, and they tremble for their new-grown tender hide. Afterwards they recover their spirits again and take a little courage and eat of the sand; but they are weak and helpless of heart until a new shelter is compacted about their limbs. (Translated by A.W. Mair)

mon process in many groups of animals, including humans. The eyestalk system in crabs is the major neuroendocrine control center, comparable to our pituitary gland, which controls not only the molt cycle but also color change, sexual maturation, light adaptation in the eyes, and carbohydrate metabolism.

In addition to regular incremental growth, crabs often change shape as they grow, which is called relative, or *allometric*, growth. Changes can be gradual with each molt or sudden at a single molt, such as that between the megalopa larva and first juvenile stage. In some groups, there is a pubertal molt that marks sexual maturity with clear anatomical changes such as when the female's abdomen widens considerably to accommodate and protect the future eggs. The development of asymmetric claw size is another example of shape change that occurs in many groups in which one claw becomes a crusher and the other a cutter. An extreme case is the increase in growth of one claw of male fiddler crabs. For most species in which the two claws are not identical, there is no preferential handedness; the exceptions are two families of anomurans, one (Paguridae) right-handed and the other (Diogenidae) left-handed.

AGING CRABS

Knowing the ages of the members of a population is important for understanding its ecology and potential future population growth. In the case of commercial species, this information also is essential for resource management. In some organisms such as trees or fish, age can be determined by examining hard parts that show growth rings that accumulate over time and can be counted to establish age. However, this is impossible with crustaceans, which discard any growth history each time they molt. It is therefore very difficult to estimate their ages accurately. By using captive individuals or tagging crabs in the field, it is possible to determine the amount of growth at each molt and how often that species molts. This allows a correlation between size and age, which can then be used to estimate an animal's age from its size. Growth curves can be used to predict future growth, but these are just estimates. Many common species like blue crabs and fiddler crabs live only for 2-3 years. Japanese spider crabs (*Macrocheira kaempferi*; see Fig. 1.14), the largest crustaceans in the world with a leg span of almost 13 feet, a carapace width of 15 inches and a weight of up to 44 pounds, are believed to live up to 100 years.

Biochemical techniques are being developed that can greatly improve the accuracy of age estimates. Se-Jong Ju, David Secor, and Rodger Harvey of the University of Maryland's Chesapeake Biological Laboratory found that the fluorescent pigment lipofuscin accumulates in the nervous system as a blue crab ages, so the amount of this pigment is proportional to the crab's age. This finely granular yellow-brown pigment is considered one of the aging or "wear and tear" pigments. These researchers determined the rate of lipofuscin accumulation in crabs of known age reared in the laboratory. Measuring the amount of lipofuscin in crabs caught in nature and comparing it with the amounts in crabs of known ages thus provides a useful technique for aging crabs. This technique should be of great use. Perhaps now we can learn if Japanese spider crabs really do live to be 100 years old.

Crabs do have many mechanisms that promote longevity, such as molting, renewal of tissues by lifelong stem cell activity, regeneration of appendages, detoxification of environmental pollutants, and isolation of pathogens and diseased tissue. Age-related diseases including cancer—despite the shared name—are virtually unknown.

CHAPTER FIVE

Behavior

To study the behavior of aquatic animals, you can either bring them into the lab or watch them in their own environment while snorkeling or scuba diving. Although an enormous amount of information has been learned about the behavior of fish by means of underwater observation, crabs tend to be more secretive and less abundant in coral reefs, where so many of the fish behavior studies have typically been done. In estuaries, the home of many species of crabs, water tends to be murky so underwater observations are difficult at best, and deep-water observations are rare and logistically very difficult. This is one reason why so much study of crab behavior has been done on semiterrestrial crabs such as fiddler crabs, which are out of the water at low tide. You can visit a marsh or mangrove area, put down a lawn chair (someplace where it won't sink in the mud), slather on your sunscreen and bug repellant, sit quietly with your binoculars, camera, pencil and paper, tape recorder, and laptop, make your observations, and collect your data. At first, all the crabs will run into their burrows, but if you sit quietly and don't make quick movements, they will reemerge and go about their business as if you weren't there.

FEEDING

Different species of crabs have very different diets: some are scavengers, some eat plankton, and many others eat primarily clams or other bivalve mollusks, or even catch fish, other crabs, or baby sea turtles. Chemoreception is an important way for crabs to detect their food (see Chapter 3). They pick up food with their claws and pass it to their mouthparts, the maxillipeds, maxillae, and the mandibles. Maxillipeds and maxillae manipulate the food, and mandibles grind it and reduce it to a size suitable for swallowing. Different types of feeding are described below.

Deposit Feeders

Deposit feeders feed on the organic matter in sediments. Fiddler crabs are considered surface deposit feeders, processing the sediments in which they live, extracting detritus, bacteria, and algae from the marsh surface. Females, with two feeding claws, can feed faster than males, which have only one feeding claw (the male's large claw is useless for picking up food). Using their small claw, or both claws in the case of females, they scoop up mud and transfer it to their mouths, where mouthparts separate edible material (algae and detritus) from sand, silt, and clay. Water floods the mouth, separating the lighter edible material from the sediment particles by flotation. Flat-tipped hairs (called *setae*) on the mouthparts sort the material, and sediment particles are returned to the marsh surface. Species adapted to sandier sediments have spoon-tipped setae that are believed to help in scouring food from the sand particles. Crabs that feed in sandy sediments have less food available than those that feed in muddier sediments with more organic material. We studied different species in Indonesia that lived near each other and found that the species in the sandiest area (*Uca vocans*) had to spend most of their time running around and feeding in different patches of sand, expending considerable resources in the search for food. In contrast, those that lived in the muddiest area could afford to sit in one place and eat occasionally, presumably because each pinch of substrate provided more nutrition. These different feeding strategies are related to appearance as well as behavior. The species in the muddy area (*Uca chlorophthalmus*; Plate 18) that hardly moved at all was a conspicuous bright red. By remaining still, they might be mistaken for a red dead leaf and avoid the attention of potential predators. A third species (*Uca tetragonon*) lived near rocks where they could feed on attached algae. This provided good nutrition, so they spent more time on other activities such as digging burrows and waving to attract mates.

Herbivores

Plant material or algae is the major source of nutrition for many species of crabs in both marine and terrestrial habitats. Some species of algae provide more nutrition than others. Some plants may be difficult to digest, unpalatable, or deficient in nutrients such as nitrogen, vitamins, and fatty acids. For many crabs, a mixed diet of plant and animal matter results in the fastest growth and greatest fitness. Herbivores may prefer certain species of algae or other plants. Loren Coen of the University of Maryland investigated plant quality and food preferences of two small herbivorous spider crabs, *Mithrax scultptus* and *Mithrax coryphe,* using seven different plant and algae species. Crabs successfully consumed seaweeds that were leathery and those that had a hard covering. Crab feeding preference among the seven different food sources was influenced by plant chemistry (amount of noxious chemicals), differences in calories, the percentage of organic matter, and water concentration.

Herbivores may play important roles in the environment in which they live. As discussed in greater detail in Chapter 6, crabs that eat algae may play an important ecological role; for example, the spider crab *Mithrax forceps* eats seaweeds that would otherwise overgrow and smother the coral *Oculina arbruscula.* Leaf-consuming mangrove crabs help process litter in mangrove forests. Grapsid crabs are common in these forests, and their eating of leaves plays an important role in leaf degradation and nutrient cycling. However, the leaves may not provide all the nutrients the crabs need, especially nitrogen. Food is often limiting for "herbivorous" land crabs where dense populations can consume all available leaf litter. In such cases, these so-called herbivores can be found, when the opportunity arises, consuming animal matter (including other members of their own species).

Scavengers

Fiddler crabs' larger cousins in the family Ocypodidae, the ghost crabs (Fig. 2.3) of sandy ocean beaches, are considered scavengers that roam the beach, looking for tasty things to eat, including jellyfish, mollusks, mole crabs, dead fish, beached whales, and smaller ghost crabs. They undergo mass movements from the burrowing areas on the beach down to the intertidal zone for feeding; these mass movements, called *droving,* and are seen in some fiddler crabs as well. Ghost crabs can also be considered predators because they prefer fresh protein whenever they can get it. Once a year, when baby sea turtles are hatching, ghost crabs enjoy a special feast. They grab the hatchlings, drag them into their burrows, and devour them, apparently unaware of their protected status as endangered species.

Some species of fiddler crabs have also been seen to be carnivorous when the opportunity presents itself. Richard Milner and colleagues from Australian

National University observed *Uca annulipes* in a mangrove area attacking shrimp that were flipping themselves over the mud as their pool of water receded and they tried to reach another pool. Crabs of both sexes and all sizes pounced on shrimp and attempted to pin them down. The crabs attempted to grab the shrimp with their walking legs, as well as claws. These investigators also observed some instances of cannibalism, as we saw with *Uca minax* in our laboratory: students witnessed a large male "stabbing" an egg-bearing female with his enormous claw and proceeding to eat her eggs. This event was so shocking that they forgot to document it with photographs. Over the course of the summer, we found several other dead crabs with slits in their carapaces, a result of stabbings. This species has been previously known to attack and eat a smaller species, *Uca pugnax,* which shares the low salinity brackish marshes with them.

Land hermit crabs are opportunistic feeders, eating what they come across. They tend to hold a food item down with the major claw and use the minor one to pick off pieces of the food and transfer them to its mouth. The large coconut crab feeds by crushing and stripping with its major claw.

Filter Feeders

Porcelain crabs and mole crabs (Plate 10; Fig. 1.5), both anomurans, are filter feeders that capture plankton and other suspended material from the water with setae on their mouthparts or on their antennae. Mole crabs use their antennae, while porcelain crabs comb plankton and other organic particles from the water using long feathery setae on their maxillipeds, then scrape off the particles and put them into their mouth. These animals will also scavenge on the bottom for detritus. Some hermit crabs can also filter-feed using setae on their mouthparts or antennae.

Predators

Blue crabs (Plate 3) are large, highly mobile, voracious predators that eat fish, clams, and small crabs, including smaller blue crabs; juvenile blue crabs can make up over 10% of an adult's diet. Clams, oysters, and mussels are mainstays in their diet, as is a small amount of plant material. Because blue crabs are aggressive predators, their prey may restrict themselves to shallow water where they are less accessible. Cannibalism is not rare among crabs: many species have been observed doing it. Juvenile king crabs in culture readily cannibalize smaller juveniles or megalopae.

Species that feed predominantly on rapidly moving prey generally have fast, but weaker claws, whereas those specializing in thick-shelled mollusks have claws that are slower but stronger. Complex shell-opening behavior or specialized claw structures can sometimes compensate for limited crushing power. Crushing a clam or mussel shell generally involves applying a series of crushes with the claws around the shell until a weak spot is found. Crabs' claws are able to crush shells by generating extremely strong forces, among the strongest measured for any animal. The crusher claw of stone crabs, for example, can exert 19,000 pounds per square inch. Crabs in the family Calappidae (Plate 4) have one claw modified in such a way that they can crack off portions of snail shells so they can get to expose the snail or hermit crab inside. This claw modification involves development of a set of heavy teeth, one projecting downward and two projecting up so that when the claw is closed the teeth fit together.

Green crabs (Fig. 1.8) can learn to manipulate their prey to reduce the time needed to consume them, and they have several different ways of attacking bivalves and snails. Studies have shown that claw strength in crabs can respond to, and thereby potentially overcome, the strength of their prey's shell. Timothy Edgell and Remy Rochette of the University of New Brunswick, Canada, investigated whether differences in a snail's shell hardness could induce changes to a crab's claw size. They gave either thick- or thin-shelled periwinkle snails to green crabs. Crabs given thin-shelled snails tended to break the shells in order to eat them, while crabs given thick-shelled snails often poked their claw through the shell opening. However, the crab's crusher claws grew stronger as they crushed more shells, and crabs given the thick-shelled snails grew, after only two molts, larger crusher claws than those given thin-shelled snails. Mollusks, in turn, grow thicker shells when crushing predators such as crabs are nearby. In this way, an "arms race" develops between predators and prey.

Jessica Reichmuth, a former graduate student in my lab, studied a population of blue crabs from the highly contaminated Hackensack Meadowlands of New Jersey, and saw, in laboratory studies, that they were poor predators compared to crabs from a cleaner estuary. They were slower at capturing active prey such as killifish or juvenile blue crabs, though they were just as good at capturing less active (or inactive) prey such as mussels and fiddler crabs. She examined stomach contents and found that crabs collected from the Meadowlands ate a diet composed largely of sediment, detritus, and algae—an unusual diet for a predatory crab. This diet probably reflected their poor ability to capture active prey, as well as the scarcity of mollusks in the Meadowlands. Nevertheless, the crabs seemed to grow as well as those from the cleaner site, so they apparently got adequate nutrition from this diet. When they were kept in our laboratory and fed clean food, or were transplanted to the clean estuary for 2 months, their prey capture ability improved, showing that it was the environment that impaired their capture rate. Similarly, when crabs from the clean site were fed Meadowlands food or transplanted there for 2 months, they became poor predators.

Omnivores

Many species are not picky eaters and eat whatever is available. Dungeness crabs (Fig. 2.5) eat a wide variety of food, including clams, fish, and crabs, as well as starfish, worms, squid, snails, and eggs from fish or crabs. They are also cannibalistic, which has been observed in laboratories and supported by examination of stomach contents of crabs in the field. Dungeness crab populations are apparently not limited by the abundance of particular foods. They appear to eat mostly bivalves their first year, shrimp their second year, and small fish the third year; this dietary shift may be related to improvements in coordination and speed as they grow, so they can take on quicker and more nimble prey. It also serves to reduce competition among age groups. It may also be a strategic advantage to decrease the amount of time spent eating thick-shelled bivalves (mollusks), which can take a toll on claws and cause breakage and wearing.

Mud crabs (Fig. 1.9) are also omnivores, with marsh grasses, algae, and detritus serving as the major components of their diet, supplemented by the occasional fiddler crab or other animal. Marsh mud crabs are considered truly omnivorous, consuming both plant and animal tissue. Individuals eat fresh plant material, leaf litter, and fungi. When animal tissue is available, the consumption of vegetation decreases, and crabs grow faster on mixed diets.

Green crabs (Fig. 1.8) are especially hardy and eat shrimp, algae, detritus, small clams, mussels, worms, fish, and living marsh grass. They live in rocky habitats as well as in marsh environments, and they are efficient and effective feeders that can out-compete blue crabs of similar size for food. Calico or lady crabs (*Ovalipes ocellatus*) eat mostly mollusks and smaller crustaceans; their diet reflects whatever is most abundant in a particular area.

Like many deep-sea organisms, red deep-sea crabs (Plate 13) are opportunistic feeders, eating whatever they can find—a wide variety of bottom dwelling (benthic) invertebrates that they find in or on top of the soft sediment on the bottom of the sea. Smaller ones eat sponges, hydroids, snails, small polychaete worms, and crustaceans. Larger crabs eat similar small animals as well as larger prey such as deepwater fish, squid, and larger worms. The ability to eat fish suggests these crabs are very quick, well-coordinated predators. The finding of sponges, hydroids, and tunicates in the diets suggests that animals that attach to solid surfaces are also preyed on; such attached organisms are common in deeper rocky areas of the Gulf of Maine and in submarine canyons. Red crabs held in aquaria were observed to eat anemones by hovering over an anemone until it extended its tentacles, then reaching down with its claws and gently pulling off and eating one tentacle at a time until there were none left.

Most hermit crabs are scavengers, eating whatever they find, mostly dead plant or animal matter. Their fellow anomurans, the terrestrial coconut crabs; Plate 1), eat primarily fruit, including coconuts and figs. However, they will eat nearly anything organic, including leaves, rotten fruit, tortoise eggs, dead animals, and shells, which provide calcium. They may also eat live animals that are too slow to escape, such as other crabs or newly hatched sea turtles. Land hermit crabs tend to feed on vegetation, fruit, and detritus, but also will eat insects and carrion. When eating fruit, the crab holds the fruit against the ground with its major claw while the minor claw pinches off pieces of flesh. Land hermit crabs are unusual in that they actively drink water.

The land-dwelling brachyuran *Gecarcinus lateralis* (Plate 6) feeds on a variety of plant material and leaf litter, though they have been seen taking advantage of carrion such as dead toads on the ground. Mangrove crabs, previously thought to get nutrition from mangrove leaves, have been found recently to derive most of their nutrition from benthic organic material, although they do eat a lot of leaves.

Wood Eaters

It is surprising that some deep-sea species utilize food originally derived from land. Apparently, enough land plant material gets to the deep sea for some animals to make a living on it. The deep-sea galatheid crab *Munidopsis andamanica* is frequently found near wood falls in the deep. While some of the wood is from sunken ships, most wood falls are natural tree debris, as well as leaves and coconuts, all of which have sunk and reached the bottom. A careful examination of the feeding appendages, gut contents, and gut lining of crabs caught near wood falls by Caroline Hoyoux of the University of Liege and colleagues revealed that this species uses wood and the biofilm of bacteria covering it as its two main food sources, making them the termites of the deep sea. Like termites, they have bacteria and fungi in their digestive system that appear to be involved in the digestion of wood.

AVOIDING PREDATORS

Not getting eaten is obviously essential in an animal's life. Strong claws are useful not only for capturing prey but also for defense. Some species with small claws use symbiotic anemones in defense (see Chapter 6). Being armored (e.g., hermit crabs) or being camouflaged are other ways to repel or avoid being seen by predators. Other common methods of predator avoidance are burying in the sand or rapid flight, seen in swimming crabs.

Juvenile king crabs use the safety-in-numbers approach. Between the ages of 2 and 4 years, red king crabs rely less on habitat for protection and tend to form aggregations, or "pods" consisting of thousands of individuals (Fig. 5.1). Podding generally continues until they are 4 years old (at a size of about 2.5 inches). These pods of juvenile king crabs can be protective for any individual not on the group's edges, as the pods function similar to a school of fish. Alaskan spider crabs have also been seen to form huge pods. While this behavior protects the crabs from predators, it would make them especially vulnerable to trawl fishing, which can sweep up thousands of crabs at once. Trawling may have contributed to population declines of red king crabs in Alaska and is no longer allowed.

Another common antipredator behavior is to bury oneself in the mud or sand. Crabs that make burrows use them as a refuge from predators. Fiddler crabs run into their burrows whenever something appears, especially something high up like a bird. Diana Barshaw and Ken Able of Rutgers found that lady crabs (*Ovalipes ocellatus*) were able to bury themselves deeper in the sand, which protected them from blue crab predators. These predators captured juvenile blue crabs more easily instead because they did not bury themselves as deep as the lady crabs.

Once grabbed by a predator, a crab has yet another type of defense—it can break off claws or legs, an ability known as *autotomy*. Autotomy is a reflex, an automatic response to injury that separates an injured limb from the body, leaving the surprised predator holding only the limb, while the rest

Figure 5.1. Pod of juvenile red king crabs (*Paralithodes camtschaticus*).
Photo by Pete Cummiskey, NOAA.

of the crab runs away. A special muscle bends the limb in such a way that it breaks along a line of weakness near the base. Having a preformed breakage plane with two thin membranes minimizes injury and bleeding. The limb breaks so that one part of the double membrane comes off with the limb, and the other part remains with the stump, sealing it off and preventing bleeding. Autotomy also occurs during fights between crabs.

Some species are more likely to autotomize limbs than others. While hermit crabs readily autotomize and regenerate limbs, mole crabs (see Fig. 1.5) are reluctant to autotomize and, in a laboratory study, had difficulty regenerating limbs that were removed artificially. The anatomy of a mole crab, with its limbs tucked in beneath and protected by the overhanging dome-shaped carapace, makes it very unlikely to lose limbs in nature, so it has little need to autotomize compared with other crab species. Another anomuran that is unlikely to lose limbs is the umbrella crab (*Cryptolithodes sitchensis*; Plate 12), whose carapace extends out to conceal the legs from view. *Cryptolithodes* means "hidden rock," and, indeed, the winglike extensions of the carapace that hide the legs and claws make the crab look more like a rock to the untrained eye. They come in a wide variety of colors and patterns from white and gray to bright orange or pink. When they are among lots of colorful organisms such as sponges, brightly colored ones such as the one pictured in

Figure 5.2. Fiddler crab (*Uca pugnax*) regenerating a claw. Photo by P. Weis.

Plate 12 can blend in and be hard to find. They can also be found on surfaces they don't match at all, which is puzzling, as their camouflage has no advantage when not matched to the proper environment.

Although having missing limbs may put an animal at some disadvantage, it certainly beats getting eaten, especially since the limbs can regenerate. Regenerating limbs start out as small projections that grow in a folded position under a thin layer of cuticle (Fig. 5.2), and unfold only after the animal molts. The new limb is smaller and generally paler in color than nonregenerated limbs, and it reaches full size after two or three molts. If a crab loses many limbs at once, the molt cycle speeds up so they can regenerate and become functional sooner. The size increase at molt for crabs regenerating limbs is smaller than for intact crabs, since some of the energy and resources for growth go to the regenerating limb. Patricia Backwell and colleagues from the Smithsonian Institution found that *Uca annulipes* males with big claws do not pick fights with males with small, regenerated claws even though they are likely to win, and during the reproductive season, females do not discriminate against males with smaller, regenerated claws. Both of these observations were surprising, but good news for those regenerating claws, which comprised a significant number of the males. One common but erroneous idea (a myth perpetuated in some textbooks) is that if the large claw of a male fiddler crab is lost, the claw on the other side will enlarge. This is untrue; the regenerated claw is not as large as it was originally, but it will grow with each molt, so that after a few molts it will have regained its original size, while the other claw stays roughly the same size.

WALKING

Most crabs can walk in all directions, but often walk sideways using their eight walking legs powered primarily by muscles of the joint between the merus and the carpus. Muscles are attached to the inner surface of the exoskeleton of the legs. A muscle can contract and pull only to bend a leg; to straighten a leg, the muscle must relax and be pulled back by another, "antagonistic" muscle on the other side. The crab's legs pivot at joints that are covered with flexible chitin, and each joint can bend in only one plane (like a human knee). But since each leg joint bends in a different plane, all the joints used in conjunction with one another allow the crab to move in all directions. However, some crabs' leg joints are in a restricted number of planes, and they can move only sideways. As Aristophanes said, "You cannot teach a crab to walk straight."

The direction a crustacean walks seems to be related to whether the abdomen is extended out like a shrimp or lobster (walk forward) or tucked under like a crab (run sideways but still able to walk forward.) Crabs are generally wider than they are long. Having many pairs of legs creates the problem of keeping them coordinated when walking forward—this is avoided by walking sideways. Unlike most brachyuran crabs, hermit crabs typically walk forward, but using only six limbs—the pair of claws and the first two pairs of walking legs. The last two pairs of walking legs are small and modified for holding onto the inside of the shell.

The fastest crabs are the semiterrestrial ghost crabs (*Ocypode*; Fig. 2.3), which run rapidly with evasive changes of direction that would be the envy of any football player. They have been clocked at speeds of around 6 feet per second. The four trailing legs provide the principal thrust as they push the crab. A crab running sideways periodically turns 180 degrees so that legs that were pulling now push, and vice versa, to give the muscles a rest. As ghost crabs run progressively faster, however, they use fewer legs, keeping the last two pairs raised to allow for greater speed as the animal "leaps."

SWIMMING

While most crabs are adapted for walking on the sand or mud at the water's bottom, one group is especially adapted for swimming: the portunids, or swimming crabs. Their last pair of walking legs are flattened into swimming paddles (see Fig. 1.1) that have large, specialized muscles used for sculling—they rotate the paddles during both the up and down strokes. As a crab swims sideways, it sticks the elbow of the leading claw ahead for streamlining and leaves the legs of the opposite (trailing) side sticking out behind the body. Swimming sideways, a blue crab is streamlined like a submarine—pointed at each end. While this shape minimizes drag, the crab also gets lift from the shape of its carapace. Swimming is also seen in some grapsids and in pinnotherids (pea crabs), although neither is an optimum shape for it and neither has paddles. Mole crabs (see Fig. 1.5) swim using their uropods, the paired appendages at the tip of the abdomen, which are hinged in such a way that they can rotate.

COMMUNICATION

Crabs communicate with one another, generally about mating or aggression, and can signal through visual, acoustic, and chemical means (see Chapter 3). Visual signals (most commonly waving a claw) are used more by semiterrestrial crabs than aquatic ones. In water, where clarity may be poor, visual signals are useful only for individuals that are close to each other. In some cases, such as fiddler crab waving, the same signal may be used to attract females and to repel other males. Some species of fiddler crabs have different kinds of waves that communicate different information.

Some crabs can also make sounds. Sound production is common in many species of fiddlers during night-time low tides. Acoustic signals—clicks or snaps made by rubbing parts of the body together, a process called *stridulation*—are useful for distant as well as close range communication. Species that use stridulation have tubercles (little bumps) on the inner surface of a joint of the claw that rub against ridges on the front of the first walking leg. Crabs may also make sounds by vibrating the walking legs, striking the ground with claws or legs, or thumping the body against the substrate. Receptors to detect these signals are located on the legs of fiddler and ghost crabs. Sounds are produced only by male fiddlers and only during the breeding season. Sounds produced by one male can stimulate others in the neighborhood to join in.

Chemical communication by pheromones can be used during the day or night. Pheromones can travel considerable distances in the water, depending on the speed and direction of the currents. Those that are sex attractants are distinct substances, different from everything else in the environment and different for each species, so there is no confusion about who the message is for (see Chapter 4). Pheromones are released by females of some species when they are ready to mate; in certain species (e.g. blue crabs) males may produce pheromones as well.

AGGRESSION

Aggressive acts may include body postures (elevated or crouched), directed movements (e.g., a rush toward the other individual), raising walking legs, cheliped (i.e., claw) display, and cheliped contact. One very effective aggressive display is to hold the claws out to the sides, which may be accompanied by spreading the walking legs as well, making the crab look bigger. Aggressive postures in hermit crabs include moving one or both claws forward so they are sticking out in front and moving walking legs out to the side. Some species use sound signals. Male mangrove-dwelling grapsid crabs and land hermit crabs produce sound by stridulation during aggressive interactions. Acoustic signals may be an important aspect of the social behavior of these crabs.

Some species are more aggressive than others—the most familiar being the blue crab, whose behavior must have been the inspiration for the term "crabby." Larger ones can do serious damage if they pinch you. Some individuals and some populations of this species are more aggressive than others. When Jessica Reichmuth was studying blue crabs and brought individuals back to our lab, we were surprised when crabs collected from a new site (Hackensack Meadowlands) managed to create mayhem, killing and maiming each other in the bucket during the brief 20-minute trip. Various factors, such as population density, scarceness of resources, and pollution may be involved in causing behavioral differences. Behaviors related to being more aggressive include being less likely to enter a crab trap; those that did so could be killed by individuals that had entered earlier. Being aggressive can have negative ramifications for blue crabs, as another former graduate student

James MacDonald found. He set up a tank with hidden food (a mussel) buried in the sand, and introduced similar-sized blue and green crabs. A common outcome of this competition experiment was as follows: On seeing the green crab, the blue crab went into an aggressive display with its claws out. Meanwhile, the green crab scuttled in and got the food. The blue crab tried to get the food, but most of the time the quicker, green crab simply hunkered down over it and did not give it up. While blue crabs initiated fights more of the time, green crabs "won" the fights more often by just holding onto the food. Of course, blue crabs do eventually get bigger than green crabs and will then gain an advantage.

Other crabs that seem to be more peaceful, such as hermit crabs, nevertheless can set up dominance hierarchies. By studying interacting pairs of individual hermit crabs, Brian Hazlett of the University of Michigan found that the largest crab in the largest shell was at the top of the pecking order.

Aggressive encounters in hermit crabs are generally fights over empty snail shells. If none are available, a crab seeking a new shell may try to evict another crab, and these fights can be vicious. In *Pagurus bernhardus*, fights over shell ownership consist of the attacker "rapping" its shell against that of the defender in a series of bouts, while the defender remains tightly withdrawn into its shell. The fight can end either by the attacker evicting the defender, or by the attacker giving up and the defender keeping its shell. Mark Briffa and Robert Elwood of Plymouth University in England, who have studied this behavior in detail, found that the vigor of the shell-rapping is critical to the outcome of such bouts. The attacking crabs that "win" rap more forcefully, and rapping is more persistent when the quality of the desired shell is high. Attackers do get fatigued after bouts of rapping, however, and the rate and power of the raps decline over time and pauses between bouts get longer. Some defenders give up quickly, particularly if the raps are powerful. These defenders tend to have lower glucose levels than those that can resist eviction and stay in their shells. Glucose provides energy and is mobilized in an attempt to resist the attacker. A typical hermit crab would rather be torn limb from limb than be pulled out of its shell. In fact these battles sometimes do result in death. The only time a hermit crab willingly leaves its shell is when it locates a more suitable one, or if it is molting. Crabs that can't find a new shell may take up residence in other things such as worm tubes, hollow stems, film cans, or soda bottle tops to protect their soft abdomens.

In general, the outcome of aggressive encounters among crustaceans is usually that the larger crab or the one with larger claws wins; in some species, males win over females, but in other species sex does not matter. Other factors that have been observed are that recently molted crabs are more likely to lose, and hungrier crabs are more likely to win. Losing crabs generally retreat before they are seriously injured, although claw loss (autotomy) is pretty common.

TERRITORIALITY

Many crabs are territorial around their home. Fiddler crabs defend their burrows and chase away intruders (unless the intruder is a female, the burrow owner is male, and it is the breeding season). Since the burrow is the focus of most of their lives, the outcome of such fights can have major effects on the ability to escape from predators and on reproductive success. When a wanderer encounters a burrow owner, fighting involves pushing and gripping, and one of the crabs may be flipped over by the other. Territory owners often respond with greater aggression to strangers than to neighbors. Because strangers are usually wanderers seeking to acquire a territory, they pose a relatively greater threat than do neighbors, who are already territory owners. Taking neighborliness one step further, some crabs may even defend burrows of their neighbors. Studying *Uca annulipes* on a mudflat in Mozambique, Tanya Detto and colleagues from Australian National University recorded many interactions of fiddlers, noting the sizes of individuals. They found that crabs will defend burrows of smaller neighbors if the intruder is intermediate in size between the neighbor and themselves. This provides an advantage to the defending larger crab, in that it is easier to have the smaller original neighbor than renegotiating territory boundaries with a larger new one. (Meanwhile, the smaller neighbor gets bodyguard service.) Richard Milner and colleagues from Australian National University found that male *Uca annulipes* also protect their female neighbors from male intruders but not from female intruders. Females sometimes mate with their immediate neighbors, so this "chivalrous" behavior may result in reproductive opportunities.

While on vacation in Fiji, we encountered a population of lemon-yellow clawed fiddler crabs (*Uca perplexa*) while walking along the beach. We stopped to watch, intrigued, and noted two different types of waving: a typical wave—up and out, then down and in, lasting about one second, and a very different wave—a very rapid, horizontal out-and-in motion, but only when other crabs were getting close to them. The regular wave seemed to mean, "This is my territory, here I am," and the second, "Get away from here!" This aggressive wave, directed toward any crab that came too close, was ignored by other species of crab but caused female *perplexa* and some of the male *perplexa* to scoot off. Other males, however, continued to approach and did the horizontal wave back. As the two crabs became close, the aggressive waves turned into a shoving match and, sometimes, a fight (Plate 22). Most of the time the burrow owner won, in some cases picking up the intruder and throwing him a distance away.

The mottled shore crab (*Pachygrapsus transversus*) is a semiterrestrial grapsid crab that lives in the intertidal zone of the Bay of Panama. Lawrence Abele from Florida State and colleagues found that these crabs occupy holes and crevices in rocks that provide food, refuge from predators, and relief from thermal stress. Predation and heat stress favor use of the holes as refuges. The hole seems to function the way a burrow does for ghost crabs on sandy beaches. Males and females move daily from the refuge rocks to flat, smooth rocks where they graze on algae. Males maintain territories on the refuge rocks, with larger males defending larger areas.

Territoriality has been studied in a number of other crabs. Porcelain crabs (Plate 10) are frequently associated with sea anemones or with sea urchins, and they may be territorial and aggressively defend the sea anemone they live in from intruders. The green porcelain crab (*Petrolisthes armatus*) is territorial when inhabiting the anemone *Condylactis gigantea*. The relatively small size of the sea anemone host means that only a few crabs can live together on one host, so resident crabs are territorial. Territorial behavior is more pronounced when anemones are scarce, but reduced when newly arriving crabs are small juveniles. The number of crab residents on the anemone depends on their size and the size of the anemone host. When the number of smaller crabs increases too much or larger crabs are present, antagonistic displays develop. Following a period when the invader and defender examine one another, defenders use their claws to push the invaders out. Sea anemones represent a relatively small and simple habitat for porcelain crab residents (such as *Allopetrolisthes spinifrons*), whereas sea urchins provide a larger, more complex habitat for their residents (such as *Liopetrolisthes mitra*). The latter species is more social, less territorial, and frequently is found together with other adult crabs of both sexes on their larger host.

Figure 5.3. Arrow crab (*Stenorhynchus seticornis*). Photo by Andrew J. Martinez.

Male Oregon shore crabs *Hemigrapsus oregonensis* indicate their territory with sounds, with larger crabs producing more intense signals. Because they live in turbid, muddy water or in burrows, acoustic communication is useful in this environment. Mangrove tree crabs (*Aratus pisonii*; Fig. 26) have well-developed social behaviors and territoriality. Males push each other with claws during aggressive encounters. Once a home range has been established, individuals may inhabit the same area for periods of several weeks to months.

The arrow crab (*Stenorhynchus seticornis*), a spider crab resident of coral reefs, is slow-moving and nocturnal, often found close to a rocky cave, crack, or crevice where it can find shelter during daylight (Fig. 5.3). It is known for being territorial and acting very aggressively toward others, including its own species. Arrow crabs look unusual because of their long, spiderlike legs, triangular body, and extremely pointed head. The legs are more than three times the length of their body. In territorial fights, the more dominant animal may pull off every leg of the loser. Those shown in the figure must be good friends or mates.

Land hermit crabs are territorial and will often act aggressively toward one another to establish a "pecking" order among their colony. This can be in the form of antennae fights or violent pushing of other crabs out of the way. This happens often in the confined space of tanks of crab hobbyists but is usually not serious enough to warrant intervention. However, if a pet hermit tries to pull another out of its shell, the owner should separate them.

GROOMING

Grooming is common in many crustaceans as a form of maintenance to rid their bodies of attached ("fouling") organisms and particulate buildup, sometimes known by the not-very-scientific term *crud*. The exoskeleton can attract fouling organisms as well as debris, sediment, and detritus. Many types of invertebrates including barnacles, bryozoans, and polychaete worms, settle on hard substrates, and a crab's carapace is especially good because it provides transportation as well as a home. Grooming is not just cosmetic, but reduces the incidence of parasitism and improves the health of the individual. Fouling in joints can interfere with movement. Fouling can affect sensory activities, since sense organs are located on the surface. Microbial fouling can develop quickly on olfactory setae, respiratory surfaces, and embryos. Blocking of different types of sensory sensilla on the cuticle can have severe consequences, so grooming behaviors are very useful. General body grooming includes scraping and brushing the carapace, eyes, and legs. It is seen often in crabs emerging from burrows that have mud sticking to them. Crustaceans molt periodically and can get rid of attached debris and fouling organisms, but the period of time in between molts can be long in older individuals or in females incubating embryos, so regular grooming is a healthy practice.

The most frequent grooming behavior involves using maxillipeds to clean the antennules, eyes, and gill surfaces, and using claws to clean the general body surface. The cleaning appendages have specialized bristles (setae) and spines. The gill chamber can be cleaned by setae or flushed by reversing the respiratory current. Land crabs may be less subject to fouling than aquatic ones, but land hermit crabs (Plate 8) are also observed to groom themselves using their third maxillipeds to clean eyestalks and antennules. Chelae and legs are used to clean one another by rubbing them together. You can see a video of a land hermit crab grooming itself at http://www.youtube.com/watch?v=r5wjI89YE8Y, or search for "land hermit crab grooming itself."

One group of spider crabs exhibits a type of behavior that is the opposite of grooming: decorator crabs (discussed further in Chapter 6) pick up material such as pieces of sponge or algae and "plant" them on their carapace where they can attach and continue to grow.

LEARNING

Learning is not really a behavior, but the ability to change response and modify behavior based on experience. Crabs are capable of learning and remembering information, just like other animals. The study showing that fiddler crabs defend burrows of their neighbors (in "Territoriality" section, above) indicates that they learn who their neighbors are. Likewise, hermit crabs are able to recognize individuals of the same species and categorize them into those that are familiar versus those that are unfamiliar.

Crabs in laboratory experiments can learn to avoid a part of their aquarium where they receive an unpleasant stimulus (e.g., electric shock)—a typical conditioning response. Hermit crabs learn to avoid food that makes them ill; this finding by Keith Wight and colleagues also demonstrates that crabs can learn from their mistakes and can retain that information so that they don't make the same mistake again. Patricia Pereyra and colleagues of the University of Buenos Aires moved a screen over the water above mud-flat crabs (*Chasmagnathus* sp.) to mimic the cues of a bird predator passing overhead. At first, the crabs ran into their burrows, but after a few times, they learned that the darkness didn't mean danger and no longer fled. This shows that crabs' reactions are not rigid reflexes, but that they respond based on what they have learned and remembered from past experiences. However, crabs were found to be like people in that they become less able to remember things when they get older.

Much of the research on learning has been done on green crabs (*Carcinus maenas*; Fig. 1.8), which show the ability to improve when tested in a maze. P. Cunningham and R. Hughes in Wales placed individual crabs into tanks with mussels or dog whelks (common food items) and observed the predatory interactions. They found that the crabs could improve in their ability to crack open dog whelks or mussels with practice, and this learning could take place over a few hours. Furthermore, skills they learned in dealing with one type of prey could be transferred to handling novel prey. Ross Roudez, an undergraduate student, examined green crabs' ability to learn the location of a hidden mussel. When tested daily over 1 wk, the crabs progressively shortened the time they needed to find the food, indicating that they learned the location within a few days. Blue crabs (Plate 3), however, did not shorten the time they took to find the hidden food, suggesting they are not "as smart" as green crabs. Patricia Ramey and colleagues at Rutgers found another behavioral difference between these two species: green crabs showed more interest than blue crabs in exploring new areas. Exploring novel localities may increase the chances of discovering new food or other resources. However, blue crabs are not all brawn and no brains; they can learn some things. Fiorenza Micheli of the University of North Carolina found that they could be conditioned to alter their initial size preference of small clams (which are easier to open and provide food sooner) over larger ones.

Another important aspect of animal behavior—courtship and mating—is covered in Chapter 4. Migration, navigation, and some other aspects of behavior are addressed in Chapter 6.

CHAPTER SIX

Ecology

Given the very different habitats in which crabs can be found (see Chapter 2), it is no wonder that their ecology is equally diverse. Following is an overview of these aspects of crab ecology, beginning with the transition from larva to juvenile, and covering hibernation, migrations, navigation, interactions with other kinds of organisms, and the effects of crabs on the environment.

TRANSITION FROM PLANKTONIC
LARVA TO BENTHIC JUVENILE

Larval stages in the plankton are particularly important for the dispersal of most marine invertebrates, including crabs. As discussed in Chapter 4, most crabs hatch into the water as free-swimming planktonic larvae. Since adult crabs generally crawl on the bottom, they do not travel great distances, so the larval stage is the principal time for dispersal. Exceptions are the swimming crabs, such as blue crabs, which can become planktonic again as juveniles and continue to disperse farther. Since many commercially important species undergo major population swings unrelated to fishing, a lot of research is being devoted to understanding the ecology of larval transport, *recruitment* (i.e., surviving juveniles being added to a population), settlement of larvae to the bottom, and predator/prey interactions after they settle. These processes are complicated, involving events during larval life, settlement and habitat selection, and after metamorphosis to the juvenile stage, all of which can have major effects on the adult population. Successful transition to life on the bottom requires that enough larvae survive in the plankton and meta-morphose in suitable bottom habitats. Environmental factors involved with year-to-year variability in recruitment of various crab species include physical factors such as currents, tides, and winds; climate change; and the nature of the bottom.

Ocean currents, tides, and wind are the major physical factors that are important in the transport of larvae. In studies of Dungeness crabs, Alan Shanks of the National Oceanic and Atmospheric Administration (NOAA) and colleagues found that climate factors affecting currents played a major role in success of returning larvae. The timing of the *spring transition*—the time when ocean currents shift and move toward the shore—was particu-larly important. In years when this transition occurred earlier, more crabs re-turned to settle. In addition, the predominance of northward currents along the Pacific Coast suggests that populations of crabs in Washington State depend on larvae from farther south. Robert McConnaughey of NOAA and colleagues found that more crabs settled in years that had relatively weak northward transport but strong landward transport. They suggested that successful juvenile recruitment reflects the proportion of larvae retained within a relatively narrow "coastal landing strip," the availability of suitable substrate within the coastal landing strip when the larvae settled, and the proportion of larvae that were moved away from the coastal area by currents. *Estuarine fronts*—regions where temperature and/or salinity change greatly over a relatively short distance—serve to concentrate larvae. On a shorter time scale, more megalopae (the larval stage preparing to metamorphose) were moved toward the shore on days with a greater tidal range (spring tides). Larvae are not completely at the mercy of tides and currents, however; megalopae can swim surprisingly well and make headway upstream against currents at speeds found in their natural habitats.

Different physical factors can be more important for different species and at different locations. Results of a study by Alan Shanks on East Coast spe-cies suggest that postlarval blue crabs (*C. sapidus*) were moved shoreward primarily by tides, but that fiddler crab (*Uca* spp.) megalopae were trans-ported shoreward mostly by wind-driven surface currents, and that spider crab (*Libinia* spp.) megalopae were moved shoreward in near-bottom waters during upwelling events. Luis Miguel Pardo and colleagues at the Universi-dad Austral de Chile studied settlement of *Cancer (Metacarcinus) edwardsii* megalopae in different location in a Chilean estuary. Their results showed that the predominant physical factor controlling the return of crab larvae to estuarine sites varied within the estuary. At the mouth of the estuary, circulation changes due to the amount of upwelling or the strength of onshore winds controlled settlement, while at a site within the estuary, settlement was affected mostly by the tides. The lack of tidal influence on settlement at the mouth of the estuary was explained by the relatively small tides in the study area and the overwhelming influence of intense upwelling. Their results also indicated that predation had negligible effects on settlement.

Effects of ocean acidification and climate change on larval transport and recruitment are also being examined. Recruitment of various species in Alaska has been low since the 1970s despite controls on fishing and appears to be related to climate shifts, which may reduce the growth of the diatoms (important phytoplankton) that early zoeal stages must feed on.

The transition from a planktonic larva to a benthic (bottom-dwelling) juvenile is a critical period, and the nature of the bottom (substrate) plays a major role. Once a larva settles on the bottom, the habitat it finds is crucial to its future success. Different species of crabs generally prefer particular types of substrates, and many species, including Dungeness crabs, blue crabs, and red king crabs, actively seek complex habitats that include vertical structures and crevices that can provide shelter against potential predators. David Eggleston and David Armstrong of the University of Washington found that recently settled Dungeness crab megalopae were much more abundant in shell habitats than in mud habitats. Experimental studies showed that they were also more abundant in areas from which potential predators had been excluded. Habitat preferences of settling red king crabs (see Fig.1.13) have also been intensively studied in the field and laboratory by Bradley Stevens of NOAA and coworkers. Red king crab glaucothoe larvae also settle preferentially in more complex habitats—sites with rocky cobble or with hydroids and algae, and they are unlikely to settle in muddy or sandy habitats. *Biogenic substrates*—that is, sites with living organisms such as hydroids, algae, or bryozoans—are especially good habitats because they are not only complex but also supply built-in food for the crabs. A complex habitat, with or without built-in food, provides protection against predators. Even in experiments using a larger red king crab as the predator (cannibalism being common in crabs), juveniles survived best in the complex structural habitat.

Settling blue crab megalopae also seem to prefer biogenic habitats; they settle preferentially in areas of eel grass (*Zostera marina*) and oysters but avoid mud or sand substrates. However, since early juvenile blue crabs can disperse again by swimming up into the water column, (post-settlement dispersal) they can later move planktonically to other types of complex benthic habitats.

HERMIT CRABS IN SNAIL SHELLS

The tail section of hermit crabs is not flat and tucked neatly underneath them like true crabs, nor is it large and extending out straight like a lobster tail; rather it is relatively large compared with true crabs and bent slightly. It is not covered by exoskeleton, but is soft and vulnerable—a good reason to keep it inside an empty snail shell for protection. The abdomen is bent like a corkscrew so that it fits into a curved snail shell (see Fig. 1.3). Hermit crabs can rapidly contract their abdominal muscles to withdraw quickly and deeply into the shell in case of danger. They then use a claw to close off the entrance and their claws are of a shape and size perfectly suited to block the opening. Claws are also used for defense and eating, the second and third pairs of legs are for walking, and the short last two pairs hold the crab in its shell. To defecate, they must bend their abdomen around to the front of their shell to release their wastes into the water, quite an acrobatic feat. Molting also requires temporarily exiting the snail shell home just long enough to wriggle out of the crab's old body shell.

The shell serves various functions. For terrestrial hermits, these include water storage: the crabs can carry water in their snail shell, which enables them to colonize relatively dry areas. All hermit crabs depend on a properly fitting shell for protection from predators. The relative size of the shell that a crab occupies can affect its survival, growth, and reproduction. Crabs in shells that are too small grow more slowly are less tolerant of air exposure and drying out, and are more likely to be eaten by a predator than those that can withdraw completely into their shell. When a crab has outgrown its snail shell, it has to look for a bigger one that fits properly. They locate shells by smell, either when the previous owner (the snail) dies and begins to decay or by detecting calcium, the major component of snail shells. The crabs do not generally kill snails to find new shells, although they may fight with other hermit crabs over empty shells, especially when empty shells are scarce. After locating a new shell, the crab investigates its surface and internal size by rolling it over and exploring it with its claws and walking legs, which move around the opening of the shell, as if measuring it for size. If it looks like a good fit, the crab withdraws its abdomen from its old shell and inserts it into the new one so quickly that it can be difficult to see. (Switching shells is risky—the crab could be attacked by a predator or lose one or both shells to other hermit crabs.)

Crabs rarely abandon their current shells without a new home lined up. However, if a crab has been buried in the sand during a storm or flooding event, it is likely to abandon its shell to return to the surface. Although abandoning its shell increases its chances of surviving such a burial, this behavior also increases the risk of predation and of being buried or injured in another flooding event.

Particular species of hermits tend to prefer certain species of snail shells, but size is the critical factor. Occupying larger and heavier shells gives them greater protection, but it takes more energy to lug a large house around. Shells often become covered with other organisms such as barnacles or algae that make them heavier and more difficult to carry. Some hermit species live in shells that get entirely covered by bryozoan colonies that eventually dissolve the snail shell, leaving the crab with a house composed entirely of the bryozoans. As the bryozoan colony grows, so too do the crabs, so these crabs have no need to change their homes.

Hermit crabs with poor-fitting shells are chemically attracted to dying gastropods and other hermit crabs where a shell may become available. In the Mediterranean species *Clibanarius erythropus,* gastropod predation sites attract dozens of hermit crabs. Elena Tricarico and colleagues from the University of Florence observed that these aggregations function as shell exchange markets: the first crab to arrive takes the empty shell, and a chain of shell exchanges among the crabs follows. They found that simulated snail predation sites quickly attracted a larger number of hermit crabs than other types of sites; therefore, aggregation is the most efficient tactic for this species to acquire new shells. In Belize, the land hermits, *Coenobita clypeatus,* (see Plate 8) have even more organized shell exchanges, in what is called a "synchronous vacancy chain" by Randi Rotjan and colleagues from Tufts University, who discovered this unique behavior. When a large empty shell becomes available, many crabs gather around it, which can take hours. As they gather, the crabs arrange themselves into a line of decreasing size, starting with the largest crab holding onto the empty shell. As though choreographed, the crabs begin shell-swapping, one after the other, a smaller crab climbing into a new shell right after it is vacated by the slightly larger crab ahead of it. What makes the synchronous chain possible is that smaller crabs linger near a too-large shell, perhaps attracting others, waiting until a bigger crab comes along, which increases their chances of getting a good fitting hand-me-down.

Most hermit crabs and most snails are right-handed (i.e., dextral) and spiral clockwise. Some species, however, such as those in the family Diogenidae, are left-handed (i.e., sinistral) and spiral counterclockwise, and they need to find snail shells that are coiled that way. Since the majority of snail species are right-handed, left-handed hermits (such as in the genus *Calcinus*) may have trouble finding left-handed snails; this may account for them sometimes being found inhabiting snail shells with remnants of the original occupant still present. Adults of the left-handed *Petrochirus diogenes*—the largest hermit crab in the Caribbean, growing to an impressive five to eight inches long—are often found in shells of the queen conch *Eustrombus gigas*. As an exception to the general rule, they will attack and eat a conch, thus obtaining both a meal and a shell.

Sometimes crabs are found in unusually shaped shells such as cowries or worm shells, which are less desirable. Catherine Bach and Brian Hazlett of Eastern Michigan University found that crabs in unusual shells initiated more shell exchanges and when given empty shells, they readily moved to standard-shaped shells. Crabs in standard-shaped shells did not move into the odd-shaped shells, which appear to not fit well. Those in the odd-shaped

HERMIT CRABS IN CHILDREN'S LITERATURE

Eric Carle's book *A House for Hermit Crab* is a popular picture book for preschool and early elementary school children. It introduces young readers to the beauty of the marine environment through the habits of the hermit crab and contains a message for small children facing the challenges of change and growing up. When the crab outgrows his first shell, he is scared. The new one he finds is big enough, but bare and uninviting. To his surprise, many undersea neighbors come to decorate and protect his new home. By the time the new house is perfect, it has become too small, and once again he must move on to a new one. But now he is more self-confident. While he is sorry to leave the familiar shell behind, he now sees exciting possibilities for the future. Children who must change schools or move to a new town can relate to the hermit crab's situation and can appreciate the message that change is not necessarily scary or negative.

OPPIAN ON HERMIT CRABS

In ca. 170 AD, the ancient Greek poet Oppian was one of the first to describe hermit crabs' search for new shells:

> The Hermit crabs have no shell of their own from birth, but are born na-ked and unprotected and weak; yet they devise for themselves an acquired home, covering their feeble bodies with a bastard shelter. For when they see a shell left all desolate, the tenant having left his home, they creep in below the alien mantle and settle there and dwell and take it for their home. And along with it they travel and move their shelter from within—whether it be some Nerites that hath left the shell or a Trumpet or a Strombus. Most of all they love the shelters of the Strombus, because these are wide and light to carry. But when the Hermit crab within grows and fills the cavity, it keeps that house no longer, but leaves it and seeks a wider shell-vessel to put on. Ofttimes battle arises and great contention among the Hermit-crabs about a hollow shell and the stronger drives out the weaker and herself puts on the fitting house" (Translated by A.W. Mair)

shells were more readily dislodged by wave surge than crabs in standard-shaped ones.

Land hermit crabs (*Coenobita clypeatus*) on the island of Bermuda have been found almost exclusively using fossil snail shells of the species *Cittarium [Livona] pica*, a species that became extinct on that island in the 1800s. These crabs modify the shell by enlarging the opening. It was thought that the diminishing supply of fossil shells would eventually doom the hermit crab population, but Sally Walker of the University of Georgia determined that hurricanes bring shells from other islands, so the frequency of hurricanes is an important factor for this hermit crab population. The snails have also been reintroduced to the island, so shells should be plentiful in the future.

HIBERNATION

During the winter, many species of crabs in temperate climates go into a dormant resting state that may be called hibernation, where they bury themselves in the bottom (or deep in their burrows) and are inactive. When the water temperature falls and the days get shorter, the blue crab (Plate 3), for example, retreats to deep water and burrows into the muddy or sandy bottom to spend the winter. It buries itself by forcing its abdomen backward into the bottom with quick snapping motions. While doing this, it will also pick and claw at the sand or mud on the bottom with its hind walking legs and flip it away with the paddles of its swimming legs. It will end up at a 45° angle in the bottom, with only its antennae, the tips of its eye stalks, and small breathing channels above the surface. Ghost crabs hibernate in their burrows, storing oxygen in specialized sacs near their gills. When it warms up in the spring, they resume their activities. In Australia, land hermit crabs hibernate underground, inland from the coast between late April and late August, the winter months in that hemisphere.

MIGRATIONS

Crabs engage in regular migrations from one area to another. While the term "migration" often implies moving a large distance, crabs undergo migrations of distances both short and long. Many of these regular movements have to do with feeding at the optimum time. Planktonic larval crabs and other invertebrates regularly move up and down in the water, moving up toward the surface at night to feed and going down into deeper waters in the daytime to make themselves less visible to predators. Semiterrestrial crabs such as fiddler and ghost crabs regularly move down to the water line to feed as the tide ebbs and then return up the slope to their burrows as the tide returns. Land hermit crabs hide under bushes or tidal debris during the daytime and move to the beach at night. They need the beach for egg deposition, and for their water and salt balance. Mole crabs (Fig. 1.5) live in the swash zone of ocean beaches, where the water from the waves washes over the beach, so they migrate up and down the beach with each tidal cycle to stay at the optimum location for filtering plankton from the water. Fully aquatic crabs such as blue crabs regularly go up onto the surface of salt marshes at high tide to feed, seek mates, and molt, and then retreat back to deeper water when the tide ebbs. Many rock crabs in the genus *Cancer* (Plate 2) undergo migrations into deeper water during the winter and return to shallow water in the summer. This migration is triggered by temperature changes. Many green (shore) crabs in the genus *Carcinus* have similar seasonal onshore–offshore migrations.

Some crabs undergo more extensive migrations associated with reproduction. For example, the Chinese mitten crab (*Eriocheir sinensis*; Fig. 2.7) is *catadromous*, meaning that it migrates downstream hundreds of miles from fresh water to reproduce. Adults migrate downstream from freshwater habitats to the salty waters of estuaries, where females carry up to one million eggs, and both sexes die soon after reproduction. During the migration, they move downstream during ebb tides and burrow during the flood tides to prevent getting washed back upstream. The larvae develop in marine waters. After a 1–2 month period as larvae, the juvenile crabs settle in salt or brackish water in late spring, then migrate back up to freshwater by moving up on flood tides and burrowing in during ebb tides.

Blue crabs (Plate 3) undergo similar downstream migrations associated with reproduction. After mating, females migrate to the mouth of the bay where they spend the winter. This migration is assisted by a rhythm in vertical swimming in which crabs move up in the water column during ebb tide and thus get pushed downstream. Months later, the female releases eggs onto her abdomen. The larvae undergo their initial development in the ocean, then juveniles migrate back into the estuary and, by going up and down at the right time to catch incoming tides, manage to go upstream without being swept back out into the ocean with outgoing tides.

Alaskan red king crabs (Fig. 1.13) migrate from deep to shallow water in late winter to mate and then return to deeper waters for the rest of the year. Some crabs have been found to migrate over 100 miles during this annual migration. Each spring, eggs hatch in shallow water, and the adults molt before beginning the trek back to deeper water. To learn more about the migration patterns of Alaskan crabs, male red king crabs were tagged and released in Bristol Bay in December 2009, while male snow crabs (*Chionoecetes opilio*) were tagged and released on the fishing grounds during the spring of 2010 and 2011. Fishermen and the public were asked to help with the recovery of tagged crabs, which will reveal their migration patterns.

Land crabs—both brachyurans such as *Gecarcinus lateralis*; Plate 6) and land hermit crabs (*Coenobita* sp.; Plate 8)—migrate miles down to the sea for reproduction. After adults congregate on land for breeding, the eggs develop on the females, which move to the edge of the water where they release their larvae and then return back inland. Migration entails much risk to both the adults migrating to and from the sea as well as the juveniles that return to shore after a few weeks as planktonic larvae. Adults may be attacked by predators, swept into the ocean, or fall off cliffs. The seaward migration of thousands of crabs at the same time has caused major disruptions to traffic on coastal roads in the tropical countries where they live. Hundreds of thousands of crabs die each year as road kill or from falling off cliffs.

The most spectacular crab migration of all takes place on Christmas Island, a small (about 85 sq mi) island in the Indian Ocean off Australia (actually closer to Indonesia, off the coast of Java). When the rainy season starts in October and November, the island becomes a red seething mass as millions of red crabs swarm across yards, fields, golf courses, sidewalks, roads, and cliffs to reach the sea to breed. The red crab *Gecarcoidea natalis* is one of many land and freshwater crab species that inhabit Christmas Island, but it is the only one in which both males and females migrate to the sea to breed. Males move to the shore first, where they establish a territory and burrow into the sand to wait for the females, which arrive a few days later and mate with the males, usually in the burrows. The females produce eggs a few days after mating and remain in the moist burrows for about two weeks while they develop. A single female can brood up to 100,000 eggs. On the last quarter of the moon at high tide, the females release their hatching larvae into the sea and start their return migration to the forest. The larvae go through several stages during about a month in the ocean, then the megalopae gather close to the shore, molt into juvenile crabs, and leave the water. The newly metamorphosed juveniles may hide under litter and share burrows before they are able to dig their own. Although less than half an inch across, the baby crabs begin their march inland. The island is again a moving red mass, as the millions of tiny crabs crawl across the island until they reach the forest. It takes almost two months for the red crabs to make their way from the forest to the sea and back again.

Though the tourist industry on Christmas Island suggests some other reasons for visiting, the primary one from the end of October through the beginning of December is to witness this migration of 50–100 million red crabs. The first part of the migration, down to the sea, lasts only 5–7 days between the end of October and the end of November, which makes it difficult to plan a trip to coincide with this small window of opportunity, especially for people coming from far away. To reduce the number of crabs killed by vehicles during the migration, "crab crossings" and tunnels built under the road have been constructed at points where thousands of crabs cross on their

LOBSTER MIGRATIONS

Spiny lobsters (*Panulirus*) undergo the most famous lobster migrations in the sea. As originally described by William Herrnkind of the University of Florida, they line up single-file to march into deeper water across the ocean floor in long lines, apparently in response to the onset of summer and fall storms and to evade the stresses of the cold, turbid waters. Spiny lobster migrations have been watched and filmed underwater. Each lobster touches its antennules to the tail of the lobster in front of it, and maintains contact throughout the migration. As with a school of fish, there is no consistent leader, but unlike a fish school, this oriented migration continues during the night. Why they go single-file is still a mystery, but it appears that vigilance, cooperative defense, and drag reduction may all contribute to the formation of queues.

Larry C. Boles and Kenneth J. Lohmann of the University of North Carolina, Chapel Hill, reported that spiny lobsters orient using magnetic fields. Their research suggests that these creatures can determine their location even when transported to an unfamiliar area. Lobsters were displaced 7.5–23 miles from their point of capture, in covered containers with seawater and transported to new locations by truck and boat, using circuitous routes. Once at the test site, the lobsters, even with their eyes covered, could tell the direction of their capture site and began moving homeward. These are the first invertebrates to display this ability known as "true navigation." In previous research, Boles and Lohmann found that Caribbean spiny lobsters (*Panulirus argus*) use an internal magnetic compass that enables them to determine the four cardinal directions: north, south, east, and west.

Clawed lobsters also undertake impressive migrations that have been studied using tag and recapture methods. Scientists compare the sites of release to the subsequent capture site and estimate the straight-line distance traveled. While most lobsters have been caught relatively close to the sites where they were released, others have traveled far: for example, more than 180 miles from the Bay of Fundy to southern Maine, and more than 120 miles from Long Island Sound offshore to Veatch Canyon along New England's Continental margin.

trek to the sea. Local authorities put up fences to keep crabs off the roads (Plate 23) and divert the crawling red mass to these crossings or tunnels. Other conservation measures used by the community are road closures and traffic detours around the major migration paths during peak periods of the migration.

NAVIGATION AND ORIENTATION

Orienting mechanisms for migrating crabs involve an internal compass that enables the animal to orient properly and the ability to remember landmarks. In addition to good spatial knowledge, there also seems to be a *kinesthetic memory*—a memory of past movements—that allows the crab to retrace its steps. John Layne and colleagues at the University of Glasgow demonstrated that crabs have a way of determining distance. They set up experiments in which fiddler crabs were made to "run home" across a patch of wet acetate, on which they slipped and had to take more steps than normal on the homeward path. Crabs whose running speed across the patch was unusually low stopped short of their burrow before getting to it, apparently thinking they should already have arrived. Meanwhile those whose running speed was not affected by the acetate did not stop short, but ran straight to their burrow entrance.

Crabs living on intertidal mudflats cannot see their burrow openings when they are more than 7–8 "eye heights" away. When ghost crabs are a few feet from their burrows, they can find them readily, even at night, but when displaced far from them, they cannot relocate the original burrow and will try to evict another crab from its burrow or build a new one. Male fiddlers may use elevated courtship burrow structures (e.g., hoods, chimneys; see Fig. 4.1) as visual landmarks. Taewon Kim found that *Uca lactea* males could orient to and find their burrows from a greater distance if there was a hood at the burrow entrance. When fiddler crabs are in the water, perhaps as a result of fleeing from mammalian or bird predators, they orient back to the shore using cues from the slope of the shore. For aquatic blue crabs, in contrast, the major factor in orientation is the breaking of waves.

Parasesarma leptosoma, an East African mangrove crab, migrates twice a day from the roots to well-defined feeding areas in the branches of the trees. Stefano Cannicci and colleagues from the University of Florence tested whether chemical or visual cues are involved in the orientation and homing of this species to reach their feeding areas. They found that altering the substrate at branch junctions in order to change possible chemical cues did not affect homing ability. In addition, crabs trained to cross an asymmetrical artificial wooden fork could still find their preferred locations after the fork branches had been switched or the whole fork had been rotated around the trunk. They were also not affected by the switching of two wide black-and-white screens that hid most of the canopy from view. It was impossible to confuse these crabs either chemically or visually; thus, they must be using other cues. Furthermore, crabs that were marked and then moved to trees 20 feet away returned to the original tree in a few days; those that were moved 50 feet away, however, tended to leave the new tree but did not return to their original tree, perhaps being too far away to find it.

INTERACTIONS WITH OTHER ORGANISMS

Interactions with Other Invertebrates

With Cnidarians
Cnidarians are a phylum of primitive animals that includes sea anemones, jellyfish, corals, and hydroids.

With sea anemones and jellyfish. Some of the most interesting relationships of crabs are with sea anemones (Plate 19). Hermit crabs of the genus *Dardanus* form a symbiotic relationship with the anemone *Calliactis polypus* with which it shares a home. The anemone attaches to the snail shell that the crab inhabits, and provides camouflage and protection. The two partners share food. Anemones have a structure called a pedal disc that they use to attach themselves firmly to a hard substrate, in this case the crab's

---

LIVING ON A LOBSTER'S MOUTHPARTS

Symbion pandora is a tiny animal about one-fiftieth ($1/50$) of an inch long, shaped like a bulbous tube with a ring of tiny hairs (or cilia) at one end and a short stalk ending in an adhesive disc on the other, which it uses to attach itself to its host. It lives on the mouthparts of Norway lobsters (*Nephrops norvegicus*), with from tens to hundreds of them on each lobster. The *Symbion* feed on small bits of leftover food and seem to be harmless to their hosts. They are unique in the animal kingdom— so much so that they are the first representatives of a totally new phylum of animals, Cycliophora, whose evolutionary history and taxonomic placement are still unclear because they were not discovered until 1995. The timing of their sexual reproduction matches the molt cycle of their host: when the lobster molts, the *Symbion* produce planktonic larvae, which can then settle on newly molted lobsters, solving the problem of a being left behind on the old shell.

---

snail shell, and normally do not move around by themselves. Where the crab goes, the anemone goes too, which helps anemones disperse. When the crab outgrows its shell, it will find a new, larger one and generally transfer the anemone onto it. This requires the cooperation of both partners. The crab can manipulate the anemone to release its pedal disc and let go of the original shell. The anemone then aids in the transfer by clinging to the new shell with its tentacles until it can turn over and reattach its pedal disc. Similar relationships and behaviors are seen with some other species of hermit crabs and sea anemones, mostly in warm temperate and tropical areas. In some cases the anemone transfers itself, taking the lead in the relationship. One hermit crab species covers itself with an anemone, using its appendages to hold it in position initially: the cloak anemone (*Adamsia palliata*) wraps itself around the shell inhabited by the hermit crab *Pagurus prideaux*; as the anemone grows, it adds to the effective room of the shell, so that the crab has space for growth and need not look for a larger snail shell.

Porcelain anemone crabs (*Neopetrolisthes* spp.) are tiny crabs that live together in pairs within the tentacles of an anemone (Plate 10). They eat planktonic food and mucus from the anemone, which they sometimes share with their more famous neighbor, the clownfish.

Some brachyuran crabs also have special relations with sea anemones. The boxer (or pom-pom) crab (*Lybia tessellata*), a very attractive, brightly colored crab that is popular in marine aquariums, carries a pair of small anemones, one on each of its small claws (Plate 20). The small white anemones look like pom-poms or boxing gloves, giving the crab its name. The claws of the boxer crab are so small that they are not effective in defense, but they are especially adapted for grasping the sea anemone's fleshy body, as these anemones do not attach with their pedal discs. The stinging ability of the anemones acts as a defense. When approached by a predator, the crab waves the anemones with their stinging tentacles. Could this be considered tool use in a crab? If a fish or another potential predator comes too close, the crab thrusts out the sea anemone. While most crabs use their claws to pull apart food into manageable chunks, *Lybia*'s claws are not strong enough to do this, and it would require putting down its anemones and becoming vulnerable to predation. So *Lybia* uses its first pair of walking legs to rip off small pieces of food and manipulate them toward its mouth. The crab may also wipe its anemones along the substrate to pick up particulate material with the sticky tentacles. Some of this material is then eaten by the crab, benefiting both partners.

Boxer crabs can use a few different species of anemones, which benefit from the small particles of food dropped by the crab during feeding and from the free transportation to new places. Sometimes the crab will lose its anemones or leave them behind when it molts. The relationship with the anemone is not essential for boxer crabs, which can be found without them, and they sometimes substitute sponges or corals.

Other crabs, including calappids (shame-faced crabs or box crabs), may also carry sea anemones on their carapace. Some small spider crabs live within the tentacles of their sea anemone partner and, like the more famous clownfish, gain protection from predators and are resistant to the host's stinging cells.

Some crabs put upside-down jellyfish (*Cassiopeia* spp.) on their backs, which provides them with defense because the tentacles of the jellyfish project upward into the water to deter possible predators.

With corals.   Some crabs have a symbiotic relationship with coral. For example, branching corals such as *Acropora* or *Pocillopora* provide a home and protection for crabs such as the tiny (0.5 inch wide) guard crabs (*Trapezius* spp.; Plate 11), while the crabs provide housekeeping duties for the coral, routinely sweeping out sediment. Accumulation of sediment on coral is known to reduce growth and increase the probability of bleaching and death. Many corals can remove some sediment from their surfaces but too much sediment can be lethal. In return for its sediment removal, the crab gets to feed on mucus secreted by the coral and on coral tissue. Hannah Stewart of the University of California, Santa Barbara, and colleagues showed the importance of the crabs by removing them from some coral specimens. This resulted in over half of those corals dying in a month, while all corals that still had their crabs survived. For the corals that survived without crabs, growth was slower, tissue bleaching was greater, and sediment load was higher. Laboratory experiments showed that corals with crabs shed more sediment and that crabs were most effective at removing sediment grain sizes that were the most damaging to the coral. These crabs may also deter predation on their host. The *Trapezius* crab living in nooks in the branching corals actively defend the coral against predators including the ravaging crown-of-thorns starfish. When a crown-of-thorns starfish approaches the coral, the crabs rush out and pinch its tube feet or spines, push it away, or actually shake the predator, which generally goes away seeking a less well-defended coral to attack.

The gall crabs of coral reefs (Cryptochiridae family) live in association with specific branched coral species that eventually grow over and imprison the small crab within a cavity in the coral. Some other species of anomuran and xanthid crabs are also found in association with corals and may also excavate a cavity in the coral.

The red-ridged clinging crab (*Mithraculus forceps*) hides within the branches of the compact ivory bush coral (*Oculina arbuscula*). The interaction is beneficial to both partners in shallow, well-lit waters where corals are at risk of getting overgrown by seaweeds and crabs are susceptible to predation by fish. John Stachowicz and Mark Hay of Georgia Tech. experimentally removed crabs from some corals and found that when corals did not have resident crabs, they got overgrown and smothered by a dense covering of seaweeds, which reduced their growth and increased their chance of dying. By reducing this overgrowth, the crab increased coral growth and survival. The crab benefits by gaining a refuge from its predators, and the coral provides it with some nutrition as well.

In the deep sea, some species of lithodid and galatheid crabs are found associated with cold-water corals such as *Lophelia*. These associations have been discovered in only the past few years, so much remains unknown about the nature of these relationships.

With hydroids.   Hydroids are small, sometimes colonial, predatory cnidarians that live attached to rocks or other hard substrates. The hydroid *Hydractinia*, a cnidarian with a thin, tubelike body, is frequently found on snail shells occupied by hermit crabs (Plate 24). Crabs appear to choose snail shells that already have the hydroid on them, and it has been assumed that the hydroid benefits the crab in some way, probably as a deterrent to predation. However, Christine Damiani of Duke University found, surprisingly, that female hermit crabs in hydroid-colonized shells had fewer eggs and more clutch failure than females living in bare shells, and William Buckley and John Ebersole of the University of Massachusetts found that hermit crabs in *Hydractinia*-covered shells were more likely to be eaten by blue crabs than those in bare shells. However, the stinging cells of the *Hydractinia* may deter some types of predators. Obviously more research is needed to learn if and how the crab benefits from this relationship, which has at least some disadvantages.

With sponges

Some spider crab species cut out portions of sponges to put on their carapace. The crab cuts and shapes the sponge (or cardboard if given it) and holds it above its carapace with its last two pairs of legs, which are tipped with needle-like pincers used to hold onto the sponges that sit on their backs. These crabs can move the sponges over the whole of their bodies for camouflage. (Instead of a sponge, *D. dormia* has occasionally been observed carrying other materials, including a hollow piece of wood and the sole of a discarded shoe.) However, holding onto the sponge means that they have only two pairs (rather than the usual 4 pairs) of legs to walk on, so they tend to also use their claws to assist in walking. Some spider crabs, such as the decorator crabs (discussed below under "Interactions with Plants"), cut off pieces of algae and sponge that they plant on their limbs and carapace; these can grow to cover the entire crab.

With Polychaetes

Some polychaete worms (segmented marine worms, related to earthworms) associate with crabs. The worm *Nereis fucata* enters gastropod shells occupied by hermit crabs, takes residence in the upper coils of the shell, and may take food from the crab by extending its head out of the shell. They also may eat some of the crab's eggs, but female crabs carrying eggs may change shells and get rid of this unwelcome visitor.

With Echinoderms

Echinoderms are marine animals with radial (often 5-part) symmetry radiating from a central area. Crabs may associate with echinoderms such as sea stars (or starfish), sea urchins, sand dollars, or sea cucumbers. Juvenile red king crabs can be found associated with sea stars. The white and dark brown striped urchin crab associates with the fire urchin or other species of urchins. The last segment of its leg forms a hook to hold onto the spines of the sea urchin. While the carrier crab *Dorippe frascone* (Fig. 6.1) carries its sea urchin on its back for protection from predators the way other species carry anemones, the small striped urchin crab (*Zebrida adamsii*) lives on top of the red sea urchin (*Astropyga radiata*) and receives protection from the spines. Three species of the porcelain crab *Clastotoechus* have a symbiotic relationship with the sea urchin *Echinometra*. Two of these species live as male-female pairs with their respective sea urchin species. The third species lives independently among individuals of a particular *Echinometra* species.

The crab *Dissodactylus mellitae* lives as a juvenile on top of sand dollars, with up to 10 individuals on one sand dollar. Sand dollars with large numbers of crabs tended to produce fewer eggs than those without crab passengers.

Figure 6.1. Carrier crab (*Dorippe frascone*) with sea urchin on its back. Photo by Andrew J. Martinez.

The swimmer crab *Lissocarcinus orbicularis* is often found on the tentacles of the sea cucumber *Actinopyga*. Both the crab and the sea cucumber are brown with white patches, so this camouflage provides protection. Since the sea cucumber does not appear to either benefit or be harmed by the relationship, it is termed a *commensal* relationship.

With Bivalve Mollusks

The bivalve *Mysella pedroana* is frequently found associated with the spiny sand (mole) crab, *Blepharipoda occidentalis,* along the Pacific coast of California and Mexico. Although sometimes free-living, the mollusk occurs most often inside the gill chamber of the crabs and appears to be commensal. Most host crabs contain one or two *M. pedroana* but over twenty have been found in some crabs. Having so many living inside the gill chamber might be harmful. Other species of mole crabs in South America were found to have mussels growing on them, but mostly on the underside, rather than inside the gill chamber. This may be an example of mussel larvae simply looking to settle on any hard substrate on a sandy beach where there is not much hard substrate to be found.

The deep sea crab *Paromola cuvieri* from various locations in the Azores (northeast Atlantic) were videotaped by submersible vehicles. Crabs were found carrying a great variety (about 60 different types) of other organisms, including sponges, hydroids, corals, brachiopods, crinoids, and oysters. Overall, 75% of the crabs were carrying live specimens of sessile invertebrates, mainly sponges and cold-water corals.

With Other Crustaceans

Crabs have been found in association with other crustaceans as well, including barnacles, lobsters, and other crabs. Crabs sometimes have barnacles on their shells, but in this case the barnacles don't have a special relationship with the crabs. Instead, their larvae just need to find a hard substrate to settle on, and a crab's carapace will do as well as anything else (Fig. 6.2). In fact, it might be better, because the barnacle can be transported to new areas. The stalked barnacle *Octolasmis mulleri* lives regularly in the gill chambers of crabs where they are protected and find a constant food supply in the stream of water coming through the gill chamber. When the crab molts, however, the barnacles are left behind, so the barnacles can mature only in crabs with a long intermolt period or in those that have had a terminal molt.

Amphipods are generally small (one-half inch long) crustaceans that are compressed from side to side. While most are free-living, the amphipod *Ischyrocerus commensalis* is considered a commensal of the red king crab, averaging about fifty per crab, and living primarily on the host's mouthparts, limbs, and gills.

Atlantic rock crabs (*Cancer irroratus*; Plate 2) and American lobsters (*Homarus americanus*) share kelp forest environments in New England, where they compete for space. When lobsters were present, crabs were found higher up on the kelp; in the absence of lobsters, crabs were more often on the bottom, suggesting that lobsters are better competitors for the space and dictate where the crabs can live. Crab interactions with other crabs similarly tend to be competitive or predator/prey. In these relationships, size generally determines who wins or who eats whom.

Figure 6.2. Juvenile Puget Sound king crab (*Lopholithodes mandtii*) with barnacles.
Photo by Dave Cowles, http://rosario.wallawalla.edu/inverts.

Interactions with Plants

Decorator crabs are various species of spider crabs (family Majidae) that live in shallow areas. These crabs, for example, the graceful decorator *Oregonia gracilis* seen in Figure 6.3, decorate themselves by putting greenish brown algae (and other things) on their backs, which helps them blend in with their environment. The algae get a good place to live, and the crabs get camouflage. Some crabs in the genus *Pugettia* are decorators, but the northern kelp crab (*P. producta*; Plate 15) relies on color change for its camouflage. Decorator crabs select pieces of seaweed as well as sedentary animals such as sponges, hydroids, and bryozoans and fasten them to hooked spines (Velcro-like bristles) on the back of their shell. These residents remain alive on the crab and benefit from the water current as the crab walks. They are able to take advantage of leftovers from the crab's meals. The invertebrates and algae in turn allow the crab to blend in with its environment and avoid predation. Decorator crabs may use the algae on their carapace as an alternate food source. When decorator crabs molt, they recycle their decorations: they

Figure 6.3. Graceful decorator crab (*Oregonia gracilis*). Photo by Dave Cowles, http://rosario.wallawalla.edu/inverts.

remove the algae, sponges, and other passengers from their old shell and place them on their new shell. This keeps them very busy for a few hours after molting. Some species will use anemones, coral, sponges, or even pebbles or wood debris to decorate themselves. However, too much decoration may slow down their activity, feeding, and escape. In some species, crabs that have grown large enough to defend themselves no longer adorn their backs. Kristen Hultgren and John Stachowicz of University of California, Davis, found that as decorator crabs grew, the hooked setae tended to decrease in many species. The world's largest crab, the Japanese spider crab (Fig. 1.14) is a decorator.

While some crab species are unselective and choose whichever algae are the most abundant to adorn their shells, others are more selective. For example, the longnose spider crab (*Libinia dubia*) camouflages itself with the chemically noxious alga *Dictyota menstrualis* in areas where this algal species is available. *Dictyota* produces a chemical that protects it from getting eaten by herbivorous fish. This chemical also stimulates decoration behavior in the crab. Crabs covered with *Dictyota* survive better than crabs covered with other algae that fish like to consume. By using this particular algal species, the crab takes advantage of the defensive chemicals of the alga to gain additional protection from predators.

Some crabs, including the coconut crab (Plate 1) climb trees. Mangrove crabs (*Aratus* spp.; Fig. 2.6) are small grapsid crabs that live out of the water on the roots, leaves, and branches of mangrove trees in tropical regions. They can be found very high up in the trees, far from the water. This mode of life protects them from most aquatic predators, but it does make them more vulnerable to terrestrial and aerial predators, such as birds.

Burrowing crabs benefit marsh grasses by aerating the soil that would otherwise have low oxygen. Alejandro Bortolus from Brown University and colleagues from the Universidad Nacional de Mar del Plata in Argentina found that the burrowing crab, *Chasmagnathus (Neohelice) granulata,* which grazes on the marsh grass *Spartina densiflora,* can increase reproduction in the plant, specifically the amount of seed production and seed viability. In addition to improving plant performance, however, the ecosystem modification (ecological engineering) by burrowers can have negative effects: Alejandro Canepuccia and colleagues from Universidad Nacional de Mar del Plata found that certain moths attacked and made holes in *Spartina* stems, and that crab activities appeared to increase moth attacks; that is, in areas with more burrowing crabs the plants had greater damage by moths. Stem-boring herbivores like these can cause mortality in *Spartina,* and activities of burrowing crabs increases this effect.

Interactions with Fish and Other Vertebrates

Most interactions between crabs and fish are predator/prey interactions, with large crabs eating small fish, and large fish eating small crabs. The presence of predators can alter crab behavior. Red king crab juveniles (*Paralithodes camtschaticus*) are generally associated with complex habitats, which provide hiding places, and the complexity of the habitat affects their survival when predatory halibut are around. In an experimental laboratory study with a fish predator, Alan Stoner of NOAA studied survival of newly settled juvenile red king crabs in eight different habitats with varying amounts and types of physical structure, open sand, gravel bottom, and habitat islands. Video observations provided insights on interactions between crabs and Pacific halibut predators (*Hippoglossus stenolepis*). He found that survival of crabs increased with the amount of physical structure and was highest in the most complex habitats and in patchy habitats with a variety of different substrates. Predators were less active in more structured habitats, which reduced their attacks on crabs, while in open sandy habitats the fish had a higher attack rate and higher capture success, so crabs had lower survival. This study found that crabs could detect the predators and change their behavior by sheltering in dense patches of habitat.

The arrow goby (*Clevelandia ios*) of North America is commonly found in the burrows of various invertebrates, especially crabs. The fish resident usually benefits the most, but having this roommate brings advantages to the crab as well. Should the goby find a chunk of food that is too large for it, it will give it to the crab. The crab chops it up as it devours its snack, allowing the goby to take some pieces back. Sometimes the gobies feed on the hosts' waste products, thus helping to clean the burrow and earn their keep.

In the cold Arctic waters around Russia, snailfish (*Careproctus*) lay their eggs in the gill chamber of golden king crabs. The number of *Careproctus* eggs increases with the size of the crab. Almost all of the crabs examined had these egg deposits.

Many species of shore birds, as well as aquatic reptiles such as some turtles and crocodiles, are known to eat crabs. There is even a saltwater crab–eating frog (*Fejervarya cancrivora*), in the Indo-Pacific mangrove swamps, the only amphibian known to enter the sea.

EFFECTS ON THE ENVIRONMENT

In addition to these specific one-on-one interactions, crabs that burrow can alter the environment and thus affect other sediment dwellers. By digging burrows crabs "stir up" the sediments—a process called *bioturbation*—bringing up previously buried sediments. This can change the chemistry of the sediments, affect other residents, and affect the cycling of nitrogen, an essential nutrient. Crab bioturbation stimulates benthic metabolism and cycling of nitrogen. Herbivorous crabs can have negative effects on marsh vegetation if they eat too much. Salt marshes may have bare patches due to disturbance by harsh physical conditions. The edges of the bare patches are subject to more grazing by herbivorous crabs (e.g., *Neohelice [Chasmagnathus] granulata*) than intact areas of the marsh. Recovery of plant growth in the bare patches will be extremely slow in the presence of crabs but will be accelerated if they are removed.

Land crabs can also affect their environment, especially when populations are dense. They can have obvious effects on the physical environment: scraping algae from rocks can accelerate erosion; extensive digging of burrows can affect soil turnover and stability and may contribute to erosion; eating leaf litter helps to keep the mangrove forest floor clear; and the crabs' waste fertilizes the mangrove trees. Abandoned hermit crab snail shells can provide reservoirs for water in otherwise arid areas. Fruit-eating crabs can serve as important dispersing agents for the plant.

A study by Gustav Paulay and John Starmer of the Florida Museum documented the extinction of a land crab, *Geograpsus severnsi,* on the Hawaiian Islands—the first crab extinction during the human era. The species was unique to the Hawaiian Islands, was the only land crab on the islands, and was the most land-adapted crab in the Pacific, expanding farther inland and to higher elevations than others. The loss of the crab likely had great impacts on the ecology of Hawaii because land crabs are major predators and omnivores, control litter decomposition, and help in nutrient cycling and seed dispersal. Their disappearance was caused by the arrival of humans to the islands and resulted in large-scale changes in the state's ecosystem.

Plate 1. Coconut crab (*Birgus latro*). Photo from rareanimalblogspot, Wikimedia.

Plate 2. Atlantic rock crab (*Cancer irroratus*). Photo from U.S. Geological Survey.

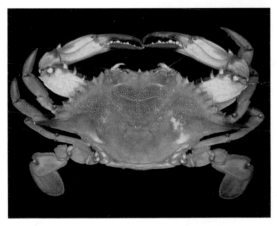

Plate 3. Blue crab (*Callinectes sapidus*). Photo from South Carolina Department of Natural Resources.

Plate 4. Shame-faced crab (*Calappa* sp.). Photo by Oliver Mengedoht/Panzerwelten.de.

Plate 5. Sally Lightfoot crab (*Grapsus grapsus*). Photo from fvqg.info, Wikimedia.

Plate 6. Land crab (*Gecarcinus lateralis*). Photo © Gregory C. Jensen.

A

B

Plate 7. Female and male pea crabs (*Pinnotheres pisum*) in bivalve hosts. *A*, Cockle; *B*, Pen shell. Photo by Carola Becker.

Plate 8. Land hermit crab (*Coenobita* sp.). Photo by ZooFari, Wikimedia.

Plate 9. Galatheid crab eating a squid. Photo from NOAA.

Plate 10. Porcelain anemone crab (*Neopetrolisthes* sp.) in sea anemone. Photo by Phil Sokol,

Plate 11. Guard crab (*Trapezius* sp.) in coral. Photo by Keoki Stender, www.MarinelifePhotography.com.

Plate 12. Umbrella crab (*Cryptolithodes sitchensis*). Photo © Gregory C. Jensen.

Plate 13. Red deep-sea crab (*Chaceon quinquedens*). Photo by Joseph Kunkel.

Plate 14. Golden crab (*Chaceon fenneri*). Photo from NOAA.

Plate 15. Northern kelp crab (*Pugettia producta*) on feather boa kelp. Photo by Kristin Hultgren.

Plate 16. Sargassum crab (also called gulfweed or Columbus crab) (*Planes minutus*) in *Sargassum* weed. Photo by Susan DeVictor/Southeastern Regional Taxonomic Center.

Plate 17. Mating green crabs (*Carcinus maenas*), with brown-phase male on top and smaller green female below. Photo by Mark Bowler, markbowler.com.

Plate 18. Fiddler crab (*Uca chlorophthalmus*). Photo by P. Weis.

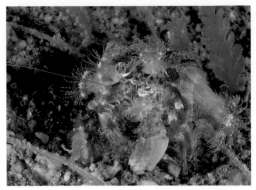

Plate 19. Hermit crab (*Dardanus* sp.) with sea anemones (*Calliactis polypus*). Photo by Nick Hobgood, Wikimedia.

Plate 20. Boxer (or pom-pom) crab (*Lybia tessellata*) with anemones. Photo by Andrew J. Martinez.

A

B

C

Plate 21 *A, B, C.* Molting blue crab (*Callinectes sapidus*). Photos from NOAA.

Plate 22. Lemon-yellow clawed fiddler crabs (*Uca perplexa*) fighting. Photo by P. Weis.

Plate 23. Red crabs (*Gecarcoidea natalis*) migrating on Christmas Island. Photo by J. Jaycock, © Commonwealth of Australia.

Plate 24. Hermit crab (*Pagurus dalli*), with shell almost completely covered by a colony of Hydractinia. Photo by Dave Cowles, http://rosario.wallawalla.edu/inverts.

Plate 25. Statue at Fisherman's Wharf. Photo from NOAA.

Plate 26. Floor mosaic in Monaco aquarium (Musée Oceanographique de Monaco). Photo by Alan Woollard.

Plate 27. Sebastian from *The Little Mermaid*. © Disney.

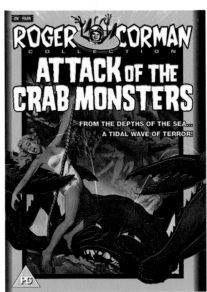

Plate 28. Poster for *Attack of the Crab Monsters* (1957).

CHAPTER SEVEN

Crab Problems and Problem Crabs

Crabs, like the rest of us, are affected by diseases, parasites, habitat loss, climate change, and pollution. On the flip side, some crabs cause problems for their neighbors and, in a few cases, for people.

DISEASES

Crabs are subject to a great variety of diseases from viruses, bacteria, and pathogenic ciliates and amoebas. For example, "gray crab" disease in blue crabs is caused by *Paramoeba* parasites, resulting in significant mortality. Fungus diseases may infect crabs and especially their egg masses, causing mortality of up to 50% of the eggs. More than thirty viruses have been reported in crabs. Bacterial diseases of crabs are caused by common pathogenic organisms such as *Vibrio, Aeromonas,* and *Rickettsia. Vibrio cholerae* and *V. vulnificus* may occur in blue crabs and may pose potential health hazards to humans who consume the crabs raw.

Shell disease—also called rust, brown spot, black spot, or burr disease—is the progressive erosion of the shell. It occurs in many species including blue crabs, king crabs, shrimp and prawns, crayfish, and lobsters (Fig. 7.1). Typically starting as little black spots on the shell, the disease progresses, and the spots become larger and deeper. Eventually they can merge and penetrate the shell completely, causing the affected areas to become soft and easily broken. In the past decade, this disease has infected shells of lobsters in Long Island Sound and southern New England, and in the worst cases it rots the

Figure 7.1. Shell disease in American lobster (*Homarus americanus*). Photo courtesy of Barbara Somers, URI Fisheries Center.

lobsters' shells entirely. Shell disease is not caused by a single type of bacteria, but rather by a combination of different bacteria that together erode the chitin layers of the shell. Any injury to the outermost layer of the shell exposes the underlying layers to opportunistic microorganisms, including fungi and bacteria. The condition is most common in stressed animals—for example, those with already damaged shells, antennae, or claws. It also appears to be more common in polluted habitats where bacteria can be high. Molting can serve to eliminate the disease along with the rotted shell, but some animals do not improve or may actually get worse after molting. If the soft tissues underneath the shell have become affected, molting is not a cure, and these animals may not even be able to separate the old and new cuticle and can therefore die during molt. In most cases, the meat of animals with shell disease is not affected and can be safely eaten.

Bitter crab disease is caused by a blood parasite, *Hematodinium perezi,* a single-celled, microscopic algae (specifically, a dinoflagellate). Once inside the crab, the parasite reproduces rapidly over 3 to 6 weeks. The crab's blood changes to a milky-white color and loses its clotting ability. The parasite consumes oxygen from the crab's blood and tissues, causing the crab to become weak and lethargic, and to eventually die. The disease is most prevalent in blue crabs in warm, relatively shallow, high-salinity waters.

Many crabs unaffected by shell disease die when they molt. This is a major problem for aquaculture operations for soft shell crabs, which keep crabs during molt. For years, this high mortality (about 50%) was attributed to the stresses of molting itself, but recently it has been found that virus infections spread in the "crab farm" contribute to the high death rate. Such infections are largely invisible, so researchers are attempting to develop a test to determine whether premolt crabs are infected. If they can find a way to do this, it will both help stop the spread of infection and benefit the business.

Not all diseases are caused by pathogenic organisms. "Black gill," a condition seen in crabs in many locations, may be caused by pollution in areas of dredging or sewage wastes. The blackened gills may be due initially to sediment accumulating in the gills, but microbes, algae, and other organisms follow and settle in the contaminated gill chamber. These organisms do not infect and cause disease; rather, they cover gill tissue and physically smother the crab.

PARASITES

A parasite is an organism that lives on or in an organism of another species (its host), from which it obtains nutrition. Parasites can cause little, moderate, or severe damage to their hosts.

Other Crustaceans

Crabs host some interesting types of parasites. Rhizocephalans are distant relatives of barnacles that spend their adult lives as parasites, living in and taking resources from their hosts. One rhizocephalan, *Sacculina*, is a particularly bizarre parasite that has an unusual structure and odd effects on the crabs that it parasitizes, essentially hijacking their reproductive system. Like barnacles, they start their lives as free-swimming nauplius larvae. But unlike barnacles, these larvae do not look for a rock to settle down on; instead, they seek out a crab host. When the larva finds a crab, it moves around until it finds a joint with soft cuticle. It then molts, injecting its soft body into the crab while its shell falls off. It settles at the rear part of the crab, at the junction of the abdomen and thorax, and grows inside the crab, forming rootlike branches that eventually penetrate all parts of the host's body, from which it takes nourishment. Roots invade all the tissues and destroy the host's reproductive system. When the crab molts, the parasite makes a hole in the new skeleton at the junction of the abdomen and the body and protrudes a portion of its own body, a large mass called the *externa*. Adult parasites consist of only the roots penetrating throughout the crab's tissues, and the externa, which protrudes from the underside and occupies what would have been the site of the brood pouch for eggs in a female crab host (Fig. 7.2). The externa becomes the parasite's reproductive system and eventually releases larvae into the water. If the host crab is male, it becomes feminized: its specialized pleopods used for copulation become like the female type, its abdomen widens, and the gonads may atrophy or become like ovaries. Because of this *parasitic castration*, infected crabs will not reproduce and are able to release only the parasite's larvae. Some rhizocephalans cause behavioral changes so that infected hosts groom, protect, and ventilate the parasite's externa as if it were their own egg mass. In addition, the parasite produces peptides that mimic the ones released from hatching crab eggs. Typically, these peptides stimulate the female to pump her abdomen to help release her larvae, but in an infested crab, this behavior results in releasing the parasite's larvae instead of her own.

Rhizocephalans are not the only parasitic castrators. Parasitic isopods (a type of small crustacean) called entoniscids penetrate through the gill chamber, migrate to the internal organs, and settle in the digestive gland, where they also act as parasitic castrators. Males infested with these parasites acquire female secondary sex characteristics, and their testes stop functioning. In areas where the parasite is common, crab reproduction can be greatly reduced. Another type of isopod, the bopyrids, occupy gill chambers, often of shrimp, and are parasitic castrators. In addition to rhizocephalans and isopods, nematomorph or horsehair worms (*Nematomorpha*) and two flatworm species are also parasitic castrators of hermit crabs.

Some crab diseases are the result of a double parasite or *hyperparasite*; that is, a parasite whose host is also a parasite. The hyperparasites that infest hermit crab parasites (mostly rhizocephalans and bopyrid isopods) were studied by John McDermott of Franklin and Marshall College, who found that rhizocephalans were themselves hosts for an amoeba and four species of isopods; bopyrid isopods were hosts for three other isopods and one rhizocephalan; and a burrowing barnacle was host for one species of isopod.

Figure 7.2. Externa of rhizocephalan parasite protruding from crab host.
Photo by Hans Hillewaert, Wikimedia.

Flatworms

Pepper spot disease, which occurs in a number of brachyurans, is an example of a disease caused by a hyperparasite. A parasitic flatworm (*Microphallus bassodactylus*), also known as a fluke, infects a crab; the fluke then becomes infected by a single-celled protist (protozoan) *Urosporidium crescens*. The very small, brownish protist multiplies inside the larval worm until the worm is completely consumed and replaced by protist spores. The flatworm parasite has a complicated life cycle, starting off in a snail, then moving to the crab. After developing within the crab, it can be transmitted to vertebrate hosts such as raccoons, in which it reaches its adult reproductive stage in the intestines, and eventually releases eggs to infect a snail and complete its life cycle. The disease manifests as tiny black specks over the body, and the large number of them has given the names "buckshot," "pepper spots," or "pepper" crabs to the condition. Crabs are not seriously affected, but pepper spot disease can make their meat appear unappetizing even though cooking kills the parasites and renders the crab meat safe to eat for humans. Predators such as raccoons, however, do not cook their food and can get infected from eating parasitized crabs.

Other Parasites

Nemertean worms in the genus *Carcinonemertes* infest a variety of crabs, as its name ("carcino") indicates. One species is named *Carcinonemertes carcinophilia*, in case there was any doubt. Up to one thousand juvenile worms live inside the gill chamber, and when a female host deposits eggs, the worms leave the gill chamber, move into the egg mass, and feed on the eggs. Because they feed on eggs, only those worms that infest female rather than male crabs can reproduce. Once the uneaten crab's eggs hatch, the worms move back to the gill chamber.

Some harpacticoid copepods, small crustaceans that are usually free-living, inhabit the gill chambers of various crabs, but they do not appear to harm the crab host, so are considered commensal (not harming the host) rather than parasitic. Certain fish and barnacles also use a crab's gill chambers. The snailfish (*Careproctus*) deposits its eggs within the gill chamber of golden king crabs. Although putting eggs in a well-aerated and safe place is clearly beneficial to the successful reproduction of the fish, in this case the presence of the eggs may damage the gill tissue of the crabs. Studies of the gill barnacle *Octolasmis muelleri,* which lives in the blue crab, found that it caused only minor increases in the crab's ventilation and respiration rate, justifying the categorization of this stalked barnacle as a commensal rather than a parasite. There is a very thin line between commensal and parasitic relationships, and whether harm is done or not may depend on the sheer numbers and size of the residents (commensals or parasites) compared to the hosts they are living in.

PREDATORS

Juvenile and adult crabs are consumed by many bottom-feeding fish such as Atlantic cod, skates, rays, cunners, tautog, striped bass, black sea bass, haddock, tilefish, conger eels, and weakfish. Other predators of juvenile crabs are lingcod, wolf-eels, rockfish, and octopus. Dungeness crab juveniles are eaten by a variety of bottom fish in the nearshore area, with flatfish (an order that includes common species such as flounder, halibut, and sole) being the most important. Adult blue crabs regularly prey on juvenile blue crabs.

Octopuses are particularly fond of crabs for dinner; humans have made their job easier by providing large numbers of crabs for them that cannot escape or hide—that is, in traps. In areas of Florida, the stone crab fishery has been affected by a horde of octopuses that climb into traps and eat the crabs. These intelligent animals have been observed going from trap to trap to dine on the contents like someone going along a salad bar. They know where the crabs are, and in some cases have reduced the catch, annoying the fishermen.

Semiterrestrial and land crabs are preyed on by terrestrial predators such as birds (e.g., rails, egrets, gulls, plovers, sandpipers, and terns) and raccoons. Most predation on fiddler crabs is on females, which lack the male's large defensive claw. A burrow does not guarantee survival because some predators can enter the burrow or dig down to capture the resident. In some areas, land crabs are prized food for iguanas. Freshwater crabs in Asia are important food for birds such as herons and kingfishers, as well as lizards, crocodiles, frogs, toads, and mammals such as otters, mongooses, civets, and macaques. Many crabs are preyed on by humans, which will be covered in Chapter 8.

HABITAT LOSS

Habitat loss is the main cause of population decline in freshwater crabs. Two-thirds of all freshwater crab species may be at risk of going extinct, with one in six species particularly vulnerable, according to a survey from The International Union for Conservation of Nature (IUCN). Freshwater crabs, which live primarily in tropical areas, are among the most threatened of all groups of animals, especially in Southeast Asia, which is one of the prime areas of crab biodiversity: For the 1280 known species, 227 are considered near-threatened, vulnerable, endangered, or critically endangered, and only one-third are not at-risk, although almost half are too poorly known to assess. The majority of those threatened are semiterrestrial species that live in habitats subjected to deforestation, alteration of drainage patterns, and pollution. Crabs contribute to freshwater systems by feeding on fallen leaves, algae, and detritus and are important food for birds as well as various reptiles and mammals noted above. Because they require clean water to survive, crabs are also excellent indicators of good water quality and are especially impacted by habitat destruction and pollution.

Marine crabs also are affected by habitat loss; for example, when salt marshes are drained for development, mangroves are removed for timber or shrimp-farm ponds, oyster reefs are overharvested, or intertidal areas are converted to jetties or hardened shorelines with seawalls or bulkheads. Over half of the original salt marshes in the United States have been filled in to create more land area for homes, industry, and agriculture. Additional marsh losses were caused by ditching for mosquito control and diking to create impoundments. Fortunately, people are beginning to realize the importance of these habitats, and federal and state laws and regulations now reflect an appreciation for the function and value of marshes and other wetlands.

At the ocean beaches in the United States, beach nourishment projects and bulldozing are performed to combat erosion. Although these short-term responses to erosion are considered preferable to "hardening" the shoreline by construction of seawalls and groins, they have a clear negative impact on ghost crab populations. Ghost crabs (Fig. 2.3) are also harmed by driving on beaches. Beach traffic not only reduces their population density but also changes their behavior—they walk shorter distances and have a reduced home range in areas where cars are allowed.

DAMAGE BY INVASIVE SPECIES

Species may be transported to new regions where, in the absence of normal predators and diseases, they may cause ecological damage; these are called *invasive species*. Crabs themselves can be the invasive species (see later in this chapter); crabs can also be the victim of an invasive species. One such example is the yellow crazy ant (*Anoplolepis gracilipes*), which arrived on Christmas Island around 1930. It is thought to have come from either Malaysia or Singapore along with produce, but did not cause major problems till the 1990s. This ant has no natural predators on Christmas Island, where it thrives, has a high reproductive rate, and forms multiqueened supercolonies in which the ants occur at very high densities, killing and displacing crabs on the forest floor. They also devastate crabs during their migration to the coast for reproduction (see Chapter 6). It is estimated that yellow crazy ants have displaced 15–20 million crabs by occupying their burrows, killing them, and eating them. Land crabs are vital to Christmas Island's tourism, as well as its biodiversity. They are an important keystone species in the forest, digging burrows, turning over the soil, and fertilizing it with their droppings, so their loss could have serious ecological and economic consequences.

The saltmarsh cordgrass (*Spartina alterniflora*) is an essential part of salt marshes on the East and Gulf coasts of North America, but it has become an invasive species on the West Coast of North America and in China. In China, intertidal areas that were invaded by this plant were examined for effects on resident crab populations. Overall, the numbers and density of crabs were actually higher in the invaded areas than in noninvaded areas because one species, *Helice tientsinensis,* was much more abundant in *Spartina*-invaded habitats. However, species richness and diversity were lower in these areas because all the other crab species had become less abundant. In contrast, *Spartina alterniflora* marshes on the East Coast of the United States are being invaded by the common reed (*Phragmites australis*). In this case, however, the fiddler crabs do not seem to "care" which plant is on the marsh surface and do not appear to be harmed by the invasive species.

POLLUTION

The products of human society can harm organisms that live near people, and for crabs, the impact is strongest in estuaries near urban or agricultural areas. There are many different types of pollutants with different effects, but of significant concern are the local areas that are contaminated by toxic chemicals such as metals, pesticides, oil, and other industrial chemicals.

Toxic Chemicals

Metals
Metals enter coastal waters through dumping, atmospheric deposition (e.g., rain), or sewage, which also brings organic pollutants and pharmaceuticals. Metals are by-products of industrial processes and include mercury, cadmium, silver, lead, copper, chromium, arsenic, and zinc. They concentrate in bottom sediments and are taken up into animals (via food, gills, or absorption from the water) and can be toxic even at low concentrations. Crabs (and other animals) have ways of dealing with metals if the concentrations aren't too great. They can eliminate them through their gills, excrete them in their urine, store them in their exoskeletons and shed them when they molt, or store them in a nontoxic chemical form. Proteins called *metallothioneins* can bind some metals; when a crab is exposed

to metals it makes more of these metal-binding proteins. Metals can also be stored in granules inside cells—the granules keeping the metals from doing damage. There are limits, however, to how much metal can be dealt with, and as more accumulates in the animal, toxic effects occur. At levels far below the concentrations that can cause death, metals can affect the sensitive chemoreceptors on the antennules (which impairs the ability to detect odors; see Chapter 3) alter oxygen consumption, retard limb regeneration and molting, impair color change, and alter behavior. Effects are more severe at low salinity and are especially detrimental at early life stages such as larvae, whose development and metamorphosis is impaired at very low metal levels.

Pesticides

Pesticides are designed to kill agricultural pests (generally insects) on land. After being sprayed on land, they wash into the water when it rains and affect aquatic and marine animals including crabs. As with metals, crabs have ways of coping with pesticides: enzymes can be made to detoxify them, but these defenses are overcome as levels increase. Chlorinated hydrocarbons such as DDT take a many decades to break down and can accumulate in animal tissue. They become more concentrated as they move up the food chain (a process called *biomagnification*). Their effects include preventing larvae from developing normally, reducing respiration and metabolism, altering limb regeneration and molting, and impairing salt and water balance. Although they have been banned for decades, chlorinated hydrocarbons still remain in sediments and organisms since they break down so slowly.

Organophosphate and carbamate pesticides, developed as "second generation" pesticides are less persistent, but still have harmful effects on crustaceans. The insecticide carbaryl (Sevin), for example, which is used to control many insects on land and used directly in the marine environment to control ghost shrimp in Pacific oyster beds, is also toxic to Dungeness crabs. Dungeness crab larvae are highly sensitive to other insecticides and fungicides as well. Malathion, the most commonly used organophosphate insecticide in the United States, slows down larval development by delaying molting. Temephos (Abate) and other pesticides affect the nervous system and behavior, making crabs more susceptible to predators.

As people have realized the widespread effects of both first- and second-generation pesticides, attempts have been made to develop new pesticides that are more specialized in their toxicity to insects. Some of these new pesticides, for example, target the molt cycle of insect larvae by mimicking their specific biology or hormones. Unfortunately for crabs, crustacean biology is very similar to insects', and pesticides such as diflubenzuron (Dimilin), a chitin synthesis inhibitor, interfere with the molt cycle of crabs, particularly of larvae that have to molt frequently. Methoprene, a juvenile hormone analog designed to prevent insects from maturing and reproducing is, unsurprisingly, toxic to larval crabs.

Oil

Components of oil pollution—including benzene and naphthalene from crude oil—are also toxic to crustaceans. They, and other water-soluble components of oil, decrease the crabs' metabolic rate, prolong their molt cycle, and affect their growth at molt. Larvae are more sensitive than adults, as usual, and their development can be retarded with low levels of exposure. Behavior is also affected, with reduced feeding and impaired chemoreception noted as direct effects of oil pollution. A rather small oil spill in the late 1960s in Cape Cod, Massachusetts, caused fiddler crabs to dig shallower burrows (probably to avoid pooled oil below the marsh surface), and over the winter they froze to death because they had not gone deep enough to escape the freezing zone. Forty years later, scientists revisited the oiled marsh site and found a substantial amount of partly degraded oil still remained below the marsh surface, and fiddler crabs burrow in the sediments where they are still getting exposed to the oil. Jennifer Culbertson from Woods Hole Oceanographic Institution and colleagues found that exposed crabs avoided burrowing into oiled layers, had delayed escape responses and reduced feeding, and were found in lower population densities than crabs in control areas. Knowledge about long-term consequences of spilled oil should be included when assessing oil-impacted areas. It will take many years (or decades) to understand the overall impacts of the oil pollution that gushed into the Gulf of Mexico from the *Deepwater Horizon* for three months in the spring and summer of 2010. Early reports found blue crab megalopa larvae with oil droplets under their cuticles; the tiny hydrocarbon droplets were visible under the transparent shells of the less than 1/8 inch–sized crabs. These crabs may lose the oil when they molt, but since so many things eat them, it is likely that the oil would move up the food web (the feeding connections in an ecological community). Adult blue crabs in the Gulf were found with a black substance in them, especially notable in their gills. A few months after the spill, effects were also found in adult deep-sea red crabs that could have been due to the oil: most crabs were dead when brought up to the surface. They apparently had enough energy to get in the trap but could no longer survive the standard trip from the bottom to the surface. Harriet Perry and colleagues found fewer red crabs in the Gulf overall; at one of their usually productive sites 12 miles from the *Deepwater Horizon*, they found no red crabs at all.

Brittany McCall and Steven Pennings of the University of Houston examined crab burrows in Louisiana marshes after the oil spill in 2010 and in 2011 and found that in 2010 the number of intertidal crabs was greatly reduced, even in marsh areas with very little oil where the marsh plants did not appear to be affected. This shows that the even when the marsh plants look good, the ecosystem may not be healthy. The following year, however, the crabs had largely recovered. This is a much faster recovery than in Cape Cod, perhaps because the oil that reached the Louisiana marshes had been weathering for several weeks in the ocean before it reached the shore so may have been less toxic.

Industrial Chemicals

Industrial chemicals such as polychlorinated biphenyls (PCBs) are also toxic to crabs, particularly larval stages, with effects on the duration of zoeal development, megalopa size, and developmental anomalies. PCBs also impair color change and physiology. These pollutants, like chlorinated hydrocarbons, are persistent in marine systems, where their concentrations and effects continue long after they are banned. They also biomagnify through food webs, and long-term effects are generally unknown.

Many industrial chemicals and pesticides can affect endocrine systems. As "endocrine disruptors," they can cause these effects at extremely low concentrations. Some pharmaceutical products that enter waterways from sewage treatment plants can also have endocrine effects on a variety of organisms. It is likely that the many chemicals that alter the molt cycle or pigmentation of crabs do so by affecting the crab's endocrine system.

Ironically, pollution can have some indirect positive effects on crabs. Blue crabs in industrialized northern New Jersey, for example, accumulate such high concentrations of pollutants such as mercury and dioxin that fishing for them is banned out of concern for human safety. Consequently, their population is growing, and individuals grow larger than in clean areas where they are still fished for and eaten by their largest predator, humans.

Eutrophication

Nutrients are chemicals that organisms need to live and grow. When in excessive amounts, however, they become a kind of pollution. An oversupply of nutrients—which come from sewage discharge and fertilizer runoff into coastal waters—cause a problem of excessive algal growth called *eutrophication*. These nutrients (primarily nitrogen and phosphorus) stimulate algal blooms that eventually die, sink to the bottom, decompose, and use up the oxygen in the deeper water. Low dissolved oxygen (DO) caused by nutrient pollution is especially damaging in estuaries with little water circulation. Large *dead zones*—that is, areas with very low DO—can extend from estuaries out into marine waters. In the Gulf of Mexico, a huge dead zone (often the size of New Jersey) appears every summer, driven mostly by runoff of nitrogen fertilizers from the Mississippi River, which drains the U.S. farm belt.

While fish may be able to swim away from areas of low oxygen, benthic animals such as crabs generally cannot escape fast enough and can die from lack of oxygen. Sometimes, in warm weather, crabs and other animals swarm into shallow water or even crawl out of oxygen-depleted water completely as they try to breathe. This phenomenon has been called a "jubilee," although the oxygen-starved crabs are clearly not happy. This may result in the crabs surviving hypoxia only long enough to be caught for dinner by the humans, who gave the name *jubilee* to this event. Excessive nutrients can harm crabs in another way beyond direct hypoxia: the nutrients cause sea grasses to decline because algal blooms cloud the water and prevent them from getting enough light, diminishing this important blue crab habitat.

Marine Debris and Trash

Abandoned or lost fishing gear can be a hazard to crabs and have significant economic impacts. In a study of lost gill nets in Puget Sound, Washington, Kirsten Gilardi and colleagues estimated the daily catch rate of a single derelict gill net, which still catches crabs although abandoned, and developed a model to predict overall mortality. They calculated 4368 Dungeness crabs would be entangled during the lifetime of a single derelict net, which is a loss of $19,656 to the fishery, compared to a cost of only $1358 to remove the net. In recent years, projects have been undertaken to remove lost fishing gear, including crab pots. Debris removal efforts have contributed to a healthier ocean and more sustainable fisheries. In addition to removing tons of debris, including thousands of derelict pots, from the marine environment, these projects have created jobs and other economic benefits along the coast. Other types of trash and litter, especially plastic that never degrades, damages marine organisms by entangling them or causing problems when the animals ingest it. There is one species that benefits though: the Sargassum crab, which is not restricted to Sargassum weed but can ride along on rafts of marine litter.

Climate Change

Global warming can have a variety of effects on crabs. Some of these effects might be considered positive, depending on location. One response, already being seen, is that the ranges of many species are shifting. Ghost crabs are being seen farther north than they used to be. Blue crabs, previously limited by colder northern temperatures, will be able to survive farther north given the warming effects of climate change, thereby increasing the fishery potential in places north of Chesapeake Bay. Blue crabs in the Carolinas become mature in only 1 year, while farther north they take 2 years. As temperatures continue to increase, they are likely to mature in 1 year in the mid-Atlantic as well, which would benefit the fishery. However, continued northern migration of species will have unpredictable effects on the communities they move into. Species that depend on cold water, such as the various commercially important crab species in Alaskan waters, will suffer from warming waters.

The predicted rise in sea level from 1 to 3 feet by 2100 could also affect intertidal crabs. The salt marsh habitats of many species will either have to move up in elevation or else move inland in order to survive. Whether these habitats can adjust their elevations in time to keep pace with climate change is uncertain. Moving farther inland is difficult if not impossible in places where there are roads and towns just inland of the salt marshes.

A compounding aspect of climate change is ocean acidification. Much of the carbon dioxide released into the atmosphere from burning fossil fuels dissolves in the ocean and becomes carbonic acid, making the ocean more acidic (i.e., lowering the pH). By some estimates, the oceans have absorbed 30% of the carbon dioxide we have pumped into the atmosphere since the start of the industrial age. This reduces its accumulation in the atmosphere and the amount of warming, but that storage comes with a price. Increasing ocean acidity especially affects organisms that make shells out of calcium carbonate ($CaCO_3$). This process, called *calcification*, is important to the biology and survival of a wide range of marine organisms, including crustaceans.

Lower pH makes it harder to build shells, and the water can become acidic enough to break down existing shell. In shell-forming organisms such as corals, there is a reduction both in the amount of shell produced and in growth rate. Lower pH negatively affected survival, growth, and calcium content of the first juvenile stage of king crabs. Not all species, however, respond in this way. Justin B. Ries and colleagues from Woods Hole Oceanographic Institution found that 7 of the 18 species they studied, including blue crab and lobster, actually built more shell when exposed to increased acidification, contrary to expectation. These surprising responses may reflect differences in the ability to regulate pH at the site of calcification, in the extent to which their outer shell layer is protected by an organic covering, or in shell solubility.

A great deal of research is ongoing to better understand effects of acidification on different species of crabs and other organisms. Effects that have been found are not limited to calcification but include altering other aspects of physiology and behavior. For example, Kate de la Haye and colleagues from Plymouth University found that hermit crabs in reduced pH seawater were less likely to change from a suboptimal to an optimal shell than those in normal sea water, and those that did change shells took longer to do so. Crabs in the low pH also showed less antennular flicking (the 'sniffing' response in decapods) and reduced movement. When a food odor was presented to them, those in the low pH water were less successful in locating the odor source. This work shows that the reduction in sea water pH damaged chemoreception, resource assessment, and decision-making processes of these crabs, reducing their ability to acquire a vital resource.

PROBLEM CRABS

In addition to having problems, crabs—as parasites or invasive species—can be the cause of problems.

Parasites

Pea Crab (*Pinnotheres*)

Pea crabs in the genus *Pinnotheres* (e.g., *Pinnotheres pisum*; Plate 7) live in the mantle cavity of bivalve mollusks, or, less commonly, in sea urchins, sea cucumbers, tunicates, and worm tubes. There are over one hundred different species of pea crabs. They are small, about the size of a pea. While they tend to be round (again like a pea), species that live in worm tubes are extended sideways to fit in the tube. Because they do not harm the worm host, some of these species are considered commensal rather than parasitic. Other pinnotherids, however, are clearly parasitic. *Pinnotheres ostreum,* found in Atlantic oysters, is considered a parasite, while the species in mussels (*P. maculatus*) is considered commensal. The crabs in the mussel feed on mucous strings by which the bivalve conveys food to its mouth. If a particular mussel is host to more than one pea crab, it is more likely to feel the strain of parasitism. When there is not much food available, pea crabs will chew on their host mussel's gills, showing that the line dividing "commensal" from "parasite" is a fuzzy one indeed. *P. sinensis* in the Pacific near China and Japan routinely damages the gills of the host, impairing its filtration efficiency. Over prolonged periods of time, pea crabs can do permanent damage to their host's gills. They may also surprise unsuspecting diners at seafood restaurants while they are eating oysters or mussels.

These parasites can do economic damage to shellfish aquaculture operations. Oliver Trottier and colleagues from the University of Auckland sampled green-lipped mussels in a farm in New Zealand and found pea crabs in about 5% of the mussels, and infected mussels weighed 30% less than uninfected ones. The researchers estimated that the loss of production on this mussel farm was about 1763 pounds. When extrapolated to total mussel aquaculture production in New Zealand, they calculated that pea crab infection causes a loss to the industry of over US$2 million annually.

Most large bivalves host at least some species of pinnotherids, which typically take up residence where they can obtain oxygen and feed on plankton or mucus made by the host. Carola Becker of the Senckenberg Research Institute in Frankfurt, Germany, found that European species of pea crabs live in a number of different hosts, contrary to the previous thinking that they were host-specific. Female pea crabs have a rather soft body and depend on their hosts for protection. Females mate as juveniles, and with each successive molt, their carapace becomes softer and more translucent. Adult males are smaller and harder than mature females. While the small males can leave and move around, the larger females generally cannot leave their host and have a very high investment in reproduction, typical of parasites.

Coral Gall Crab (*Hapalocarcinus* spp.)
Coral gall crabs live inside corals and were previously thought to be filter feeders. However, Roy Kropp of the University of Maryland took scanning electron micrographs of the crabs' mouthparts and found that they were not suited for filter feeding but rather for collecting coral mucus, and he deter-

CRABS BEHAVING BADLY IN HOLLYWOOD MOVIES

In the 1957 B-movie *Attack of the Crab Monsters* (a "camp" horror movie made by Roger Corman; Plate 28), a U.S. Navy seaplane delivers a team of scientists, led by nuclear physicist Dr. Karl Weigand, to a remote Pacific atoll to study the effects of atomic fallout from nearby H-bomb tests. This team replaces a previous research expedition that had disappeared. As supplies are being unloaded, a seaman falls overboard and is decapitated by something in the surf. In the team's laboratory, Weigand reads the journal left by the previous team and learns that they had noted an increase in the size of the island's creatures due to atomic radiation. There isn't a sign of life on the island, but the researchers hear voices calling to them at night, and when they investigate they are captured and eaten. The gigantic mutant crabs (with human-type eyes rather than stalked ones) absorb the brain tissue and intelligence of their victims and can speak in their voices. Members of the current expedition are systematically attacked and eaten by the crabs, which are invulnerable to most weapons because of their mutation. The scientists discover that the crabs are causing earthquakes and landslides that are destroying the island. As the remaining expedition members struggle to survive on the island, they must find a way to stop the crabs before they reproduce and invade the oceans of the world. Any knowledge of crustacean biology, other than their use of claws in capturing food, is non-existent in this movie.

Jules Verne's *Mysterious Island* (1961), produced by Charles Schneer and directed by Cy Endfield, is about Union prisoners of war from the Civil War who escape a southern stockade in a hot air balloon, which encounters a violent storm and crash-lands on an unknown island. After being attacked by a giant crab, the fugitives discover that this unusual island has been previously inhabited and they are being watched. It turns out that the island is inhabited by Captain Nemo, captain of the submarine *Nautilus*, from *20,000 Leagues under the Sea*. He is experimenting with ways to end starvation in the world—which explains the enormous crabs, bees, and birds that the castaways encounter. Before he can accomplish his goal, however, he is destroyed by the island's volcano, while the others manage to escape in the *Nautilus*. Despite the fantasy, the giant crabs in this movie are anatomically correct and look like gigantic land crabs, but the black tips of the claws suggest that they are stone crabs.

A giant crab appears in *Land of the Lost* (2009), directed by Brad Silberling and produced by Sid and Marty Krofft and Jimmy Miller. This movie, based on the 1974 TV series of the same name, is a comedy science fiction movie about a pompous paleontologist who finds a way to travel back in time with colleagues. The crab plays only a cameo role and is generally upstaged by a variety of dinosaurs, a pteranodon, a race of lizard men, and Will Ferrell. Nevertheless, in its big scene, the crab walks forward rather than sideways.

mined that some species make their living from the coral itself. One species collects coral mucus by fanning or scratching the coral with its legs. Another uses its claws to collect mucus and other debris or to snip pieces of coral tissue. The third uses its mouthparts and claws to make a mucous ball and sweep it along the coral surface to pick up mucus and debris. Kropp therefore considered these species of gall crabs as parasitic rather than commensal.

Invasive Species

When non-native species arrive in a new location, most are either harmless or do not survive the changed conditions they encounter. But some new immigrants do flourish, and the small percentage that thrive and reproduce may end up becoming invasive by outcompeting, eating, or parasitizing native species. There are many crabs that have become invasive in various parts of the world; a few are described below.

Green Crab (*Carcinus maenas*)

The green crab (Fig. 1.8) is native to the Atlantic coasts of Europe and Northern Africa where it lives on protected rocky shores, pebbly beaches, mud flats, and tidal marshes. It thrives in a wide range of both salinity and temperature, and has invaded South Africa, Australia, and both coasts of North America. Its larvae spend about 2 months in the plankton, dispersing many miles along the coast. Then they are swept by tides and currents into coastal waters and estuaries where they molt and settle out as juveniles. If conditions are suitable, they will survive and reproduce, establishing a new population. Green crabs arrived on the U.S. Atlantic Coast in the 1800s, probably on fouled ship hulls, and found suitable habitat in coastal bays from New Jersey to Cape Cod; in the early 1900s, they began spreading north, and their arrival in Maine coincided with dramatic declines in the soft clam fishery. Green crabs are a major predator of soft-shelled clams and quahogs, which are shellfish that people favor. The second major invasion was detected in 1989 in San Francisco Bay, where they probably arrived as larvae in the ballast water of commercial ships or in sea grass or kelp used for shipping lobsters and bait worms to the West Coast. Their arrival was associated with losses of up to 50% of the Manila clam stocks in California.

The green crab is an effective forager—it is able to crack open clams and mussels faster than other crabs—and an adept competitor for the food of native crabs, fish, and birds. It also feeds on oysters, worms, and small crustaceans. Kyle Matheson and Patrick Gagnon of Memorial University of Newfoundland learned that newly arrived green crabs in eastern Canada could outcompete other crabs as well because, surprisingly, they can consume bivalves just as well after losing one chela, while another species (rock crabs) reduce their consumption (as would be expected) when they have only one functional claw. They also found that low temperatures reduced feeding to the same degree in both species. Furthermore, Melanie Rossong and colleagues set up competitions for food between green crabs from newly invaded Canadian areas versus those from areas where the crabs had been living for a long time. Recent invaders from Newfoundland were significantly superior to long-established invaders from Nova Scotia and New Brunswick. As the green crab continues to move northward on the Pacific coast, it is of concern to Dungeness crab, oyster, and clam fisheries in the Pacific Northwest.

On the East Coast, snails and mussels that have been living with green crabs for over a century have developed thicker shells as a defense, making them harder to crush than shellfish that have not been exposed to green crab predation. Melanie Rossong and colleagues from Memorial University of Newfoundland found that the green crab also has negative effects on lobsters. In the presence of green crabs, juvenile lobsters, which use shelter to avoid predation, in laboratory aquaria spent more time in their shelter and fed less. The small juveniles also spent less time feeding and handling the food but took longer to locate food sources. Green crabs in North America have fewer parasites and grow larger than they do back home in European waters, traits that may contribute to their success in the New World.

Chinese Mitten Crab (*Eriocheir sinensis*)

The Chinese mitten crab (Fig. 2.7), also known as the hairy crab, is a burrowing crab native to the Yellow Sea in Korea and China that gets its names from the dense patches of hair on its claws. They are believed to have been accidentally released in ballast water in the early 1900s in Germany. In the 1920s and 1930s the population exploded, and the crabs rapidly expanded into many northern European rivers and estuaries. The Thames River in England has also had a population explosion. Economic impacts in Europe from fishery losses due to mitten crabs are estimated at around 80 million Euros.

Adults migrate downstream to reproduce in estuaries, and after 1 or 2 months as planktonic larvae, they migrate upstream to freshwater. They are estimated to take 2 years to reach maturity and live for 4 years. Juveniles eat mostly vegetation, but as they grow they prey more on worms and clams. Many animals prey on them, including raccoons, river otters, wading birds, and fish, but they apparently do not have enough predators to slow down their invasion.

Considered a delicacy in Asia, mitten crabs have been imported illegally into seafood stores in California for the Asian market, which—if not from ballast water—may have been the source of the U.S. introduction. Mitten crabs became established on the U.S. West Coast in the 1990s and are considered a threat to native invertebrates, to the ecological structure of freshwater and estuarine communities, and to some commercial fisheries in the San Francisco Bay area. They may imperil the state's threatened and endangered salmon populations due to their appetite for salmon eggs, and there is concern that they may move north to Oregon, Washington, and British Columbia. They can walk on land and easily enter new rivers to disperse far and wide. In the summer of 2006 they were found in Chesapeake Bay, and by 2007 were spotted in Delaware Bay and the New York–New Jersey vicinity. New York and New Jersey have issued alerts for crabbers to report any sightings. In low-salinity tidal areas, they burrow into banks during low tides, and there is concern that this may increase erosion and make riverbanks unstable. Another problem in California is their impact on water diversion and on fish salvage facilities. In San Francisco Bay, one trawler reported catching over 200 crabs in a single tow on several occasions, a time-consuming and costly distraction. Facility operators and biologists were surprised at the magnitude of the invasion: they had expected a population boom, but not 10,000 crabs a day clogging up systems. Since the crabs are edible and are a valuable commercial species in China, some scientists are encouraging people to eat them to minimize potential problems, using the "if you can't beat 'em, eat 'em" approach. As reported in *National Geographic News*, Philip Rainbow of London's Natural History Museum has called on commercial fishermen to target them in England: "The Chinese love them, especially when they're full of gonads during the breeding season. The carapace of a large one measures eight centimeters (about three inches) across—that's a decent-sized meal."

Asian Shore Crab (*Hemigrapsus sanguineus*)

The Asian shore crab (Fig. 4.6) was first observed in New Jersey in 1988, after likely arriving as larvae in ballast water. It has since extended its range to Maine and North Carolina, becoming very abundant in pebbly intertidal and shallow-water habitats. These crabs have a long breeding season and reproduce readily in a wide range of environmental conditions. They are found in very high densities, and actually seem to have displaced green crabs from some areas, possibly because *H. sanguineus* prey on small *C. maenas* recruits. Asian shore crabs also began to appear in France in the late 1990s, where they have spread and developed dense populations, competing with the area's native green crabs.

Control of Asian shore crabs by predators seems unlikely because there is little evidence that they have major predators in the United States, unlike in their native range. (There is some good news, however: a recent study by Kari Heinonen and Peter Auster of the University of Connecticut showed that, in the laboratory, crustacean-eating fish [cunners and tautogs] readily preyed on Asian shore crabs, and even preferred them over native crab species.) Furthermore, Asian shore crabs have very few parasites in their introduced range. April Blakeslee and colleagues from the Smithsonian Institution found only one parasite species infecting *H. sanguineus* on the U.S. East Coast compared to six species in its native range. In contrast, the invasive green crabs were host to three parasite species on the East Coast compared to ten in its native range. The amount of parasite infection was lower for both invasive crabs in their introduced area, but the difference was greater for shore crabs than for green crabs. Factors such as time since introduction (200 vs. 20 years) or distance from native range (Europe vs. Asia) may contribute to the success of Asian shore crabs, which are displacing green crabs in some areas. Another factor contributing to the displacement of green crabs by Asian shore crabs is that in the presence of shore crabs, green crabs shift their diet from primarily animal material to primarily plant material—a shift that reduces their reproductive output.

Asian shore crabs like the moist, shady environment created by cordgrass and mussels in salt marshes. The cordgrass attracts ribbed mussels by giving them something to attach themselves to; the mussels, in turn, give the crabs crevices in which to avoid predators—this is termed a *facilitation cascade*. The cordgrass also provides valuable shade for both mussels and crabs. In this case, the crabs' exploitation of the habitat does not seem to crowd out native species such as periwinkles, small crustaceans, blue mussels, and barnacles. Field studies by Andrew Altieri of Brown University showed that the more *Hemigrapsus* crabs there were, the greater the number of native species. It is encouraging that the salt marsh habitat may be able to accommodate this new resident without severe problems.

It is curious that the species has not become established on the Pacific Coast, which seems like a more likely invasion site, especially since there is suitable habitat as well as considerable shipping back and forth from Asian ports. Unlike the Atlantic Coast, however, the Pacific Coast is home to two native species of *Hemigrapsus: H. nudus* and *H. oregonensis.* Mia Steinberg and Charles Epifanio of the University of Delaware wondered if the presence of these related species might make the Pacific Coast more resistant to invasion by Asian shore crabs, and they studied competition among the three species. Shelters, made from a section of PVC pipe that was cut in half lengthwise, were glued to the bottom of the container with the concavity downward. The size of the shelter was such that only one individual could fit beneath it. They found that juvenile *H. sanguineus* were outcompeted for shelter by both of the native species, which may partially explain why this species has not successfully invaded the Pacific Coast.

Other Nonindigenous, Potentially Problematic Species

Tropical porcelain crabs have recently been found on oyster reefs in southern U.S. states. They were observed in Florida during the 1990s, and have since appeared in large numbers in coastal waters of Georgia and South Carolina as well. Unlike native crabs that eat oysters, the green porcelain crab (*Petrolisthes armatus*) is a filter feeder, extracting its food from the water much as oysters do. Although it does not attack oysters, it may compete with them for food. The presence of porcelain crabs appears to reduce the growth of oysters through competition for food, according to Amanda Hollebone and Mark Hay of Georgia Tech. However, many native fish and crabs feed on the invasive crabs rather than on young oysters, which gives the young oysters a better chance of surviving. The long-term effects of this invasion on the oyster reef ecosystem and the balance of positive and negative effects, however, remain to be seen.

Charybdis hellerii is a small Indo-Pacific portunid crab that has invaded areas in the Mediterranean Sea via the Suez Canal and invaded the South Atlantic and Caribbean down to Brazil via ballast water. It is spreading fast and, although negative effects have not yet been reported, is considered a potential threat to native crabs because it may compete with them and inflict changes in natural benthic communities. It may also affect crab fisheries if it displaces native species or reduces their numbers. *C. hellerii* is itself commercially important in southeast Asia, but no market exists for it in the United States. Perhaps if one were developed, these worries about potential harm would be assuaged.

Percnon gibbesi is one of the most widespread grapsid crabs (one of two species called "Sally Lightfoot"; Plate 5), and is found on both sides of the Atlantic Ocean, and on the Pacific Coast of North America where it ranges from California to Chile. It was first observed in 1999 in the Mediterranean Sea near Sicily and has rapidly spread since then, expanding its range throughout the Mediterranean and into the Aegean and Ionian Seas. An opportunistic feeder, it feeds primarily on algae high up on rocky shores. Its planktonic larvae are very long-lived, which enables long-range transport and survival in ballast water and so may contribute to its invasive success.

The red king crab (*Paralithodes camtschaticus*; Fig. 1.13), native to the Okhotsk and Japan Seas, the Bering Sea, and the northern Pacific Ocean, was introduced in the Barents Sea in the 1960s to establish a fishery. It currently inhabits an extensive area and numbers over 40 million. As a large generalist predator, its potential impact on native bottom communities is expected to be high. Britayev and colleagues studied its impacts and found effects on the bottom communities of the Barents Sea were not as dramatic as was expected given the crab's high feeding activity and wide diet. They believe that the crab's wide diet likely distributes its predation pressure among various groups of organisms and prevents elimination of any one species. However, the red king crab was also introduced from the northern Pacific to the Russian Murman coast during the 1960s and 1970s and has become established in northern Norwegian waters. As an active predator on benthic fauna in deep soft-bottom environments, it has reduced soft-bottom fauna, both at and below the surface, including echinoderms, nonmoving burrowing and tube-dwelling polychaetes, and most bivalves.

In the Antarctic, as the climate warms, king crabs (*Neolithodes yaldwyni*) are moving into new areas. Sven Thatje and colleagues from the University of Southampton, England, have collected digital images of hundreds of crabs moving toward shallow coastal waters that were previously protected from such predators for more than 40 million years by the cold waters. They ran transects up the slope and discovered hundreds and hundreds of king crabs, which could translate into millions across broad expanses of coastal Antarctica. King crabs can now disperse across the Antarctic shelf and reproduce in at least some Antarctic shelf waters. One species of king crab has moved about 75 miles across the continental shelf in West Antarctica and established a large, reproductive population in the Palmer Deep along the west Antarctic Peninsula. Crabs had not lived in coastal Antarctic waters previously because it has been too cold. Bottom-dwelling mussels, clams, snails, brittle stars, and sea urchins in this area have thinner shells and have not developed the usual defenses against shell-crushing predators because they have never encountered this type of predation. In the absence of crabs, worms and mollusks that usually burrow into sediment tend to spend more time on the surface. This also suggests that these predatory king crabs will have a feast and cause a major reduction on seafloor biodiversity as they invade Antarctic habitats because they appear to be eating all the echinoderms in the Palmer Deep. As king crabs move into an ecosystem with bottom fauna inexperienced in dealing with this predation pressure, the crabs' prey will need to adapt to survive.

Our native species may become disruptive invasives elsewhere. The estuarine mud crab (*Rhithropanopeus harrisii*), native to estuaries along the East Coast of North America, has spread to at least twenty-one countries, causing varying degrees of both environmental and economic damage. This crab has the potential to disrupt local ecosystems, invade inland lakes, and harbor diseases. It also fouls pipes and preys on fish caught in gill nets. Atlantic rock crabs (*Cancer irroratus*; Plate 2) were transported in ballast water and arrived in cold Nordic waters off Iceland sometime in 2000, where they are multiplying rapidly and eating eggs of native crabs. Researchers at the University of Iceland are worried that the crabs will quickly outcompete native crabs. Individuals that have been caught are as big as some of the biggest caught in their natural habitat, suggesting that the non-native crabs are thriving.

The blue crab, beloved on the U.S. East Coast, established itself about a century ago in the Mediterranean, which is especially prone to introductions of non-native species via the Suez Canal, commercial shipping, and aquaculture. There, the blue crab was recently named one of the "100 worst invasive species" due to its potential effects on biodiversity and fisheries, even though such effects have not yet been observed or studied. A commercial fishery has been established for them, however.

Native species may become problematic in their native areas, too, under certain circumstances. Christine Holdredge and Mark Bertness of Brown University found that marsh crabs (*Sesarma reticulatum*; Fig. 1.11), which eat cordgrass (*Spartina alterniflora*), are depleting the marsh grasses on Cape Cod, Massachusetts—an explanation for the mysterious dieback of the wetlands that had been going on there for the past several years. The crabs are proliferating because their natural predators—blue crabs, striped bass, and tautogs—have declined because of increased recreational fishing as more homes and marinas are built in the area. This has led to an imbalance in the marsh ecosystem.

Not all alien species become invasive. The Asian portunid *Scylla serrata* was imported to the United States in an attempt to start fisheries in Florida and Hawaii. This species is commercially harvested in areas where it has become established. Its ecological impacts are unknown, but like other portunids, it is active and aggressive, and it feeds on mollusks, crustaceans, and polychaetes. Commercial fishing keeps the population under control and the species is not considered invasive.

CHAPTER EIGHT

Crab Fisheries

People living on the coast have depended on living marine resources for many thousands of years. Millions earn their living in commercial fisheries, and many people still depend on seafood as their primary source of protein. The very high catch rates of modern industrialized fishing fleets have had widespread effects on fished species, nontarget species, and marine habitats. Overfishing continues to be a major threat to marine ecosystems and vulnerable species throughout the world. Although dwarfed by fisheries for finfish, crab fisheries are important in many countries.

HISTORY OF CRAB FISHERIES IN THE UNITED STATES

As early as prehistoric times, blue crabs (Plate 3) were collected for subsistence living. Evidence suggests that Native Americans used spears to catch blue crabs in shallow water and may also have used simple traps. During colonial times, some settlers survived by catching blue crabs, and since the mid-1800s, blue crabs have been caught commercially in the Chesapeake Bay, the largest estuary in the United States, surrounded by Maryland and Virginia. They are now caught from the mid-Atlantic region to Florida and in Gulf states as far west as Texas. Records from 1850 indicate that a market for soft-shelled blue crabs had developed on the East Coast. In 1870, the first toothless dredge called a "crab scrape" was patented for taking soft-shelled blue crabs, and fishermen wading with scoop nets or seines collected hard-shelled crabs. The crab scrape is a lightweight oyster dredge with a bottom bar that glides along the bottom rather than digging into it. It collects eelgrass with its inhabitants, including the molting crabs (called "peelers") that seek protection in that habitat. The invention of the ice machine and availability of ice played a major role in the development of the commercial fishery, allowing live fresh crabs to be shipped by rail to distant cities.

Chesapeake Bay is the center of the blue crab fishery. In Virginia, in the lower half of the bay, the concentration is on catching and extracting meat from hard-shelled crabs, whereas in Maryland, the focus is on the more difficult soft-shelled crabs, which must be caught prior to molting and monitored through the molting process. The crabbing industry has a lifestyle and even a language of its own. Crabbers are called "watermen," crabs are known as "jimmies" (legal-size males), "she-crabs" (immature females with a V-shaped abdomen), "peelers" (crabs about to molt), and "sooks" (mature females with a round abdomen). The United States is the leading crab-consuming nation in the world, with annual catches that range from 250 to 350 million "whole crab" pounds, with the blue crab making up 50% of the nation's total crab catch.

Dungeness crabs (Fig. 2.5) have played a similar role in the culinary history of the West Coast. Although Native Americans and others caught and ate the crabs for centuries, in 1848, the first commercial industry opened in Dungeness, Washington, a village at the tip of the Olympic Peninsula. The Dungeness crab, named after the village, has become a major commercial fishery on the West Coast and is important in the history of San Francisco. Shortly after the turn of the century, fishermen began catching Dungeness crabs near San Francisco's Golden Gate Bridge, and an area known as Meiggs Wharf was set aside by the state legislature in 1925 for the fishermen's use. Some fishermen began to sell their catch directly to the public from their boats or stalls on the sidewalk, the precursors of the present-day Fisherman's Wharf restaurants (Plate 25). The first wood-fired crab boilers appeared on Fisherman's Wharf in the 1920s. The popularity of the cooked and cracked crabs and "take-out" cocktails helped to turn fishermen's shacks into thriving seafood restaurants.

Commercial king crab fishing in Alaska officially began in Adak, a western island in the Aleutians, in 1960. The following year, the king crab fishery in Dutch Harbor opened at the port of Unalaska in the eastern part of the island chain. Five years later Dutch Harbor experienced a record 33 million pound harvest. In keeping with the boom and bust pattern of Alaska, what was once the second most lucrative commercial fishery in the state has fallen on hard times due to overfishing and other problems and as yet shows no signs of real recovery.

COMMERCIAL CRABBING WORLDWIDE

Crabs make up 20% of all marine crustaceans that are caught, farmed, and consumed worldwide, amounting to 1.5 million tons annually. Swimming crabs (also known as portunids) are the most important group. The horse (or gazami) crab (*Portunus trituberculatus*), found from Hokkaidō to South India, throughout the Malay Archipelago and as far south as Australia, accounts for 20% of that total. Other commercially important portunids include the blue swimmer crab (*Portunus pelagicus*), the blue crab (*Callinectes sapidus*), the Indo-Pacific swimming crab (*Charybdis* spp.), and the mud or mangrove crab (*Scylla serrata*). Several spider crab species in the genus *Chionoecetes,* and the cancroids the brown crab (*Cancer pagurus*) and Dungeness crab (*Metacarcinus* [or *Cancer*] *magister*) also each yield more than 20,000 tons annually.

Four dominant crab fisheries exist in North America. Besides the aforementioned brachyuran crabs—the blue crab (Plate 3) and Dungeness crab (Fig 2.5)—there are also queen or snow (tanner) crabs (Majidae: *Chionoecetes* spp.; Fig. 8.1), and the anomuran red king crab (*Paralithodes camtschaticus*; Fig. 1.13), which was the single most lucrative crustacean species until about 1970. The dominance of these groups has decreased as stocks have been overfished and diminished. The most productive region for crab fisheries is the North Pacific; the blue crab is the only significant crab harvested on the Atlantic Coast.

Dungeness and Other Cancer (or Rock) Crabs

The Dungeness crab (Fig. 2.5) ranges from Alaska south to Mexico, living in eelgrass beds or in sandy or muddy bottoms, in which it lies buried with only its antennae and eyes projecting up. The most important crab species in the Pacific Northwest, Dungeness crabs are usually caught in water 12–120 feet deep, but they are tolerant of salinity changes and can also be found in estuaries, although they tend to avoid low salinity except when they are hungry. They scavenge along the sea floor for organisms that live partly or completely buried in the sand, including shrimp, mussels, small crabs, clams, and worms. Males reach maturity in 3 years, while females spawn at 2 years of age. Each male may mate with more than one female. This may be important in maintaining the viability of this species because only males can be harvested.

Figure 8.1. Tanner crab (*Chionoecetes bairdi*). Photo from NOAA.

On much of the West Coast, Dungeness crab is a winter fishery, beginning in San Francisco in November where the harvest typically peaks in January; in Oregon and Washington, the season extends into the spring. In British Columbia, the peak season starts much later—in April; while in southeast Alaska, it is mainly a summer fishery. The first historical reference to the Alaska Dungeness crab fishery was in 1916; they were canned at Seldovia in 1920. Today, Dungeness crab is processed by both shore-based and floating processors, and they are sold whole or in sections, fresh or frozen. They are caught commercially in circular pots baited with herring, squid, or clams, but only hard-shell males may be taken according to regulations. This crab supports both a commercial fishery and a personal use fishery in Alaska. Crab pots similar to those used in the commercial fishery, ring nets, dip nets, and hand lines can all be used for personal use (see section on Gear, below).

In the winter of 2010–2011, the National Oceanic and Atmospheric Administration (NOAA) reported that large quantities of California Dungeness crab were being sent to China in quantities that were more than 20 times greater than those of the previous year. Exporters shipped 939,001 pounds of live, fresh, salted, or brined Dungeness crab to China in 2010, up from just 41,502 pounds in 2009. Techniques of shipping live crabs overseas are a closely guarded secret because it is critical to minimize the time from when the crab is caught to when it reaches the market. Many crabs are chilled, packed into Styrofoam boxes with an oxygen supply, secured in plastic bags, and placed in the cargo section of passenger planes bound for China.

Several other cancer (or rock) crab species related to Dungeness crabs are caught by commercial and recreational fishermen. In southern California, where Dungeness crabs are less abundant, other rock crabs including the yellow crab (*Metacarcinus* [formerly *Cancer*] *anthonyi*), the brown rock crab (*C. antennarius*), and the red rock crab (*C. productus*) are caught and sold.

Minor fisheries also exist on the East Coast for Atlantic rock crabs (*Cancer irroratus*; Plate 2), Jonah crabs (*C. borealis*), and red deep-sea crabs (*Chaceon quinquedens*; Plate 13). Red deep-sea crabs occur in large numbers from Nova Scotia to Cuba on the edge of the continental shelf, and are often caught accidentally in lobster pots or offshore lobster trawls. They can be taken in lobster pots, but until recently were not part of a commercial fishery because if not chilled, they are difficult to keep alive during the trip home. The advent of onboard refrigeration systems enabled the development of the fishery and processing plants for them.

Brown crabs (or "edible crabs") (*Cancer pagurus*), an important commercial species in Western Europe, are found in the North Sea, North Atlantic, and Mediterranean Sea. They are reddish-brown, robust crabs with an oval carapace with a characteristic serrated edge and black claw tips. They eat benthic invertebrates, particularly bivalves, small decapods, and barnacles. Adults, especially females, undertake extensive seasonal migrations, which are thought to be associated with reproduction. The brown crab fishery is economically very important for Scottish vessels with a value of £10 million. It is illegal to catch crabs below a certain size (carapace width of a bit over 5 inches) in Britain, a conservation measure dating back to the 1870s.

King Crabs

King crabs live in southern Alaska up to the northern Bering Sea and on the Asiatic coast. They can weigh up to 25 pounds, although the average weight of crabs in the fishery is about 10 pounds. Commercial fisheries exist in Alaska, Canada, Russia, Japan, and Korea as well as in the southern hemisphere in New Zealand, Australia, South Georgia and Falkland Islands, Argentina, and Chile. Canneries started in Japan in the late 1800s, and in the United States in the 1920s and 1930s.

In Alaska there are three commercial king crab species: red, blue, and golden (see Table 2). Red king crabs (*Paralithodes camtschaticus*; Fig. 1.13) are the most important of Alaska's crabs and occur from British Columbia to Japan, with central Alaskan populations at Bristol Bay and the Kodiak Archipelago. Blue king crabs (*P. platypus*; Fig. 8.2) live from southeastern Alaska to Japan, with the highest abundances at the Pribilof and St. Matthew Islands in the Bering Strait. Golden king crabs (*Lithodes aequispinus*), are found from British Columbia to Japan, with the Aleutian Islands forming Alaska's central population. Red king crabs can grow to be larger than the blue and golden kings, with a carapace width of about one foot. Males

Figure 8.2. Jeff Sleer, federal fisheries observer, holds a blue king crab (*Paralithodes platypus*), caught as part of the Alaska King Crab Research and Rehabilitation Program. Photo by Celeste Leroux, Alaska Sea Grant College Program.

are larger than females, and only males can be legally sold. King crabs eat a wide variety of food: worms, clams, mussels, snails, brittle stars, sea stars, sea urchins, sand dollars, barnacles, other crustaceans, fish parts, sponges, and algae. Juveniles are eaten by Pacific cod, sculpins, halibut, yellowfin sole, skates, octopuses, other king crabs, and sea otters.

Historically, the red king crab fishery has been Alaska's top shellfish fishery and is currently one of the most valuable in the United States overall. Since statehood in 1959, nearly 2 billion pounds, worth $1.6 billion, have been caught, mainly in the Bristol Bay area. In 2008, over 27 million pounds of red king crab were caught, with a value of $120.2 million. Because of concerns about overfishing, managers implemented the Crab Rationalization Program in 2005 to decrease fishing capacity (i.e., to reduce the number of fishing vessels) to improve conservation. The program is administered by the National Marine Fisheries Service, and is a limited-access system that allocates crab resources among several groups that depend on these fisheries, including harvesters, processors, and coastal communities. Prior to this, NOAA's National Marine Fisheries Service implemented a buyback program in 2004 to reduce excess capacity and reduce overfishing. In this program, the Fisheries Service paid participants for withdrawing their vessels from fishing and turning in their fishing licenses.

Snow and Tanner Crabs

Snow crabs and tanner crabs are spider crabs that are abundant in deep waters in the Bering Sea and elsewhere in Alaska, but may occur as far south as Oregon. Tanner crabs (*Chionoecetes bairdi*; Fig. 8.1) and snow crabs (*C. opilio*) form the basis of a thriving fishery from southeastern Alaska north through the Bering Sea. They are fished for by Japanese and Russian fishermen in the eastern Bering Sea. They feed on worms, clams, mussels, snails, crabs, other crustaceans, and fish parts; they are eaten by fish such as Pacific cod, halibut, sculpins, skates, and humans. Their migration patterns are not well understood, but it is known that the sexes are separated during much of the year and move into the same area during the reproductive season. The Alaska Tanner crab fishery began in 1961 and is a fishery of major commercial importance. Crabs are taken by vessels ranging from small inshore boats to new "super crabbers" in the Bering Sea, using pots similar to those used for king crab, which are baited with chopped herring and soaked for 1–3 days. This fishery is the focus of the popular television program *Deadliest Catch* on the Discovery Channel.

Other Fisheries

A minor fishery exists for Florida stone crabs (*Menippe mercenaria*; Fig. 1.10) from North Carolina to Florida and in the Yucatan, Cuba, Jamaica, and the Bahamas. The large Florida (or southern) stone crab is usually fished with pots near jetties, oyster reefs, or other coastal rocky areas. This is the most sustainable of all crab fisheries because only the claws are harvested (and will grow back), much like fruit is gathered from a tree. (The word *harvest* is often used to refer to what is caught in a fishery; however, that term implies that something has been planted there, which is not the case, except for in managed aquaculture products.) One claw is removed from each crab, and the animal is released alive so that it can regenerate the missing claw. It is legal to take both claws, but this would leave the crab with few defenses against predators and decrease both its chance of survival and the possibility of a secondary harvest. Although a clawless crab can still find some food, having a single remaining claw enables it to obtain more food in a shorter time. Its survival depends on the skill of the fisherman, who must separate the claw from the crab's body properly. If the joint is pierced or snapped properly, the crab's autotomy reflex (see Chapter 7) contracts its muscles and drops the claw cleanly. If, however, the claw is broken in the wrong place, more blood is lost and its chances of survival decrease. Gary Davis and colleagues from the National Park Service found that about one-fourth of experimentally (and presumably properly) declawed crabs died in captivity. The rate is probably higher in the wild, where crabs have to compete for food and avoid predators. Next to the spiny lobster, the stone crab is the most important commercial species in the Florida Keys. About half of the 3 million pounds caught statewide are produced in the Keys and harvested mostly in Florida Bay.

European spider crabs (*Maja squinado*) are found in the northeast Atlantic and the Mediterranean Sea. They are the subject of commercial fishery, with about 5000 tons caught annually, 70% off the coast of France. The European Union has a minimum size restriction, and some countries have additional regulations, such as a ban on landing egg-bearing females in Spain and a closed season in France.

In Asia, various portunid (swimming) crabs are the subject of commercial fisheries. Collected mainly by trawls, beach seines, cylindrical wire traps, folding traps, pots, and drop nets, the total catch reported for blue swimmer crabs (*Portunus pelagicus*) for 1999 was almost 134,000 tons. Widely distributed in eastern Africa, Southeast Asia, Japan, Australia, and New Zealand, this species is commercially important throughout the Indo-Pacific, where it may be sold canned, frozen, or fresh, either in hard-shelled or soft-shelled form. Another major fishery in the Indo-Australian region is mangrove (or mud) crabs (*Scylla serrata*). These large, active crabs are widely distributed in shallow waters with a mud bottom from northern Australia, east to Samoa and Fiji, north to the Philippines, and west into the Indian Ocean, across

Figure 8.3. Land (mangrove) crab (or swamp ghost crab)
(*Ucides cordatus*). Photo by Pancrat, Wikimedia.

to Africa. They are found in sheltered waters, especially estuaries and mangroves. They are collected by hand at low tide or with a hook, traps, and gill
nets at high tide. They were introduced into Hawaii, where a commercial
fishery was developed.

Horse crabs (*Portunus trituberculatus*), also known as gazami crabs or
Japanese blue crab, are widely fished, with over 300,000 tons caught annually, 98% of it off the coast of China. They are found from Japan to South
India throughout Indonesia and as far south as Australia, on shallow sandy
or muddy bottoms. There they eat seaweed, small fish, worms, and bivalves,
and they may reach 6 inches wide. In the Indo-West Pacific, the red frog
crab, Kona crab, or spanner crab (*Ranina ranina*)—a species with a broad,
tapered body and flattened legs—is another valued food item, usually taken
in nets. Another unusual species is the long-eyed swimming crab (*Podophthalmus vigil*), which has eyestalks so long that when they lie horizontally
in a groove along the front of the body, they extend almost across the whole
body. These crabs live in soft bottoms of estuaries and river mouths, where
they are caught in trawl nets in India.

In Brazil there is a commercial fishery for the terrestrial mangrove crab (or swamp ghost crab) (*Ucides cordatus*; Fig. 8.3). A recent study by Karen Diele and Volker Koch provides information for the sustainable management of the fishery and confirms that the species is slow growing and long-lived (>10 years), suggesting high vulnerability to overfishing.

LOBSTER FISHERY

Only a few types of lobster are caught commercially, but they are some of the most frequently collected and valued crustaceans and generate a multibillion-dollar industry, with over 200,000 tons of annual global catch. The lobsters that most people know are the American and European clawed lobsters *Homarus americanus* and *Homarus gammarus*, which are cold-water species. Tropical lobsters are also widely consumed; these are the small-clawed spiny and slipper lobsters and South African rock lobsters (langouste). These warm-water species are harvested by diving or trapping. Commercial traps are weighed down with cement and include an escape panel that degrades over time. Traps may damage bottom habitat if they are deployed on coral reefs, sea grasses, or hard bottom.

Lobsters have not always been considered good food. In the seventeenth and eighteenth centuries, they were often used as fertilizer and considered "poverty food," served to children, prisoners, and indentured servants. It was so commonly used as a food for servants and prisoners that Massachusetts passed a law forbidding people to feed servants lobster more than twice a week. It wasn't until the nineteenth century that lobsters gained their status as a luxury food item. Improvements in transportation in the late–nineteenth and twentieth centuries brought fresh lobster to distant areas, and its reputation as a delicacy grew.

The lobster fishery is an important part of the state of Maine's economy, with a boat price of over $425,000,000 in 2011, the highest since they have been keeping records. Fishing is the major source of mortality for lobsters and can reach 90% for legal-sized lobsters in Maine. Newly molted animals actively seek food and may be trapped more easily than hard-shelled lobsters that feed in a smaller territory. Maine produces the most lobsters and has many regulations, including licensing, use of traps with escape vents, maximum and minimum sizes, and prohibition of removing egg-carrying females (which are marked with a notch) or scrubbing off eggs. There are also limitations on the number of traps on a single line and on fishing season and hours. Despite heavy fishing, the lobster population is booming, perhaps as an indirect effect of the depletion of cod—which eat juvenile lobsters.

Populations of commercially important lobsters elsewhere are thought to be declining, and overfishing in Europe is taking a toll. Since the 1990s, the spiny lobster fishery in the Caribbean has shown signs of overfishing, and abundance has declined. Standardization of data and better data collection should allow for more accurate determination of the status of the fishery. Spiny lobsters are difficult to culture because of their 6–7 month larval life, so there is interest in developing aquaculture technologies for the Caribbean species *Panulirus argus*. An open-ocean aquaculture operation in the Caribbean has successfully collected lobsters settling on submerged sea cages. A small number of these lobsters were used in a study demonstrating that they could, indeed, be farmed

GEAR

The most common way to capture crabs commercially is by using various types of traps, also called pots. Lines, trawls, and dredges are also used in certain crab fisheries.

Pots

Baited traps (called "pots"), made of wire or wood, are the most commonly used gear for catching crabs, which tend to be omnivorous bottom-dwelling scavengers. The baited crab pot used in estuaries and coastal waters for blue crab is a large, square trap with two internal chambers constructed out of galvanized chicken wire or PVC (polyvinyl chloride)–coated wire (Fig. 8.4). The bottom chamber, or "downstairs," has two or four entrance funnels, known as "throats" that allow the crab to enter but not exit easily. In the center of the bottom chamber is the "bait box" made of fine-mesh galvanized wire so that the crab cannot get the bait. The top chamber is the holding area, known as the "parlor" or "upstairs." Crabs enter the parlor through funnel-shaped holes in the floor of the parlor making it difficult to go back out. Crab pots exploit the crab's escape instincts in order to trap them. Crabs smell the bait and enter; once inside and unable to reach the bait, they swim up toward the surface to escape, but instead end up inside the parlor where they are trapped until removed through a special opening along one of the

Figure 8.4. Crab pots. Photo from NOAA.

top edges. Most people attach bricks or metal to the bottom of their pot to anchor it down. Commercial watermen frame the bottom of their pots with steel reinforcement rods, which also make them more durable. A long line and a floating buoy with bright colors and identifying markings are attached to the pot.

A "condo" trap is an effective means of capturing the golden crab (*Chaceon fenneri*; Plate 14) from deep waters. This is a large (2½ ft × 4 ft × 6 ft) box-type wire trap with a bait-holding cylinder and two tapered openings at opposite ends. Traps are set by using a long line at depths of 1140–2880 feet. The traps are retrieved from the depths with grappling hooks and mechanical pulleys, which is dangerous work.

King crabs are most commonly fished using large 600- to 700-pound steel frames covered with nylon webbing. Each pot is baited with chopped herring and dropped into the water where it sinks to the bottom. When fishing for red or blue kings, the pot soaks for 1 or 2 days, but longer (up to 3 days) when fishing for golden kings. Buoys attached to the heavy pots with strong line are retrieved and lifted onto the boat by powerful hydraulic systems. Boats fishing king crabs are 40–200 feet long, and may cost several million dollars. In years past, king crabs were also caught in tangle nets and trawls, but these types of gear were prohibited in 2007 because they caught too many females and young males in addition to the desired large males.

In commercial fishing, part of the catch (sometimes a large part) includes marine animals that were caught unintentionally, which are known as *bycatch*. Crab pots, like other gear, can trap other species such as fish and sea turtles. In East Coast estuaries, for example, diamondback terrapins are frequently caught in traps meant for blue crabs and they can drown if the trap is not tended to daily. The problem of bycatch is exacerbated because as many as a fifth of the pots used in Chesapeake Bay each year are lost due to storms or boat propellers that cut the lines between pots and their buoys. Derelict crab pots—the term for these lost pots—can remain on the bottom for many years because they are made of wire and steel and covered in vinyl and, unlike wooden and cloth net traps or galvanized steel traps that were previously used, do not decay rapidly. During this time the derelict pots continue to entrap crabs, fish, turtles, and other sea life—a process known as *ghost fishing*. Once trapped, animals are doomed to live in the confined space of the trap until they die. Abandoned or derelict crab pots can also be snagged by fishing lines or nets, and they can be a navigational hazard when snagged by passing boats and entangled in propellers. The pots can travel long distances and may wash up on shore, along beaches, riverbanks, and estuaries. Dungeness crab traps and floats lost off the coast of Oregon during the 2006–2007 fishing season were recovered 4 years later in the Northwestern Hawaiian Islands.

Because of these dangers and waste, programs have been set up to locate and remove derelict crab pots; some states are asking residents to help in pot removal and to report derelict pots. NOAA's Chesapeake Bay Office discovered that side-scan sonar, used to map the bottom, can locate derelict pots. A cooperative program involving NOAA personnel, commercial fishers, and scientists was developed to provide supplemental income for fishers and to help restore the crab fishery. In this program, watermen were trained in the use of side-scan imaging and employed to remove derelict crab pots. Integrating commercial fishers into the planning and management of the project helped to increase their trust of the regulatory agency and scientists. Watermen were able to earn income and removed over 28,000 items of derelict fishing gear over a 3-year period.

Another approach is to use pots with bycatch reduction devices (BRDs) that greatly reduce the bycatch of terrapins and other species without reducing the number of crabs trapped. The device, which is attached to each funnel opening, creates a bottleneck to exclude the larger, nontargeted species while letting the smaller crabs in. These devices are required for recreational and commercial crabbers in many coastal states. There have also been efforts in the snow crab fishery in Newfoundland and Labrador to reduce bycatch of small undersized individuals. Paul Winger and Philip Walsh of Memorial University (Newfoundland) found that installing escape mechanisms into traditional traps resulted in the capture of about 40% fewer undersized crabs, with no significant difference in the capture of large crabs. Another approach being used is to use escape panels made of biodegradable twine.

Line

A trotline is a large-scale commercial version of recreational crabbers' hand line. It is the only permissible gear in some areas of Maryland's eastern shore. This line, over a mile in length, is anchored with heavy weights, baited at intervals with eel or other bait, and allowed to sink to the bottom. The waterman starts at one end of the line, pulling it up and draping it over a roller attached to the side of the boat. As the boat moves down the line, the line, bait, and (hopefully) the crabs, are slowly raised toward the surface where the waterman scoops up the crabs with a dip net (a bag net with a handle).

Crab Tiles

Laying down artificial materials on the shore to create a refuge to attract crustaceans is a technique used mainly in South America and the United Kingdom, where this method is called *crab tiling*. It involves laying down roof tiles or other materials such as sections of drain pipe in intertidal estuarine areas to provide habitat for green (shore) crabs (*Carcinus maenas*), which are harvested from underneath the tiles at low tide for use as bait. The shelters are often used by crabs that are molting, so can be used for harvesting soft-shelled crabs. Crab tiling has the side effect of reducing the numbers and diversity of mud-dwelling invertebrates from around these tiles, which are prey for wading birds and fish.

Dredge

Crabbers in lower Chesapeake Bay (in Virginia) use a dredge during the winter to collect dormant crabs that are partially buried in the sediment. The crab dredge, which is pulled behind a boat, is about 6 feet wide and weighs 250 pounds. It has a metal frame and a *bag* consisting of netting made of chain in its lower half and twine in the upper. It has long teeth that can be set at various angles to rake the bottom, forcing up mud or sand like snow in front of a road plow. The rudely awakened crabs (mostly females with fertilized eggs who have migrated down to the lower parts of the bay) are caught in the bag. The *crab scrape*, a modified dredge, operates by cropping eelgrass and whatever crabs are in it. Most of the ones that don't escape are either "peelers" (i.e., getting ready to molt) or "doublers" (i.e., male-female pairs waiting for the female to molt). The scrape is operated from a skipjack boat, a traditional sailing boat originally designed for oyster dredging.

Trawl

A *trawl* is a long, conical net dragged along the sea bottom. Chile and a few other countries have trawl fisheries for crabs, such as galatheids (squat lobsters), in which nets are pulled along the bottom. Because this method is nonselective, the amount of bycatch is extensive, and many nontarget species are discarded. In many cases, the bycatch is a greater proportion of the catch than the target crustacean. About 150 species have been documented in the bycatch, with the hake (*Merluccius gayi*) being the most frequent victim.

Researchers in Chile are working to develop new net designs to reduce by-catch by changing the size and shape of the mesh at the end of the net and building in escape panels that allow the fish to escape.

Getting Soft-Shelled Crabs

Soft-shelled crabs are obtained in a number of ways. In the early part of the season, female crabs that are preparing for their pubertal molt are lured into traps containing adult males. "Jimmy potting" is the placement of two or three males in the upper section of the pot, which attract females by their behaviors and pheromones. Using the same type of sexual lure, "Jimmy crabbing" involves tying a string around the leg of a male, releasing him on this leash, and allowing him to attract and embrace a premolt female. The crabber gently pulls up the line and dip-nets the couple together. Later in the season, males that are preparing to molt can be captured in bare pots (without bait). A bare pot in an area without sea grass will attract these males when there are no other good refuges in which to molt. Environmental factors may cause large numbers of crabs to molt at the same time. Once premolt crabs are collected, they are stored in "shedding floats" (floating rectangular boxes that are anchored in the water) with good water circulation, where the crabs are watched and checked as they approach the time of molting. While many die in the process, millions of pounds of soft-shell crab are produced annually; soft-shell crabs are worth much more money than crabs with a hard shell.

REGULATIONS AND MANAGEMENT

Fisheries management in the United States is overseen by the National Marine Fisheries Service, part of NOAA. Specific details are managed by regional Fisheries Management Councils and by the individual states. For example, the New England Fishery Management Council regulates deep-sea red crabs, and the Gulf of Mexico council regulates stone crabs. The Mid-Atlantic council oversees the blue crab fishery, but because the species is estuarine, individual states regulate it. Under the traditional regulatory system, there is a total catch limit allowed each year, but it is not allocated to individuals. As a result, fishermen often race each other to catch as many crabs as they can before the total limit is reached under complicated regulations dealing with where and when they can fish. This process increases expenses as fishermen use more boats and gear than necessary in an attempt to maximize their catch. Such systems also encourage people to fish in bad, unsafe weather. This system can result in too many crabs reaching the market at the same time, reducing prices and increasing spoilage and waste. From time to time the competition between Maryland and Virginia watermen over blue crab rights has caused considerable friction. After blue crab catches plummeted from about 120 million pounds in the 1990s to 44 million pounds in 2007, Maryland and Virginia together requested disaster status for the blue crab fishery and imposed new regulations to restrict catches, infuriating watermen in both states.

Maryland is considering switching to a different approach for the blue crab fishery called "catch shares" or "individual transferable quotas." This system has worked in many other fisheries, and, although controversial, NOAA is encouraging U.S. fisheries to move to this approach. Under a *catch share program*, a total maximum for the year is established, and shares of the total are given out. The program divides the total allowable catch in a fishery into *shares*, which are allocated based on historical participation in the fishery and assigned to individuals, cooperatives, communities, or other entities who are then allowed to fish up to their assigned limit. Usually shares can be bought and sold. Crabbers would therefore be able to fish when and how they choose as long as they did not exceed their own quota. Under this system, the participants have a stake in the fishery—if the crab population increases, the total maximum allowable catch increases, and everyone's shares are increased. This gives them a financial interest in conservation and growth of the population, like owners of stock in a corporation. Maryland's blue crab fishery would be a good choice for this system because crab population estimates are quite accurate. The annual blue crab winter dredge survey is a precise indicator of abundance. Survey results allow scientists to estimate the number of crabs that can be caught while leaving enough to maintain a healthy population. Setting an annual quota is relatively straightforward. The difficult part of a catch share program is determining how to allocate the shares. Rules to determine how the catch would be divided would be based in part on past catches, but other factors could be considered as well. A difficult aspect of the blue crab fishery is that it has thousands of either full-time or part-time participants; other fisheries that have switched to catch shares have had fewer people involved.

Red king crab stocks in the Aleutian Islands and eastern Bering Sea are managed cooperatively by the federal government and the State of Alaska through the North Pacific Fishery Management Council's Fishery Management Plan (FMP). This plan defers management of crab fisheries to the State of Alaska, with federal oversight. The crabber's cooperative (alliance) credits catch shares, which started in 2005, allowing the crabbers to work cooperatively and to adopt more efficient, environmentally friendly fishing gear. In the red king crab fishery, pot usage dropped from 50,000 to 12,000 pots. New sorting systems use flumes (open artificial water channels), mechanized hydraulic tables, or conveyor belts that allow crabs to be sorted quickly with less handling and mortality. Five years after the catch share system was introduced, it had achieved resource conservation, economic stability, and reduction of bycatch, excess harvesting, and loss of life and injuries.

The popular TV documentary program *Deadliest Catch* focuses on Alaskan crab fishing in the face of hurricane force winds and monstrous waves, and has brought attention to the dangers of crab fishing. Alaskan crab fishing is more dangerous than other commercial fishing because of the conditions of the Bering Sea, and it is truly one of the riskiest occupations. The U.S. Coast Guard rescue squads stationed at Kodiak frequently rescue crew members who fall victim to the harsh conditions. The death rate during the season averages nearly one fisherman per week, while the injury rate on most crab boats is nearly 100% due to severe weather conditions and the danger of working with heavy machinery on a constantly rolling boat deck. The series follows eight to ten fishing boats and their crews through the October king crab season and the January tanner crab season. Filming episodes of *Deadliest Catch* is a dangerous occupation in itself for the camera crews on the boats, who run into dangers not normally encountered when filming a documentary. One cameraman got out of the way just seconds before a 900-pound crab pot swinging from a crane crossed the place where he had just been standing. In another incident, a cameraman accidentally stepped into an open hatch on the deck and broke three ribs. The Dungeness crab fishery is also dangerous, with about two deaths per year, often due to boats capsizing and crew members not wearing life vests. New, less cumbersome life vests have been developed that more fishermen are willing to wear.

OVERFISHING AND OTHER PROBLEMS

As with finfish, crab fisheries have been declining at an alarming rate around the world. Many factors are involved, including uncertainty of population estimates, bycatch, and ghost fishing. Climate change, overfishing, and ecological interactions have been implicated in collapses of crab stocks around the world. For example, the collapse of red king crab (Fig. 1.13) fisheries in Alaska in the 1980s led to speculation about the roles of climate change, increases in predators, habitat alteration, and overfishing by large fleets of vessels. In 2008, 27 million pounds of red king crab were caught, down from 130 million pounds in 1980. In 2008, steps were taken to restore populations. The Crab Rationalization Program limits the number of crabs caught each season, in contrast to the previous free-for-all system that limited only the length of the season. Under the new system, there are fewer vessels and fewer jobs. The Bristol Bay red king crab fishery is still one of the most valuable in the United States. The 27 million pounds of red king crab caught in 2008 had a value of $120.2 million. Bycatch in the fishery includes females, males under the legal size, and nontargeted crabs. Pots have been modified to reduce bycatch; escape panels and rings are included to prevent ghost fishing in case the pot gets lost. Most stocks of red king crabs in Alaska have still not recovered. The blue king crab fishery also fell on hard times due to overfishing. The lone stock classified as overfished—Pribilof Island blue king crab—hasn't been fished since 1999. Under the fishery management plan for the Bering Sea and Aleutian Islands (BSAI), the state Department of Fish and Game sets the harvest level after a joint state–federal team of scientists determines the overfishing limit. At its October 2010 meeting, the North Pacific council approved the current state control over harvest-setting. The crab industry has supported the state's approach to Bristol Bay king crabs.

Approximately half of all king crab sold in the U.S. market is imported from Russia, where it is fished in the Russian Far East and the Barents Sea. Far East populations are low, a situation made worse by overfishing and illegal fishing. In 2006–2008, and again in 2010, scandals erupted over illegal Russian fishing for king crabs, and people involved with importing Russian crabs were arrested. In 2007, people involved with Eastern Fisheries Holding Co., a consortium of about twenty Russian Far East crab fishing companies were charged with illegally exporting over 15,000 tons of king crab, worth about $200 million. Spokesmen for the Bering Sea crab industry asked for a prohibition of U.S. marketing of Barents Sea king crab caught illegally by Russian vessels. By some estimates, the amount of poached crab caught in the Russian Far East is more than double the legal catch. The small size of some Russian crab legs sold in the United States indicates that undersized crabs have been part of the haul. In September 2010, Arkadi Gontmakher, the largest

U.S. crab importer, was arrested and jailed in Moscow, accused of money-laundering and participating in a poaching operation that illegally exported millions of pounds of king crab to the United States. In the first half of 2010, his company brought in 20 million pounds of Russian king crab—roughly equal to the year's entire Alaska red-king-crab harvest. Gontmakher was subsequently acquitted of all charges. Now officials are wary about buying crabs from Russia, and Russian officials have pledged reforms and a crackdown on poachers. At the same time, the Bering Sea crabbers fear that high prices will stimulate more illegal harvests, and a flood of illegal crab could collapse their markets again. They say that producers, the state of Alaska, and crab sellers lost about $500 million due to illegal and unreported crab fisheries over the past 10 years.

Tanner crabs (*Chionoecetes bairdi*; Fig. 8.1) were once an integral part of the economy in Kodiak, Alaska, but, due to a sharp population decline, their fishing fleet has been idled. Humans are the primary predators of adult Tanner crab through both fishing and ghost pot catches, but other factors could be involved in their sudden decline. Crabs are prey for many other species and are susceptible to parasites. Weather patterns may also play a role, as could oceanic thermal fluctuations in the North Pacific.

Blue crabs (Plate 3)—the most important commercial fishery in Chesapeake Bay and valued at over $65 million annually—had major declines along most of the Atlantic Coast since the 1990s. The percentage of crabs removed annually from the population approached 70% in some years and exceeded an overfishing threshold of 53% in most years. The decline is also due to other factors, including water quality, loss of important habitat such as submerged aquatic vegetation and oyster reefs, and changing climate. The population declined 70% since the early 1990s, leading to historic low harvests in 2007. In 2008, the governors of Maryland and Virginia set a framework to manage the fishery sustainably. The framework set a limit that should not be exceeded (46% of the population) and extended a spawning season sanctuary to achieve a minimum safe level of abundance of spawning adult males and females (86 million crabs), so that the population will be able to reproduce adequately. Additional restrictions aimed to cut the harvest of females by one-third. Buying back commercial licenses reduced the number of watermen fishing for crabs, some of whom were hired to recover lost traps.

After considerable controversy and opposition by angry watermen, Virginia listened to scientists and closed its winter crab dredging season in 2010 and 2011 to conserve female crabs, most of which had not yet spawned. The winter dredge uses rakelike dredges to haul up gravid female crabs that have moved down the bay in the winter. The state said that this fishery jeopardizes the biological health of this resource. A subsequent survey showed that, despite degraded water quality and the presence of many predators such as striped bass, there was a huge increase in crabs from 2008 to 2010, with increases in females, males, and juveniles, indicating that the saved females had reproduced successfully and boosted the population. Through these management actions, one of the world's largest crab fisheries was brought from near collapse to a healthy population in just 3 years. Shortly after the survey, the watermen in Virginia successfully lobbied their state legislature to end the moratorium on the winter dredging and allow them once again to remove the hibernating gravid females from the bay bottom. They did not make enough money picking up abandoned crab pots compared to dredging out the crabs.

The Dungeness crab (Fig. 2.5) fishery along the U.S. West Coast is more stable, but also has had some ups and downs, but not necessarily due to fishing. Several decades of population declines started in the 1950s. Studies by Alan Shanks and G. Curtis Roegner of the University of Oregon suggest that the population size is determined by variation in larval success, namely the return of megalopae, which depends largely on the timing of the "spring transition"—a seasonal shift that occurs when the ocean changes from a downwelling state to an upwelling state. *Downwelling* is when surface water moves downward, while *upwelling* is the movement upward of nutrient-rich deeper water. The beginning of upwelling can occur any time between March and June. Generally, the earlier the upwelling, the greater the productivity, since upwelling brings up nutrients to stimulate plankton growth in surface waters and thus the whole food web. Early spring transitions lead to more returning Dungeness megalopae.

As salmon and other fisheries have declined, the Dungeness crab fishery has become more important. In December 2010, the Oregon Dungeness crab fishery (regulated by the state) was certified by the Marine Stewardship Council as "sustainably fished," the first West Coast crab fishery to be so certified. This certification is valued because it suggests that the fishery is not overexploiting the resource or severely damaging the environment. The fishery's sustainable approach includes returning undersized males to the ocean, releasing all females, and using equipment that minimizes bycatch. Size restrictions have been in place for over a century, and catching females was banned in the 1940s. In 1995 they limited the number of vessels, and, as vessels got bigger and used more pots, they limited the number of pots as well. For whatever reason, 2011 was a banner year for Dungeness crab, and, despite the abundant supply, prices remained high. Private buyers, many of whom export to China, purchased much of the catch. Demand also is up in Europe after the Marine Stewardship Council's "sustainable fishery" designation. The secret of success, says Al Gann, an Oregon crab fisherman who has fished for 36 years is "a good boat, the best gear, the best bait, and you need to be willing to fish the worst weather."

Fishermen in Washington state, however, face additional regulations. In 1974 a court decision allotted Native American tribes 50% of the catch shares, forcing the nontribal fishing fleet (which was already at excess capacity) into a smaller area. Three-fourths of the nontribal crabbing in Washington is now restricted to a 38 mile stretch of coast. Ray Toste, the president of the Washington Dungeness Crab Fisherman's Association complains, "There's 30 of them [Native American crabbers] and 228 of us, and there's the disparity." Toste helped push for a state law that prohibits fishing out to 200 miles off the Washington coast without a commercial fishing license, and stops Oregon and California crabbers from going north, thereby eliminating 20,000 traps from the Washington coast and preserving the state's boats and jobs. State legislation also set trap limits, eliminating another 35,000 traps. Toste also helped set up a program to retrieve lost crab traps, and wants the federal government to offer a buyback program to further reduce the fleet, which would mean more crabs for the remaining crabbers. Toste wants to secure a future for his children and grandchildren, and he thinks the fishing industry should adopt policies to use resources wisely. He is a unique voice for commercial fishing interests on the board of the highly respected Marine Fish Conservation Network.

In California, legislation was introduced in 2011 aimed at making its Dungeness crab fishery safer and more competitive, based on recommendations from a Dungeness Crab Task Force (DCTF) created in 2008. Dungeness crab is one of the most profitable and productive fisheries in California, so the demands of fishermen and consumers are increasing. The DCTF was concerned that state money used to mitigate lost fishing opportunities in the salmon fishery was being reinvested in the Dungeness crab fishery, thereby increasing pressure on the crab. There is pressure for fishermen to set more pots to increase their potential catch of the limited number of crabs, creating an "arms race." Boats from Oregon and Washington exacerbate the problem by coming to California to put out crab pots, responding to pot limits in those states. The legislation attempts to ease this rush at the beginning of the crab season when fishermen race to catch as much as possible in the shortest period of time. Recommendations were to cap and then reduce the number of pots to reduce the capacity of the fishery.

The mangrove (or giant mud) crab (*Scylla serrata*) is an important commercial crab in the Western Indian Ocean that is exploited by local fishermen for subsistence, consumption in local hotels and restaurants, supply to regional and national markets, and commercial export. The fishery is important in the mangrove swamps of western Madagascar, where crabs are collected using hand-collection, nets, and scoops. Demand is growing rapidly, particularly from commercial export markets. Evidence suggests that, owing to the largely unregulated nature of the fishery in Madagascar, crab stocks are being rapidly depleted.

On the other hand, U.S. importers of blue swimmer crabs (*Portunus pelagicus*) took steps in 2011 to improve the sustainability of that fishery in Indonesia and the Philippines. The National Fisheries Institute's Crab Council adopted a minimum size requirement designed to end harvesting of undersized crabs. Eleven U.S. companies, representing over 60% of the U.S. market for blue swimmer crabs, now require that the carapace measures at least 3 inches across. The government of Indonesia has officially recognized this limit and has instructed fisheries officials to enforce them on all exported crab.

Land crabs are caught in many tropical areas. The coconut crab (Plate 1) has long been collected for food in the tropical Pacific. On many Pacific Islands, it is getting scarce, and conservation measures are needed. In Niue Island of Polynesia, scientists recommended that no egg-bearing females be taken, that there should be a minimal legal size, that spawning areas be closed to public access during the breeding season, that exports be stopped, and that a public awareness campaign be initiated. Unfortunately none of the recommendations were acted on. Other islands such as Vanuatu are somewhat more proactive, and public education programs have resulted in coconut crab seldom appearing on menus. In Guam, regulations specify that no egg-bearing coconut crabs or crabs less than 4 inches in carapace width can be taken.

For many species, fishing changes the population structure because only large males are harvested. Male-only fishing decreases male size and skews the sex ratio toward females, resulting in more mating opportunities for smaller males, which have less sperm. This can result in "sperm limitation," in which females in fished populations do not receive enough sperm from the remaining males. In the (male-only) spiny king crab *Paralithodes brevipes*, fishery, the catch has declined in recent years, male size has decreased, and the sex ratio has become skewed toward females. Female reproductive success in years with more fishing was lower than in years with less fishing. In this case, the small males and the few remaining large males in the population could not provide adequate sperm to females.

In blue crabs (*Callinectes sapidus*; Plate 3) only 8% of mature females survive to spawn for a second season. Their average size has declined significantly, although it is not clear if this is because of the removal of larger individuals or possibly the warming temperatures. Male size declined locally due to removal of large crabs, and sperm limitation may occur. The focus on conserving females while intensively fishing males appears to alter the sex ratio to 3:1.

AQUACULTURE

Aquaculture is the aquatic equivalent of agriculture: the farming of aquatic organisms such as fish, crustaceans, mollusks, and aquatic plants. Crustacean aquaculture is feasible but difficult because crabs and lobsters tend to cannibalize tank mates, especially after they molt. Feeding habits are critical, and herbivores are easier to culture than carnivores because eating closer to the base of the food chain means that food is more available and cheaper, and animals are less likely to eat each other. Feeds for different species in culture are being developed. There is no large-scale culture of crabs comparable to that of shrimp. As with aquaculture of any organism, crowded conditions increase problems with water quality and disease. *Polyculture*—that is, raising different species together—enables the raising of compatible species that use different foods and niches in the tanks. This is likely to provide more dependable success and income.

Swimming Crabs

In the Indo-Pacific, the large mangrove (or mud) crab *Scylla serrata* is cultured in fish ponds, where it eats shellfish and some of the farmed fish, but produces sufficient income to supplement that from the fish in the ponds. This species is widely distributed in mangroves and estuaries. A study by

Lee Parkes from Bangor University in the United Kingdom and colleagues showed some differences between hatchery-reared and wild crabs. Wild crabs were heavier and had thicker spines, and hatchery crabs had a higher incidence of deformities in the shape of their abdomens. Initially, hatchery-reared crabs had less burying behavior, but after a few days of exposure to sediments, this defensive behavior increased to match that of wild crabs.

In the United States, the blue crab is cultured for limited periods of time (generally a few days to weeks) when it is in premolt, so it can be harvested as soft-shelled crab, which is of higher value than a hard-shelled crab of the same size. Doug Watson of the University of Alabama and colleagues may have found a way to induce molting and thus make soft-shell crabs available year round. His team has isolated the receptor for the hormone that inhibits molting and will test compounds designed to block the receptor and induce molting. They will need to develop an injection or food pellet to distribute the receptor-blockers. However, crab mortality in soft-shell production facilities is high: about a quarter of all crabs die due to stresses from harvesting and handling, plus a high incidence of infectious disease that occurs when many animals live in a confined area. Research aimed at preventing the introduction of viruses to crabs in hatcheries may reduce the number of soft shelled crabs that die before reaching the market.

Scientists have long been able to raise various species of crabs from eggs to early adult stages in the laboratory. Partial lifecycle culture of blue crabs is being developed for enhancing the depleted stocks in Chesapeake Bay. Yonathan Zohar and colleagues from University of Maryland have developed culture techniques for raising larvae and juveniles for release in the wild. Juveniles have been produced year round, with excellent survival. During 2002–2006, cultured crabs were tagged and released into nursery habitats. Cultured crabs survived as well as their wild counterparts, increased local populations at release sites, grew quickly to sexual maturity, mated, and migrated from the release sites to spawning grounds, contributing to the breeding stock as soon as 5–6 months after release. By producing juveniles 3–4 months earlier in the year than occurs naturally, the released females were able to spawn the same year they were released, while wild crabs of the same age did not spawn until the following year. Therefore, releases of cultured juveniles could speed up population recovery, and using hatchery juveniles to replenish breeding stocks in Chesapeake Bay is feasible. This practice is commonly used by finfish hatcheries to supplement wild fish populations, although studies have shown that hatchery-raised fish do not avoid predators or grow as well as wild fish. Eric Johnson and colleagues from the Smithsonian Environmental Research Center, however, found equivalent survival rates of hatchery-reared and wild blue crabs in the field. Hatchery-reared and wild juveniles also showed similar growth rates, indicating that hatchery blue crabs, unlike hatchery fish, are not at a disadvantage when released into the environment. In Japan, the horse (or gazami) crab (*Portunus trituberculatus*) is similarly being cultured for stock enhancement.

King Crabs

Larvae of king crabs are being cultured in Alaska as part of a program to refine techniques that might one day be used to rebuild their depleted stocks around Kodiak Island (red kings) and the Pribilof Islands (blue kings). Unlike the other species, king crabs live in cold water and grow slowly. However, larval culture in Russia has had high (30–90%) survival rates. Researchers are learning to hatch and rear red and blue king crab larvae in a large-scale hatchery setting. The Alaska King Crab Research, Rehabilitation and Biology Program (AKCRRAB) is a partnership among Alaska Sea Grant, fishermen's groups, communities, NOAA laboratories, the Alutiiq Pride Shellfish Hatchery and Chugach Regional Resources Commission, and the University of Alaska. The larvae they are currently raising are not being released into the wild, but are being studied to learn what and how much to feed them; what artificial habitat, water flow rate, and temperature are best for optimum survival; and whether hatcheries can play a role in rebuilding these crab stocks. In 2010, 2.7 million red king crab larvae successfully hatched from 18 females. Scientists are designing experiments to learn how hatchery crabs might fare in the wild and are developing methods to identify hatchery-raised king crab using tags. Modeled after efforts in Chesapeake Bay, they are testing crab survival and retention of tags after molting for a range of juvenile crab sizes. Golden king crabs are attractive candidates for culturing because their larval period is relatively short and all larval stages do not need to be fed (i.e., they are lecithotrophic; see Chapter 4), one of the major issues for most aquaculture operations.

Mitten Crabs

Chinese mitten crabs (*Eriocheir sinensis*; Fig. 2.7) (also known as hairy crab) are popular in China because of their sweet meat and rich roe, although this same species is a despised invader in Europe and the United States. After the 1980s, populations in China declined sharply due to overfishing, pollution, and dams that blocked migration. Since then, the crab has become an important cultured species in China, with an annual production of 500,000 tons valued at $2.2 billion in 2005, according to the Food and Agriculture Organization. It accounts for two-thirds of all crab aquaculture production worldwide (the rest being *Scylla* and other portunids). The species is robust and its omnivory makes it easy to provide food. The market is primarily Asia, with most of them being consumed within China itself. Its culture started with the release of small wild crabs into lakes that had been isolated from rivers by water-gates in the late 1970s. Most mitten crabs are farmed in two lakes—Lake Tai and Lake Yangcheng—in Jiangsu Province. Juveniles are obtained from the mouth of the Yangtze River and transferred to the lake, where they are confined at the lake edge in netted-off areas and fed maize, seaweed, and snails. Lake Tai is fed by the mountain streams that bring rich nutrients. The local government is very strict on the water quality of the lake, and all feeds must be approved. The young crabs hibernate in the winter in burrows. In the spring, they are transferred to large pens in the middle of the lake for grow-out. From the collection of juveniles to the final harvest, it takes about 2 years to get the crabs ready for export to major markets in Shanghai and Hong Kong. Shortly before eggs hatch, gravid crabs are transferred to a larval rearing tank.

Mitten crabs also can be reared through their whole life cycle. The density of the newly hatched zoea larvae is controlled at 200,000–300,000 per cubic meter (a cubic meter is approximately one cubic yard). The gravid crabs are transferred to another tank once this density is attained. Larval rearing takes about 3 weeks, during which the zoea molt five times to reach the megalopa stage. Salinity is reduced gradually to almost freshwater levels when the megalopae are 2–3 days old. Older megalopae are stocked in seed crab rearing ponds for the grow-out in net enclosures.

In contrast with crab and lobster aquaculture, shrimp aquaculture has been developed on a large scale in many areas, especially Asia and South America, in some cases causing some environmental problems. Thailand and Ecuador have chopped down extensive mangrove forests for their shrimp farms, and wastes flushed from the farms have ruined the water quality in nearby bays. Progress has been made in developing less polluting systems. Another controversial issue is the use of fish meal to feed the shrimp, which contributes to depletion of forage fish species. Manufacturers are developing shrimp food based on vegetable protein such as soy, reducing the amount of fish meal used. If crab aquaculture eventually becomes as successful as shrimp farming, some of the same problems could arise unless environmental impacts are taken into account during the planning process.

CHAPTER NINE

Eating Crabs

Crabmeat, like fish, is a nutritious food, low in calories and fat but high in protein and omega-3 fatty acids, which help prevent heart disease. These fatty acids are especially important for women who are pregnant or breast-feeding because they are needed for their child's developing nervous system. Omega-3s, which are higher in crabmeat than in shrimp, may also reduce inflammation, enhance immune function, and even lower the risk of certain types of cancer. Crabmeat is also rich in vitamins and minerals, with high levels of vitamin B-12, a vitamin critical for healthy nerve function. The composition of fresh crabmeat is about 75% water, 20% protein, 0–6% fat, and 1–2% minerals. Caloric value of the cooked meat is 25–35 calories per ounce. Principal minerals include phosphorus, magnesium, and calcium, and crabmeat is also a good source of zinc and copper.

LIVE CRABS

Some crabs are shipped to be sold alive. However, crabs may be damaged in the process of being caught, including physical damage to the carapace and limbs by fishing gear and physiological stress from exposure on deck. The ability to assess whether a crab will live or die is important when crabs are sorted for sale. External visible injuries are not a useful prediction alone as a crab's survival must account for internal or physiological injuries, which are difficult to detect and more likely to occur in recently molted crabs. Testing reflexes is a better method to assess internal injuries because reflexes are a measure of nervous system activity and reflect damage from both injury and environmental stress. In a study of Bering Sea snow and tanner crabs, Alan Stoner and colleagues from the National Marine Fisheries Service found that a suite of reflexes, including movements of the mouth, eyestalks, claws, and legs, could dependably predict future mortality.

In Nanjing, China, there are vending machines that sell live crabs. One Chinese mitten crab (called "hairy crab" in China) costs the equivalent of $1.50–$7.50, depending on its size. Crabs in the vending machine are kept at a cold temperature that causes them to become dormant and remain alive. Eating them can be a tedious process, requiring special utensils to pry open the shells and dig into the flesh after they are cooked. Many people dip the meat in vinegar made in Jiangsu Province. The brilliant, reddish-orange *roe* (eggs) of the mitten crab is prized for its delicate, creamy flavor.

Mitten crabs used to be widely sold in the United States but are now largely banned as an invasive species (see Chapter 7). In New York, sales are prohibited whether the crabs are dead or alive. But in California you can fish for them if you have a permit. The crabs are also invasive in some European countries (e.g., the Netherlands) where they are caught and sold. Eating invasive species once they have been established and cannot be controlled, however, does make sense: "If you can't beat 'em, eat 'em."

PROCESSING CRABMEAT

Crabs deteriorate rapidly after death due to the growth of microorganisms and the action of enzymes. While the crab is alive, the enzymes are under biochemical control, but when the crab dies, they begin to degrade the quality of the meat. Digestive enzymes break down the flesh, reducing yield and destroying the compounds that impart the fresh crabmeat's flavor. Deterioration is much more rapid than for fish, so crabs must be kept alive until they are processed. The usual method of holding crabs on a fishing vessel is to place them in a flooded hold or in large tanks through which seawater is continuously pumped. The pumping rate must be sufficient to maintain enough dissolved oxygen to keep the crabs alive and healthy. The Alaska Sea Grant program provides advice for king and snow crab fisheries. They advise that water temperature should be kept as close as possible to the natural environment and that all surfaces that crabs can contact, particularly the insides of holding tanks, should be smooth, resistant to corrosion, and cleaned often. Water circulated over crabs must be free from contamination. Crabs can be held on deck for 24 hours and, under very good conditions, up to 48 hours. Increased time on board increases death in both king and snow crabs. Colder temperatures do help to ensure the quality of the meat, and it may be helpful to chill the crabs before processing to decrease microbe populations.

Pasteurization of crabmeat—by quick heating followed by immersion in ice water—was developed in the mid-twentieth century. This valuable process allows refrigerated crabmeat to last for 6 months to a year, rather than only 10–12 days. It is particularly useful for stockpiling crabmeat when more crabs are caught than can be processed and eaten. Pasteurization is a useful short-term method of storing crabmeat, which is packed into enameled cans with double-seamed lids. The closed cans are immersed in a bath of 175°F water for about 70 minutes for a half-pound can or just over 100 minutes for a 1-pound can so that the meat at the center of the can reaches 170°F for at least a minute to destroy any bacteria. Pasteurized cans should be kept cold (33–35°F) during storage. The process seems to have no effect on the color, smell, or taste of the crabmeat.

Processing plants cook, pick, and package the crabmeat. Red crab and Dungeness crab may be partially butchered before cooking to remove the viscera and gills. Three marketable products are produced: whole crab, crabmeat, and crab waste. Since most crabs are processed only for meat, a lot of waste is produced. This waste used to be discarded, but now the byproducts can be marketed, including shell pieces, chitin, protein concentrate, and waste meal, which can be used as fertilizer and farm animal feed.

Crab-processing operations in the Chesapeake Bay involve crab-picking "houses" (Fig. 9.1) that cook the blue crabs in enormous vats or kettles that can hold baskets with about a thousand pounds of crab. After cooking, they are ready for the "picking room" where they are split, quartered, and dissected for their meat. Crab-picking houses are traditionally staffed by local women, often wives of watermen, who remove the meat and sort it into lump, claw, back fin (i.e., the muscle that powers the swimming legs), and other smaller bits with remarkable speed. They work rapidly to stab at the back, pull off the carapace, cut away the eyes and mouth section, remove the gills and the stomach, cut off the legs, pierce and remove the muscle from the posterior body section including the prized back fin, and flick out the smaller "flake meat" from the more anterior parts with the point of a knife. Finally, they whack off the claws and break them apart to extract the meat. They work quickly because they are paid by the pound. Some can pick 3–4 pounds of meat in 15 minutes, and since the meat is only a small percent-

Figure 9.1. Crab-picking house in Maryland. Photo from NOAA.

age of the whole crab's weight, this means dissecting twenty to thirty crabs in 15 minutes, or one to two crabs per minute.

Many seafood-packing operations are located along Maryland's eastern shore. Smith Island has many dedicated female pickers, many of them wives of watermen, who work at a co-op, a State Health Department–approved hall, where they work at long tables, receiving crabs from the watermen who operate on a small dock nearby and who started the Smith Island Crab Meat Cooperative in 1996 to save the threatened crab industry on their small (population: 75) island in Chesapeake Bay. Most picking houses are still staffed by women, but rather than local wives of watermen, they are now more often foreign workers with temporary visas. There have been problems in getting enough workers and some crab houses have closed. Big-time agri-business companies have entered into the previously low-key crab-processing field, threatening the locals. Mrs. Paul's was one of the first companies to enter, building a plant in Crisfield, Maryland, to make frozen deviled crabs, and later branching out into all kinds of crab products and processing from breading and frying to freezing and packaging. The Duffy-Mott company (of applesauce fame) opened a packing company on Tilghman Island for frozen crab cakes. In Georgia and the Carolinas, there are other large-scale companies that are replacing the traditional processing operations.

The canning process for crabmeat was first developed in the late 1870s. After being cooked and picked, the extracted claw and body meats are separated because canners pay the highest price for lump meat and lowest for small pieces of leg meat. The meats are rinsed, dipped in a mild acid solution (acetic or citric acid) to prevent discoloration, and packed into parchment-lined or enameled cans, with claw meat lining the top and bottom, and body meat in the middle. An acid-brine dip made from salt brine and citric acid has been developed to prevent discoloration when protein molecules react to the heat required for canning by releasing copper and forming blue copper oxide. Dipping the meat in a solution of sodium chloride, lactic acid, and aluminum salts stabilizes the copper so no blue color is produced. Cans are lined with parchment or given a special enamel finish to prevent discoloration through chemical reaction of the crabmeat with the can itself. The lids are crimped on the cans, the first stage of the can-closing process, and cans are heated to 212°F for 10–30 minutes. The cans are then fully sealed and heat processed for over an hour.

WAYS TO EAT CRABS

Unlike lobsters and shrimp, crabs do not have a muscular tail (abdomen) forming a large piece of meat. Instead, smaller muscles that power the claws and legs are eaten. Claw rather than leg meat may compose a significant portion of the meat in species with large claws such as stone crabs (Fig. 1.10). The hard exoskeleton makes it difficult to get at the meat without tools like nutcrackers and picks. Cancer crabs such as Dungeness crabs have a very thick shell, while the portunids (swimming crabs) have thinner shells that are easier to crush. Swimming crabs have enlarged muscles for the swimming paddles; back fins are prized for eating. Even though Dungeness crabs lack back fins, about one-quarter of their weight is meat. Many people on the West Coast have a tradition of eating Dungeness for Thanksgiving, Christmas, and New Year's.

The easiest way to prepare crabs—boiling them in water—is the most difficult way to eat them, requiring knives, mallets, and nutcrackers to break open the shell, followed by various messy ways of trying to get the meat to and eat it. A small wooden mallet is often used to crack the claws to remove the meat. Males have a slim abdomen ("apron") on the underside, which can be used as a tab, similar to a beverage can. The apron is pried up with the knife, pulled back, and cut off, revealing an area in the rear of the crab where the knife can be inserted to pry the upper and lower shells apart. The meat is then pulled out and eaten, but because the interior is a series of compartments separated by a somewhat pliable but still sharp shell, removing the meat is also a lot of work for the relatively small amount of edible crabmeat. It is easier to do this with your hands than with any implement provided. Sometimes the whole crab is served in a sauce. While this can be even tastier, the sauce does compound the messiness. It is no wonder that restaurants provide a plastic bib for customers who order whole crab. Extra napkins, fingerbowls, and wet wipes are indispensable. Most diners are not nearly as expert as the crab house workers, and for some, eating crabs is more time and trouble than it is worth, because without a meaty tail section, crabs are a whole lot of work for relatively little meat.

Many chefs and humanitarians have been concerned about the way crabs are killed. Traditionally, they are dropped alive into a pan of boiling water and take several minutes to die. A more humane method would kill the shellfish almost instantly. Entrepreneur Simon Buckhaven has created a device named the Crustastun, which uses an electric current to stun and painlessly kill the animals. According to its inventor, the meat tastes better as well.

Blue crabs are most often eaten in the hard shell. Steaming them in large pots with water, vinegar, and seasoning is the norm on the East Coast. The crabs are placed on a raised tray in large cooking pots, and are layered into the pot with a lot of seasoning between the layers. Places such as New Orleans tend to boil them in water with heavy Cajun or "crab boil" seasoning. The pot is then covered and kept boiling until the crabs turn red. The cooked crabs are cracked by hand, but most diners use a small knife to pry open the shell and remove the unwanted parts such as the gills. The crab's digestive gland (hepatopancreas), known as the *tomalley*, is usually removed but considered a delicacy by some. In many Asian cultures, the eggs (and sometimes the ovaries) of female crabs are eaten.

The eastern shore of Maryland has many informal crab restaurants with brown paper tablecloths where diners manipulate a wooden mallet in one hand and a paring knife in the other. Your hands get slimy to the wrist (or elbow) with crab innards and spicy sludge, along with melted butter—but you enjoy yourself. Crabs measuring from 6 to 6½ inches across are listed on large chalkboard menus at crab houses as "jumbos." Smaller "mediums" and "larges" are available all season, but the best time to get jumbos is late summer and early fall, when the crabs that have been lucky enough to survive the season begin to prepare for hibernation.

Blue crabs undergo their first molt of the season in the late spring. Watermen call them "peelers." The molting process takes place a number of times during the summer as the crabs grow. Crab-packing houses can temporarily keep peelers in water baths until they molt and are soft, meaty, and ready for distribution. Graded and priced by size, they range from *mediums,* 3½–4 inches wide, to *primes,* more than 5½ inches. Soft-shell crabs are prepared by first cutting out the gills, front ("face"), and guts. They can be sautéed, baked, broiled, or grilled but are most often battered in flour, egg, and seasoning and fried in oil until crispy. They can be served as an entrée or in a sandwich, and the entire crab is consumed, legs and all. While fancier restaurants might sauté soft-shells in light butter and garlic, the usual preparation in the crab houses is deep-fried and stacked on a roll or white toast with mayo and tomato.

The picked meat, especially the large chunks from the back-fin area, can also be used to make crab cakes, crab soup, crab dip, and other dishes. Traditionally, crab cakes were fried, but many health-conscious people today prefer them broiled or grilled.

King crabs are delivered live then cleaned, leaving the legs, which are cooked in boiling water then dipped in cold water, both slightly salted. The legs, termed "sections," are then frozen and shipped. The meat can be eaten hot or cold; plain or with melted butter, garlic, or sauce; or put in salads.

Surimi

Surimi is a fish-based product that mimics the texture and taste of the meat of lobster, crab, or shrimp. It is typically made from white-fleshed fish such as pollock or hake that is pulverized to a paste, pressed, treated with a natural binder, and becomes rubbery when cooked. The gelatinous paste is then mixed with various additives such as starch, egg white, salt, vegetable oil, sorbitol, sugar, soy protein, and seasonings, and flavored with "juice" from crabs (or shrimp). An antioxidant found in crustaceans called *astaxanthin* is often added for color. Unlike most processed meat, the chemical additions to surimi are mostly derived from natural products. The gel can be molded, shaped, and cut into thin strips which, when rolled together, mimic the texture of real crabmeat. The most common surimi product in the Western market is imitation crabmeat, which often is sold as "sea legs" or "krab" in the United States, where it was introduced in the early 1980s, though the Japanese have been using surimi products for hundreds of years. Technology developed in Japan in the early 1960s promoted the growth of the industry, based on the Alaska pollock (or walleye pollock). Subsequently, this species was supplemented with others, including cod and tilapia. The industrialized surimi-making process was refined by scientists at Japan's Hokkaidō Fisheries Experiment Institute to process the increased catch of fish, and better methods of preservation were developed to extend

CRAB PRODUCTS OTHER THAN FOOD

Chitin, a major component of shells and a waste product from crab-processing plants, can be processed for the substance *chitosan*. Chitosan is used in a myriad of products and processes, including dialysis, photographic emulsions, artificial fabric, printing inks, adhesives, cosmetics, and anticoagulants. It is used in agriculture as a seed treatment and plant growth enhancer and as an ecologically friendly biopesticide that boosts the innate ability of plants to defend themselves against insects, fungi, pathogens, and other diseases. Chitosan is able to promote natural defenses of pine trees against the devastating mountain pine beetle. It can be used in water processing as a part of filtration, where it causes fine sediment particles to bind together and removes phosphorus, minerals, and oils from the water. It is sold in tablet form at health stores as a "fat attractor" with the claim that it attracts fat from the digestive system and expels it from the body so that users can lose weight without eating less. Research suggests that these diet claims are untrue. Chitosan does slow down the emptying of the stomach, however, so if the user gets hungry later than usual after eating, it might indeed contribute to weight loss.

In addition to chitosan, the shells from Maine lobsters are used to manufacture decorative tiles, trivets, and drinking-glass coasters. Work is under way to use them in countertop production. Prototypes of biodegradable golf balls and plant pots made of ground-up lobster shells have been developed. An additional bonus is that the plant pots have a high calcium content, which is beneficial to flowers and vegetables planted within them. Turning seafood waste into products with commercial value benefits the seafood industry.

the shelf life. Currently, 2–3 million tons of fish from around the world, amounting to 2–3% of the world fisheries supply, are used for the production of surimi-based products. Imitation crabmeat is popular in the United States, with annual sales of over $250 million. It is cheaper than real crabmeat, which may account for its popularity. The technology continues to improve, saving crustacean lives and making use of food that might otherwise be wasted.

FAMOUS CRAB DISHES AND THEIR ORIGIN

"The crab who walks too far falls into the pot" (Haitian proverb).

She-Crab Soup

Charleston, South Carolina, is famous for She-Crab Soup. This rich, creamy soup, a cross between a bisque (thick creamy soup) and a chowder (chunky, with potatoes or other vegetables), is made with blue crab meat, and is considered the city's signature dish. It is named because of the addition of crab roe (eggs) to the soup, which may also include butter, cream, sherry, and seasonings such as mace, shallots, or onions. The addition of the crab roe is credited to William Deas, a cook for R. Goodwyn Rhett, former mayor of Charleston (1903–1911). According to the local story, President William Howard Taft was being "wined and dined" by Mayor Rhett, and the Rhetts asked their cook to "dress up" the pale crab soup they usually served. The cook added the orange roe to give color and improve the flavor, thus inventing this Charleston delicacy.

Baltimore Crab Cakes

This classic American dish is composed of crabmeat and ingredients such as bread or cracker crumbs, milk, mayonnaise, eggs, onions, and seasonings. Occasionally other ingredients such as red or green peppers are added, at which point the cake is then sautéed, baked, or grilled and then served. Crab cakes are traditionally associated with Chesapeake Bay, in particular Maryland and the city of Baltimore. Many restaurants that offer Maryland crab cakes will offer to have the cakes fried or broiled. They may be served with a sauce, such as a remoulade, tartar sauce, mustard, or ketchup and vary from the size of a small cookie to as large as a hamburger. Some particularly tasty ones include claw meat in addition to the heftier meat from the back fin and body. Sweeter in taste and fibrous in texture, the claw meat balances out the richness of the heavier meats. Although any species of crab may be used, the Chesapeake blue crab is traditional and considered the best. Crab cakes are popular along the coasts of the Mid-Atlantic States, the Gulf of Mexico, and the Pacific, where the crabbing industry thrives. On the West Coast, the native Dungeness crab is often the main ingredient.

Other Crab Dishes

Soft-shell crab is prepared by brushing the crab with a sauce of oil, fresh parsley, lemon juice, nutmeg, soy sauce, and Tabasco sauce and then grilling the crab at a moderately high temperature until lightly browned, turning it over to cook the other side.

Crab bisque is a rich soup that contains minced onion, butter or margarine, flour, shellfish or chicken stock, half-and-half or cream, crabmeat, and salt. The onion is sautéed in butter, the flour is added, and the stock and half-and-half (or cream) gradually stirred in. After about 5 minutes, the crabmeat is added to the broth, which is salted to taste, heated thoroughly, and garnished with parsley.

Crab jambalaya is made from crabmeat, bacon, chopped onion and green pepper, flour, cooked rice, canned tomatoes, Worcestershire sauce, paprika, and thyme. The bacon is cooked until crisp, the onion and green pepper are added and cooked until tender, and then the flour and the other ingredients (except crab) are added and cooked while stirring for a few minutes. Finally the crabmeat is added. Cracked crab legs are put over a rice mixture, covered, and cooked over medium heat for about 5 minutes or until the crab is thoroughly cooked.

FOOD SAFETY ISSUES

Spoilage

As mentioned before, crabmeat spoils rapidly if it is at room temperature for too long. Spoiled crabmeat is sticky, has an ammonia odor, and is yellowish in color. Do not buy crabs if the meat looks off color or dried out. Crabmeat should remain fresh for 3 to 5 days in the coldest part of your refrigerator. If you are planning to cook crab at home, it is best to buy live crabs and consume them when they are as fresh as possible, preferably the same day, although they will keep in the refrigerator for a day or two. Buy your crabs from a known and reputable fish store or supermarket and ask how long the crabs have been in the tank. If it is longer than a week, they should be avoided. Choose crabs that are lively and active. They should smell fresh and salty, without a fishy smell and especially not a smell of ammonia. Don't buy crabs that are dead because the meat will likely be bad when you cook it. If you are buying live crabs, put them in a bowl or a container where they can still breathe, cover them with damp paper towels or a damp cloth, and put them in a cold area of your refrigerator. Check on them from time to time; if they die, cook them immediately.

Frozen crabs are okay, although frozen seafood never tastes quite as good as fresh. Experts suggest that frozen crabmeat be prepared in crab cakes, casserole, or soup because freezing fresh crabmeat toughens and dries out the meat. Prepared dishes can be stored in the freezer for 3–6 months, but the longer crab is stored, the more it will toughen and dry out. Soft-shell crabs can be frozen successfully by removing the front, carapace, inner organs, and gills, then washing and wrapping the crabs individually in an air-tight freezer wrap.

Contamination

Concerns about seafood safety include the possibility of chemical contamination. Fortunately, unlike tuna or swordfish that are high on the food web, crabs seldom accumulate pollutants such mercury or PCBs to the point of being unsafe to eat. One of the big concerns with eating a seafood-rich diet is exposure to mercury. Crabs tend to be low in mercury, making them a good seafood choice. However, there are highly contaminated urban locations such as the Hackensack Meadowlands of New Jersey where there is a ban on catching blue crabs (and fish) because they have accumulated high levels of pollutants such as dioxin and mercury.

Toxins

A handful of xanthid crab species are highly toxic, and dangerous to humans who eat them. These poisonous crabs include the mosaic reef crab (or white spotted reef crab) (*Lophozozymus pictor*), demon crabs (*Demania* spp.), jewel crab (*Zosimus aeneus*), crested reef crab (*Platypodia granulosa*), and green egg crab (*Atergatis floridus*), which are native to the Indo-Pacific. The consumption of any of these crabs, even if well cooked, is extremely dangerous and has proved fatal in several instances. All these species belong to the family Xanthidae and have distinctive color markings, which may function as a warning to potential predators.

Crabs may accumulate toxins from toxic algae, similar to what occurs with shellfish such as clams and mussels. Mud (xanthid) crabs in particular appear to be able to accumulate saxitoxin, the cause of paralytic shellfish poisoning (PSP). Saxitoxin is manufactured by microscopic algae, such as dinoflagellates of the genus *Alexandrium*.

Saxitoxin is a neurotoxin that interferes with nerve/muscle transmission. Getting PSP from eating crabs is not uncommon in the Pacific but rare in the Atlantic, where it is much more common from eating clams or mussels. Dungeness crabs have sometimes been found to have PSP in their internal organs, so people are advised not to eat the tomalley (hepatopancreas), where the toxins accumulate. Mud crabs are omnivores, and the source of toxins in these crabs is not always clear and not necessarily *Alexandrium*. Bacteria and some species of red calcareous algae have been implicated as sources of toxins. Some xanthid crabs may carry enormous amounts of paralytic shellfish toxins: one *Zosimus aeneus* was reported to have enough toxin in its body to kill hundreds of people. Since 65–100% of the individuals of this species can be toxic, they should be avoided.

After eating toxin-containing shellfish, people experience symptoms within 30 minutes. Early symptoms include tingling of the lips, numbness, weakness, and poor coordination. A burning or tingling sensation starts in the lips and face, then extends to upper body extremities and to fingers and toes. Gradually the body becomes paralyzed with voluntary movements becoming increasingly difficult. As the toxin continues to exert effects, it paralyzes the diaphragm, which is the muscle used in breathing, causing victims to die of suffocation. A lethal dose can cause death within 12 hours. There was an outbreak of PSP in Southeast Alaska in the summer of 2010. Several of the victims had eaten Dungeness crabs, and some apparently ate internal organs, which are more likely to accumulate the toxin than the muscle. There were five cases of PSP reported, possibly from Dungeness crab, including at least two deaths. The Department of Fish and Game and the State Health Department warned Alaskans not to eat internal organs of crabs.

Domoic acid is a neurotoxin produced by another type of microscopic algae, the diatom *Pseudonitzchia*. This toxin produces amnesic shellfish poisoning. When mole crabs (filter feeders) eat the toxic plankton, they become toxic to birds, otters, and fish that eat them. Fortunately, people don't generally eat mole crabs.

There have been reports of people getting ill after eating coconut crabs. In some regions coconut crabs eat certain plants that contain mild toxins. It is believed that these plant toxins build up in the crab's body and may cause the reported effects in people. In addition, plant toxins may be involved with presumed aphrodisiac qualities that are said to come from eating this crab.

Parasites

If crabmeat is eaten uncooked, for example in sushi, there is a slight chance of transmission of some parasites to humans, particularly trematode flatworms (also known as flukes), although this is rare. There are several species of the lung fluke, *Paragonimus,* that infect humans through the consumption of raw or undercooked crustaceans. These parasites are more common in freshwater than in marine crabs. After ingestion, the parasite penetrates the intestines and migrates through the abdomen, the diaphragm, and eventually to the lungs; at that point respiratory symptoms begin: cough, chest pain, and bloody sputum. In 2006, the Orange County (CA) Health Care Agency had an unusual situation where several people were diagnosed with lung infections from *Paragonimus.* The source of the infection was found to be restaurants that were serving Sawagani crabs, a freshwater species imported from Japan. Apparently, the infected patrons had been eating the small crabs raw. After 6–10 weeks, they developed a cough, difficulty breathing, diarrhea, abdominal pain, fever, and hives. The presence of the parasite was medically confirmed. A danger with *Paragonimus* is that during its migration in the body, it can end up in other organs, the most serious being the brain.

Allergies

Food allergies are common, and allergies to shellfish are one of the more common types of food allergies. A crab allergy is an adverse reaction by the body's immune system to crabs or food containing crab. The symptoms may not occur immediately after eating the crab and may last varying lengths of time from hours to weeks. The body's immune system produces immunoglobulin E (IgE; an antibody) and histamine in response to contact with the allergen. Someone who is allergic to crabs may or may not be allergic to other types of seafood but will usually be allergic to other crustaceans such as lobster or shrimp but probably not to clams, mussels, or finfish. An allergic reaction to crab can be severe or mild. Symptoms include skin rash, which can appear anywhere; asthma or difficulty breathing is a more severe symptom, and in such cases a physician should be contacted immediately. Shortness of breath can quickly become serious because it is probably caused by swelling that blocks the windpipe. Other symptoms may include dizziness, headache, abdominal upset, vomiting, diarrhea, and anaphylaxis (a potentially lethal reaction). The best approach for those with such allergies is to avoid eating crabs, but if a severe or anaphylactic reaction occurs, an adrenaline injection is recommended. Antihistamines and bronchodilators are recommended for asthma. People who are allergic to crabs should also avoid eating surimi because it includes a bit of crab for flavoring. Allergies do not come only from eating crabs; some workers in aquaculture facilities and crab-processing plants who received extensive occupational exposure, especially to newly molted crabs, developed asthma. Apparently, some people are allergic to chitin, a major constituent of crab shells.

CHAPTER TEN

Crabs and Humans

People most commonly encounter crabs casually on a dinner plate or at the beach ("Ouch, my toe!"). But some people, especially children, find the crabs they encounter at the shore a source of wonder, and scoop them up and put them in plastic pails to study. Others, perhaps some of these same children decades later, spend much of their lives studying various aspects of crab biology, which is called *carcinology*.

CRAB WATCHING

In a similar manner as a zoo or museum, a public aquarium and a tank in a pet store that sells tropical fish can provide a wonderful learning experience and an avenue for people to become familiar with these fascinating creatures. While public aquaria tend to have more exhibits of fish, birds, and marine mammals, there will generally be some crabs and other invertebrates as well. Some have a *touch tank*—a shallow tank with fish and invertebrates (usually including hermit crabs) that encourages hands-on exploration. Public aquaria may be affiliated with research institutions or conduct their own research, sometimes specializing in species from local waters. Aquaria, like zoos and museums, have a great potential to communicate conservation issues to the public. Children and adults can learn about the marine environment, from species identification and habitat to conservation techniques. Aquaria can enlighten the public about the oceans and freshwater systems and their inhabitants. Some even have beautiful mosaics on the floor (Plate 26). Some of the most impressive crab exhibits include the huge Japanese spider crab (*Macrocheira kaempferi*; Fig. 1.14), such as "Crabzilla" (see Chapter 1). There is a medium-sized individual of this species at the Atlantis Marine World Aquarium in Riverhead, New York, which, despite being only medium-sized, is nevertheless very impressive.

People can also watch crabs by snorkeling or scuba diving; crabs are not as easy to observe as the brightly colored fish that are much more conspicuous on coral reefs, but with keen eyes, patience, and determination, they can be seen. An underwater camera can record your observations; many of the photographs in this book were taken this way while snorkeling or scuba diving (others are of captive crabs in aquaria). The camera need not be expensive, and there are underwater housings available for many "point-and-shoot" digital cameras. If you don't like to get wet, in many tropical areas tour operators run glass-bottom boat trips that go over a reef and permit observers to watch the colorful reef life while staying dry. A submersible vehicle that can stay under water many hours and can visit previously inaccessible deeper parts of the ocean is a more expensive option. Overall, for crab watching, it is easier to watch semiterrestrial and terrestrial crabs on

---

WATCHING CRABS IN ART

Though not among his most famous works, Vincent van Gogh painted a crab on its back in 1889 and another of two crabs, recognizable as cancroid crabs, which were popular food items in Europe. After his release from the hospital in Arles in January 1889, van Gogh painted a series of still lifes, including these crab studies. The two crabs paintings may show the same crab right side up and on its back. The one on its back is at the Van Gogh Museum in Amsterdam, and the two crabs painting is at the National Gallery in London. Rembrandt used a crab in a still life of a breakfast on a table; this piece is in the Hermitage Museum in St. Petersburg, Russia. Several other artists also created still lifes with crabs. Franz Snyders' painting, however, entitled "Still life with Crab and Fruit" actually depicts a lobster.

Aside from "fine art," crab images in popular culture abound. Many areas in which crabs are an important fishery have turned crabs into pop cultural symbols, with t-shirts, napkins, key chains, posters, jewelry, paintings, sculptures, and other objects with crab icons available as souvenirs. Some countries have put crabs on their postage stamps, and crab jewelry designs are plentiful. There is a crab statue on Fisherman's Wharf in San Francisco (Plate 25) and a beautiful mosaic of a crab on the floor at the Monaco Aquarium (Plate 26).

land. If you sit quietly, they will get over their initial flight and go about their normal behaviors.

RECREATIONAL CRABBING

Beyond watching, another way of interacting with crabs is to catch them. This provides an opportunity to watch their feeding behavior, notice their disposition, and—should the crab get away—watch them swim. The blue crab's abundance, coloration, and flavor make it a favorite of recreational crabbers, despite its well-deserved reputation for nastiness. One of the most popular methods is to use baited hand lines about 7 feet long from a dock or a boat. The most common baits are menhaden (bunker) and chicken necks (hence the nickname "chicken necker" for these crabbers), but any fish will do. Throw the baited line into the water and slowly pull it across the bottom. When a crab is felt, pull up the line slowly and steadily until the crab is close enough to be scooped up with a long-handled dip net.

There are also various traps that are effective when used from a bridge. The *ring net* is a simple, inexpensive trap that consists of two rings, each of a different diameter connected by netting. When baited and lowered to the bottom, the trap lies flat on the bottom, and the crab will start to feed on the bait. When the trap is pulled up, the top ring is lifted first, thus trapping the crab. The drawbacks are that it works only in relatively calm water with a flat sandy or muddy bottom and that it must be lowered very slowly straight down. Pyramid (folding star) and box traps are made of metal and have sides that swing down (open) when resting on the bottom. They are more expensive and complicated but can be used in stronger currents and on bottoms covered with small rocks. The pyramid trap folds completely flat but is cumbersome to use, while the box trap is bulkier but works consistently and well.

Crabs can also be caught without a trap with a *scoop net* (a net or mesh basket held open by a hoop) when the shallow waters are clear and calm. Crabs can be scooped up from around marshes or bridge pilings and bulkheads. To avoid receiving a painful pinch, it is advised to wear gloves and to pick up the crab from behind; however, blue crabs can reach over or under their bodies to get at you, so beware! The safest way to pick them up is to hold an elbow or swimming paddle in each hand. Blue crabs, however, seldom cooperate in letting you do this, and it may be easier to dump them from the net right into a bushel basket or bucket with a lid without touching them. But the crabs will probably grab onto the net and be difficult to dislodge. Keep the basket damp and cool and avoid leaving crabs in direct sunlight, especially during the summer. They should not be put in a bucket of water because they will soon use up the dissolved oxygen and die. On the West Coast, crabbing is popular in Puget Sound. Each year, recreational crabbers there catch over a million pounds of Dungeness crab, using pots, ring nets, and—in the case of waders or divers—bare hands. The safest place to hold a Dungeness crab is its back. Although the crab is commonly picked up from behind, their claws can sometimes reach the holder's hand.

Each state that has crab populations has its own regulations for collectors. In Maryland, there is a season, but no license is required. There is a minimum size limit for both hard and "peeler" crabs, and a daily catch limit of 1 bushel per person. There are regulations on how many feet of line can be used, how many hand lines, and how many traps. Crab pots need to have a turtle reduction device attached, to allow turtles to escape. In many states, all commercial-style crab pots must include a biodegradable panel designed to create an opening to allow crabs and other animals to escape if the pot is lost or abandoned (see Chapter 8). Washington has size limits and seasonal restrictions for Dungeness crabs, and a license is required. All sport crabbers in Puget Sound and the Strait of Juan de Fuca must report their Dungeness crab catch on record cards at the end of each season.

CARCINOLOGY: THE STUDY OF CRABS

Why Study Crabs?

I posed the question "Why do people study crabs?" to a number of crab biologists to learn what got them interested in these creatures. I received varied and interesting responses, which I share below to give a sense of what makes crabs fascinating to budding biologists and what entices them to make the study of crabs their life's work.

John Christy of the Smithsonian Institution wrote,

> I was trained as a vertebrate terrestrial behavioral ecologist. I had intended to study monkeys and spent my first summer as a grad student doing so in Costa Rica. However I quickly became tired of watching partial silhouettes of what I thought were howler monkeys doing uncertain things high in the canopy and decided to open my lawn chair on a tropical beach and watch thousands of fiddler crabs fight, court, and mate in plain view instead.

Cristy is a well-renowned fiddler crab behavioral ecologist.

The late Patsy McLaughlin of Western Washington University wrote to me a couple of months before she died. She had a job with the U.S. Fish and Wildlife Service to study the benthic fauna in Alaskan waters that are eaten by king crabs.

> Among all the samples that came into my office were a multitude of hermit crabs, which my boss said I needn't bother with as there was only one species of hermit crab in the eastern Bering Sea. As the specimens I was looking at certainly seemed like more than one species, I pursued the matter further, and ultimately wrote my PhD dissertation on the 31 species that inhabited the eastern North Pacific from the Chukchi Sea to the Columbia River. After that, hermit crabs became a "way of life," and these many years later, their diversity continues to fascinate me.

McLaughlin made many significant contributions to our knowledge of hermit crabs.

Linda Stehlik of the National Marine Fisheries Service had a colleague who studied mollusks and was interested in their predators, which inspired her to look into blue crab abundance and migrations. "Then I became fascinated by their diets. Opening a crab's stomach is like opening a grab sample of what lives in the bottom, and the crab has collected it nicely for you, so you don't have to sieve it." Stehlik has contributed much to our knowledge about blue crab biology.

Don Mykles of Colorado State got interested in crabs as an undergraduate in an invertebrate physiology lab:

> We studied the effect of serotonin on the crab heart. It was my first introduction to crab anatomy and I was fascinated by what I saw—the circulatory system with blue-grayish blood, the large stomach with its grinding teeth, the powerful claws for crushing prey, and the calcified exoskeleton that provided protection and articulated joints for movement. It got me wondering about how an animal with a rigid exoskeleton can replicate precisely a new, larger exoskeleton, which provides space for tissue growth. It requires a sophisticated coordination of physiological processes that culminates in shedding of the old exoskeleton and inflation of the new exoskeleton by a rapid uptake of sea water. I am still trying to understand how crabs do it!

Mykles is recognized for extensive work on the biochemistry and physiology of molting.

Jorge Golowasch of New Jersey Institute of Technology appreciates their nervous system:

> Crabs afford a much simpler (at least in number of neurons) system to explore basic mechanisms of neuronal function. In particular, crabs have a small ganglion on the dorsal surface of their foregut of only 25–30 neurons that drives several different rhythmic patterns of activity necessary for the digestion of food. The generation of these rhythms, their regulation by multiple factors, as well as their ability to recover the rhythms after their loss due to trauma makes this system a great simple model system to study that has shown a number of basic principles that have already been proven to occur in other animals (such as mammals). Other advantages are their low price, availability, and the large size of the neurons, which allows for easy manipulations of different sorts.

Charles Epifanio of the University of Delaware was originally pre-med:

> I majored in biology, joined a fraternity, captained the varsity soccer team, and seemed well on my way to the country-club life that would attend a successful surgeon. But around the middle of my junior year, I had the opportunity to work on a research project with one of my professors. The project didn't involve crabs—in fact we were studying digenetic trematodes—but I contracted a life-long case of the "research bug." I went on to Duke University to study marine biology—sounded sexy at the time—and ended up in the Costlow/Bookhout Lab, which was probably number 1 in the small world of crab larvae. The rest (as they say) is history.

He has made many important contributions to crab ecology, particularly of larval stages.

In graduate school, Tom Wolcott of North Carolina State studied the physiological ecology of limpets along the rocky shores of California; then he moved to North Carolina.

> Inasmuch as rocks had not been invented on NC shores, it seemed clear that I would need to pursue the principles I'd seen on California's rocky coast on a sandy one instead. We promptly made a trip to the beach and were stunned: "But . . . where are the animals?" Instead of the abundance and diversity to which we were accustomed, there seemed to be only a handful of common macroinvertebrates: coquinas (butterfly clams), beach hoppers, mole crabs (*Emerita*), and ghost crabs (*Ocypode*), with their gray suit, white "face," and yellow legs that tiptoe along at amazing speed. An undergraduate asked for a "directed study" project, and I suggested that he find out if fiddler crabs and

ghost crabs have an oxygen problem when they plug their burrows during high tides. He dutifully went to the library. At our next meeting, he expressed frustration. "I can't find any literature on ghost crabs!" "Hmmm!" quoth I, "how interesting. . . ." The next summer was spent watching these fleet, elegant little crabs by day and by night—an essential discipline to find out what they really do for a living, and what their physiological challenges are.

His wife and collaborator, Donna Wolcott, was trained in cell and developmental biology and took some time off with their children. When she was ready to return to science, Tom was working with land crabs. She concluded that she wasn't about to push little dishes of nucleic acids around a lab bench while her husband was off cavorting on some tropical beach, and she brought her cellular and molecular expertise into collaborative projects.

Linda Mantel, formerly of City College and Reed College, wrote,

> Well, the story I tell students is that when I was a little girl and went to the beach, I was wading in the water and felt something on my foot. I looked down, and there was a crab hanging on to my heel! So I shook my foot, the crab fell off (so, far, true), and I shook my fist at it and said, "I'll get you!!" (not so true). Years later, when I was at the Marine Biological Laboratory in Woods Hole, I was casting about for something to work on and through a long series of serendipities, settled on blue crabs. After starting with blue crabs, of course, I quickly came to realize what special, amazingly adapted organisms crabs are—from the trees to the swamps to the ponds.

Mantel has made important contributions to the understanding of osmoregulation.

Peter de Fur of Virginia Commonwealth University also had formative childhood experiences. "I spent summers on the beach in Connecticut, turning over rocks to find crabs scurrying about—I was fascinated. Maybe the last straw was the following: While snorkeling at the breakwater, I peered into an opening to see a large blue crab, claws raised, swimming at me in what looked for all the world like a frontal attack! I was hooked." de Fur has made contributions to crab physiology, pollution physiology, and is active in environmental protection.

Penny Hopkins of University of Oklahoma said,

> I am afraid my answer to your question is pretty mundane—I study crabs because I couldn't study crayfish! I was able to find a good supply of crabs but couldn't get anyone to collect the crayfish that I studied in graduate school and send them to me. I like to think that what I study applies to all crustaceans. But

I must say that over the years I have fallen in love with *Uca pugilator* [the sand fiddler crab; see Fig. 2.1]. It is a beautiful animal and wonderful to work with.

Hopkins has made major contributions to the understanding of the cellular processes involved in limb regeneration.

Women in the Field

There is a long history of scientists studying the natural history of crabs, and it is interesting that there have been an unusual number of women in this field compared to many other disciplines. One of the earliest was Mary Jane Rathbun (1860–1943) who identified nearly 1000 crab species (a record), including the blue crab, *Callinectes sapidus* Rathbun, 1896. (This may be the only species named after its good taste; that is the meaning of "sapidus.") When her brother was working at the U.S. Fish Commission, she accompanied him on a trip to the commission's summer laboratory at Woods Hole, Massachusetts, where her interest was stimulated, and she volunteered to work for the commission without pay. In 1884 she became a clerk in the Fish Commission and then was appointed to a position as "copyist" in the Division of Marine Invertebrates of the National Museum, where she later became assistant curator. Her most important works are four large monographs on the grapsid, spider, cancroid, and oxystomatous crabs of America, published as Bulletins of the U.S. National Museum between 1918 and 1937. For much of her active life she held relatively minor positions, which was typical for women in those days, but nevertheless, she managed to make major contributions.

Jocelyn Crane (1909–1998) joined the New York Zoological Society as a research associate in 1930. She descended with William Beebe in the bathysphere to depths of up to 0.5 mile off Bermuda and wrote articles on the results of these dives. She spent much of her career studying the morphology and behavior of fiddler crabs, culminating in her monograph *Fiddler Crabs of the World* (1975). Torben Wolff related an anecdote about her resourcefulness in an article in the November 2000 issue of *The Ecdysiast,* the newsletter of the Crustacean Society:

> On her way back from Puerto Rico, Dr. Crane brought with her, for further study in New York, a bunch of fiddler crabs which were very much alive. Obviously, she was stopped by a brusque officer when passing through customs which particularly in New York may be a punctilious affair (I know from experience!). The man knew his regulations regarding introduction of living animals which are (or at least were) classified according to number of legs: Two Legs and four legs (e.g., birds and mammals)—no way! Six legs

and eight legs (insects, spiders, etc.)—definitely not! Many legs (millipedes, etc.)—equally impossible! Having jointly considered these five categories, Jocelyn sugarly asked the officer to count the number of crab legs. Since 10 was not included in any custom regulation list she picked up her crabs, sent the officer a charming smile, and passed without further hindrance.

Dorothy Skinner's interest in crustaceans grew out of her student experiences at the Marine Biological Laboratory in Woods Hole. Her training in both biology and chemistry allowed her to pursue lines of research as diverse as control of molting and regeneration, structure of the crustacean integument and muscle, and characteristics of satellite DNAs, in which she published dozens of landmark papers in crustacean biology.

Dorothy Bliss (1916–1987) earned a doctorate from Harvard and spent most of her career at the American Museum of Natural History, which she joined in 1956, where she was appointed Curator of Invertebrates in 1967. She made landmark contributions to the study of neuroendocrine control of molting, was editor-in-chief of the ten-volume work *The Biology of Crustaceans*, and served as president of the American Society of Zoologists. It is interesting that so many women had successful careers in carcinology during a time when relatively few women had scientific careers in any field of study.

How Crabs Are Studied in Nature

Originally, the only ways to study crabs were those available to recreational observers—either to bring crabs into the laboratory and study them in aquaria or to watch intertidal or shallow water species in their native habitats. Snorkeling is another way of observing shallow-water species in their habitats, though many crabs are shy and will not remain visible to observers for long. Research vessels can collect crabs from deeper waters, and survivors can be studied in the laboratory. In the past several decades, however, technology has provided scientists with new ways of observing crabs where they live. Scuba (originally an acronym for self-contained underwater breathing apparatus, but now accepted as a word) allows divers to observe deeper-dwelling crabs. Species living within the range of scuba gear (about 100 feet deep) can be observed by divers, but because of limited air supply, scuba divers must pay attention to the time and may have to ascend just when their subject is doing something really interesting. Now it is possible to go down beyond the range of scuba and stay down longer in submersibles—research submarines such as *Alvin*. There are also remotely operated vehicles (ROVs) and autonomous underwater vehicles (AUV) that send video back up to a ship or to laboratories on land, where scientists can observe the deep sea without having to go down in the vehicle—not as exciting, but much safer. Nonpropelled vehicles called *gliders* can stay in the ocean for several months and are wonderful for studying its physical properties, but currently their sensors are too limited for detailed studies of living organisms. Current underwater robots are fast and have sophisticated sensors, but their batteries drain in a day, leaving researchers with only brief snapshots of ocean life. A new long-range underwater robot that can function for months has been developed by the Monterey Bay Aquarium Research Institute (MBARI) and introduced in 2010. It will allow scientists to study marine life hundreds of miles from shore. This robot, called *Tethys*, has the speed of existing robots and the range of gliders and can follow organisms while simultaneously recording the physical and chemical properties of the water. *Tethys* will help scientists learn more, while reducing costly and time-consuming ship voyages, because scientists can modify its mission and receive data via satellite. Scientists are currently building a second version of *Tethys*, and hope eventually to deploy a team of robots to simultaneously track different organisms in the food web.

Telemetry—referring to technology that allows measurement to be made at a distance—is another approach, and radio tags on free-ranging blue crabs have been used by Tom and Donna Wolcott to reveal details of foraging, mating, aggression, molting, and migrations. It is possible to tag adult crabs but not the much smaller larvae. To study how larvae manage to return to the area where they were spawned, Tom Wolcott created a tracking device that behaves like a larva. The "Plankton Mimic" is a robot drifter that can be programmed to behave like a larva and swim up and down, but it has a global positioning system (GPS), a pinger, radio- and light-emitting diode (LED) beacons, and a satellite transmitter so it can pop up periodically and "phone home" with its current location.

CRABS AS PETS

Land hermit crabs (Plate 8) are frequently kept as pets. They are omnivorous or herbivorous, and eat a variety of foods. Popular species kept as pets include the Caribbean land hermit crab (*Coenobita clypeatus*) and the Pacific hermit crab (*C. compressus*). Less common species include *C. brevimanus, C. rugosus, C. perlatus,* and *C. cavipes.* In the Caribbean, land hermit crabs are used for races, in which they are placed in the center of a circle, and people place bets on which one will get to the outside of the circle first. Unlike race horses, the crabs don't know they are supposed to go in a straight line, or where they are supposed to go, or that they are in a competition, so some will not move at all while the bettors yell in excitement.

Crabs may be sold in pet stores but also in souvenir stores where the salespeople may not know much (or anything) about the proper care of these animals. To counteract the misinformation that may be disseminated, there are organizations, discussed below, to help pet owners care for their crabs properly. There was a discussion about this a few years ago on the "crust-l" listserv. Someone wrote: "I was in a souvenir shop and they had a display of live crabs, plus accessories. A woman had bought one for her daughter and, along with it, a small wire cage, a sponge which would provide the crab with water, and a shell for a food dish. When asked what they ate, she was told to feed it anything. Pizza crusts, pasta, steak, basically any type of food they ate, so would the crab. I did manage to speak with the woman after she left the shop, but I think the info I gave her on the proper care of the crab fell on deaf ears. Most likely, it will be dead in short order. Sad, really."

Crista Wilkin of hermit-crabs.com, hermitcrabassociation.com, and land-hermitcrabs.com responded:

> The way I see it, there are always going to be people who "take a shine" to land hermit crabs as pets. Most people see them for sale at the beach and view them as a live souvenir they can bring home to keep. Some organizations go all out to make these wonderful animals look like toys. Before 2003, you could only purchase two species of land hermit crabs in the United States: *C. clypeatus* and *C. compressus*. Then an importer in Texas imported a large amount of *C. brevimanus*, *C. rugosus*, *C. violascens* and *C. perlatus*. The importer had no idea how to care for the animals and thousands of them died before even reaching the market. . . . In 2001 I co-founded an organization to teach others how to properly care for the animals while they are in captivity. I (and the majority of adult hermit crab enthusiasts out there) do not care for decorated shells so much as we care for providing the crabs with a good life in captivity. . . . I have come to the conclusion that land hermit crabs should not be kept as pets. The mortality rate in captivity is about 80% during the first year of ownership. It just isn't worth it for us to keep exploiting these animals. I ceased buying them in pet stores years ago and only take in adoptees from people trying to get rid of them.

Carol Ormes of Crabworks has a different opinion: "My two hermit crabs have been in my care for 34 plus years, just completed a perfect molt, which takes a lot longer these days—2–3 months. They are known as the oldest living hermit crabs raised in captivity in the world. The key to success: lots of humidity and warmth (80/80), good exercise (they walk my apartment every evening for about four or five hours), separate moist coconut-fiber molting tubs with monitored temps, different foods almost every night, lots of love. Who knew in 1976 that they would be so healthy and live so long? I adore them as much today as I did all those years ago." She is also concerned that many people buy them without adequate information about how to take care of them, and that some people go overboard in buying large numbers. Although hermit crabs live in groups in the wild and do need company, up to six together are more likely to have a successful life in captivity than dozens together that can't find hiding places for molting or space to exercise.

The Hermit Crab Association is available online (hermit-crabs.com) to assist pet owners with answers to questions. It promotes proper crab care,

---

INFORMATION ABOUT PET HERMIT CRABS

- *Crab Street Journal.* An online magazine featuring articles, frequently asked questions (FAQ), care sheets, shopping tips, and much more. www.crabstreet journal.com

- Epicurean Hermit. All about feeding hermit crabs, including nutrition information, food lists (safe, unsafe), recipes, and more. http://pets.groups.yahoo.com/group/epicurean_hermit/

- Hermit Crab Cuisine. A reference site on food for hermit crabs, allowing owners to look up the nutritional value and safety of various foods. www.hermitcrabcuisine.com

- Naturally Crabby. Up-to-date care information, fabulous photography, and more. www.naturallycrabby.com

- Land Hermit Crab Owners Society (also known as the "Hermies" group). An online community (through Yahoo! Groups) for hermit crab owners to exchange information. http://pets.groups.yahoo.com/group/hermies/

- "Hermit Crabs—Easy to Care for Pets or Mistreated Animals?" A video that discourages the use of hermit crabs as pets. http://www.youtube.com/watch?v=UgLuONHYCWI

Figure 10.1. Land hermit crab (*Coenobita* sp.) in Costa Rica meets Emily Miner (*Homo sapiens*) of California. Photo by P. Weis.

from handling and care sheets to posting reports of recommended pet stores throughout the world. Land hermit crabs are not difficult to house, but the right temperature and humidity are essential. Hermit crabs in the wild are omnivores, eating a bit of everything. Feeding them in captivity is fairly easy, especially with a commercial hermit crab diet as the base of the diet, supplemented with a good variety of fresh foods and treats. Hermit crabs should be provided with a variety of shells so that they can choose one that they like. It can take a bit of experimentation to make sure your hermit crabs have shells that they like. But do not buy the painted shells sold in many pet stores. Hermit crabs are not toys, nor are their shells. There are many other online resources for hermit crab owners wanting information.

It is also possible to interact with land hermits without having them as pets. Visiting tropical countries where they live gives tourists an opportunity to watch and hold them for a while and then put them back (Fig. 10.1).

Some species of marine hermit crabs are popular in reef tanks, including the scarlet hermit crab (*Paguristes cadenati*) and the Marshall Island electric blue hermit crab (or elegant hermit) (*Calcinus elegans*). Brachyurans, both

marine and terrestrial, are also becoming more and more popular aqu
pets, and they feed on dried blood worms, brine shrimp, or dried flake fo
Crabs that are kept as pets include fiddler crabs ("gold fiddlers"), which, lik
all other fiddlers, are semiterrestrial brackish-water crabs that need some salt
in their water as well as access to air and dry land. Unfortunately, some pet
stores keep fiddlers in a freshwater aquarium and recommend the same to
buyers. They may survive in freshwater for weeks, but will eventually weaken
and die. They also need access to land and air. Providing a sloped bottom to
the tank with part of the sand out of the water works well, as does a partly

CRABS IN ASTROLOGY AND DREAMS

Cancer the crab is the fourth astrological sign in the zodiac, originating from
the constellation of Cancer. The sun enters Cancer at the summer solstice, June 21,
and leaves it around July 22. Astrologers consider people born under this sign con-
servative and home-loving. They are said to appear formidable on the outside—
thick-skinned, unemotional, and tenacious—sometimes with a philosophical side.
They are also thought to be prone to fantasy and to appreciate art and literature,
especially drama, and may have considerable literary or artistic talent.

How does any of this relate to a real crab? According to some astrologers, there
are a number of similarities: A crab is able to walk or run sideways. Similarly,
Cancer individuals can "move about" in life, in a figurative sense, in an indirect
manner. The crab's body is covered by a shell, and Cancer individuals are considered self-protective and sensitive, and often retreat into themselves when hurt.
Crabs can resist changes in the environment, protecting themselves in various
habitats. Likewise, Cancer individuals are thought to avoid too much change and
to be on the defensive. Some crabs conceal themselves by decorating their bodies
with plants and animals, and Cancer individuals tend to try to blend in with their
environments, preferring not to make a big splash in life.

In dream interpretation, a crab initially seems to be a negative symbol, representing an unpleasant or "crabby" personality. The claws could symbolize a
clingy person with too much dependence. The crab may also symbolize the inability to effectively move forward and address problems (since crabs often move
sideways). Some folklore says that the crab is an omen of poor health. A more
positive interpretation for the crab in dreams, however, is that it represents the sea
and the nourishment that can be obtained from the sea, in addition to intellectual
nourishment.

CRABS IN FOREIGN MYTHS AND CULTURE

In Chinese culture, the crab signifies prosperity, success, and high status, perhaps because the Chinese word referring to its shell is a pun on the term used for the highest score possible on the Chinese Imperial Examinations (a system used in Imperial China designed to select the best administrative officials for the state's bureaucracy). Crab symbolism includes attributes such as trust, emotion, protection, and transformation. The Chinese words for crab and for harmony are pronounced the same way. The crab symbol is used on charms that express a desire for peace. The golden crab is said to help prevent pitfalls and dangers and to solve professional problems. The ability of the crab to hold things firmly is thought to help people pursue their goals, and its claws symbolize strength and vigor. The crab is quick-thinking, deft, observant, and agile. Its sideways movement represents success and the ability to stand out, bring distinction, and achieve career success. Students appreciate the crab, with hopes that it will help them get good grades.

In a Malaysian myth, Cancer was a giant crab that lived thousands of years ago in a deep hole, and its comings and goings were responsible for the tides. This is reminiscent of the role of crabs in the "Just So" short story by Rudyard Kipling, "The Crab that Played with the Sea" (see "Crabs in Kipling's *Just So Stories*," page 82).

In Greek mythology, the crab was rewarded with a place in heaven by Hera after the crab's involvement in the battle between Hercules and Hydra, the nine-headed serpent. Hera sent the giant crab to help Hydra, and the crab bit Hercules on the foot and was then stomped to death. Hera, who was opposed to Hercules, rewarded the crab with immortality and placed him in the zodiac. (Her hatred of Hercules may be because he was the son of one of Zeus' paramours and threatened her rule.) The crab in this myth uses the classic indirect approach: while Hercules is struggling with Hydra, the crab snaps at his feet rather than confronting him directly.

---

filled tank with large rocks in the middle on which the crabs can climb out of the water but not out of the tank. There is also a small market for "rainbow crabs," which appear to be *Gecarcinus* land crabs, and for "red claw" crabs, which are a semiterrestrial species of *Sesarma*. Some other colorful crabs such as boxer crabs (with their anemones; see Plate 20) are also available in the pet trade.

CRABS IN POPULAR CULTURE

Films, Cartoons, and TV

Crabs are featured in films and television programs. In the 1989 animated Disney film *The Little Mermaid*, Sebastian the crab is the servant of King Triton. Officially, he is the court composer and music teacher for King Triton's daughters, but he is also supposed to keep an eye on the headstrong daughter, Ariel. This character was developed for the film, and was not in the original Hans Christian Andersen story. Aside from being a crab, Sebastian, whose full name is Horatio Felonius Ignacious Crustaceous Sebastian, is also known for his Caribbean accent and singing the popular song "Under the Sea." Sebastian has released two reggae albums for children under the Walt Disney Records label. He is also available as a bean bag, clip art, t-shirt, computer screen wallpaper, and various other products. Given his ambiguous appearance, there was some debate about whether he was a crab or a lobster, but the Disney company says that Sebastian is, indeed, a crab. He looks like a type of anomuran, probably a galatheid, given the appearance of his abdomen (see Table 2; Plate 27).

SpongeBob Square Pants, is a popular American TV program for children that began in 1999. SpongeBob is sea sponge who lives with his pet snail, Gary, in a fully furnished, two-bedroom pineapple in the town of Bikini Bottom, on the bottom of the sea. His dream in life is to be the ocean's ultimate fry cook. His employer is Eugene Krabs, a miserly red crab obsessed with money, who is the owner of the Krusty Krab restaurant. Mr. Krabs is so greedy that he will do almost anything for profit, usually without regard to the safety or well-being of others (or even himself).

Sherman's Lagoon, a nationally syndicated daily comic strip by Jim Toomey, appears in many U.S. newspapers and around the world. The comic strip not only entertains but also educates about conservation issues such as shark finning, overfishing, and the importance of marine protected areas. Toomey created the strip as a means of getting readers to think about marine conservation, and he has won awards for his advocacy from the National Oceanographic and Atmospheric Administration. In July 2010 the cartoon had a storyline in which the undersea denizens got involved with the devastation from the BP spill in the Gulf of Mexico. Sherman's lagoon itself is located by the island of Kapupu in the South Pacific. It features a dimwitted Great White shark named Sherman, his sea turtle sidekick, and an assortment of

Figure 10.2. *Sherman's Lagoon*, featuring Hawthorne the hermit crab.
© 2011 Jim Toomey. Distributed by King Features Syndicate.

other coral reef residents—including a crab—who team up to battle the encroachment of humans on their remote tropical paradise. Hawthorne the hermit crab is described as "a toe-pinching, penny-pinching, party pooping, macho, beer can–dwelling, woke-up-on-the-wrong-side-of-life hermit crab." Unlike other hermit crabs, he prefers a beer can over a snail shell. In earlier strips, he would shed his shell once a year and strut around naked, mooning his friends and scuba divers. His interests include scamming the other members of the strip out of money or resources and cracking jokes and insults (Fig. 10.2). A recurring storyline is his get-rich-quick schemes and business ventures, usually designed to rip his friends off. He seems similar in personality to Mr. Krabs—neither of them are very likeable.

It is clear that crabs play an important role in human society and culture. Knowing more about their lives and biology, as described in this book, should help people appreciate them for what they really are—remarkable living organisms—rather than as symbols of various things. They are extremely diverse and have adapted to life in a great variety of habitats, probably more than any other basically marine animal. They undergo major developmental

CRAB FESTIVALS

Many U.S. coastal states have annual crab festivals, which include games, music, arts and crafts, souvenirs, and—most important—food featuring crabs.

Alaska. The annual spring Kodiak Crab Festival includes a photo exhibit, sporting events, a boat tour, artisan tents, a carnival, foot races, live music, and a cook-off in which contestants enter their favorite recipe, which is judged on the use of Kodiak seafood products, nutritional value, originality, and taste. Galleries sell Crab Festival posters, and there is an art show, a sidewalk book sale, poetry reading, a parade, a marathon, a 9.3-mile Pillar Mountain race, and an "Ididarock" triathlon (bicycle 41 miles, run Pillar Mountain, and swim a mile in the community pool). Other crab festivals concentrate more on the food and less on the exercise.

California. San Francisco starts the Dungeness crab season in November with the Slow Crab Festival, a dinner featuring 3 prized commodities: locally caught Dungeness crab, and locally produced wines and beer. Festivities include cooking classes, crab tours, fishing excursions, crustacean-and-wine dinners, and a crab cake cook-off and wine tasting.

Florida. The village of Panacea is a quiet town except for one weekend when they have a celebration of the blue crab. Thousands of visitors come every year for a day of fun, shopping, entertainment, and down-home hospitality.

Maryland. Crisfield, Maryland, is known as the "Crab Capitol of the World" because the town's main industry is crabmeat. The locals continue to ply the water, shipping both live crabs and picked steamed crabmeat around the world. Their crab festival is on Labor Day weekend, and event include a famous crab derby, another name for a crab race. Crabs from all over compete in the run for the Governor's Cup. The festival includes parades, beauty pageants ("Miss Crustaccan"), boat races, arts and craft exhibits, a crab cooking and picking contest, a swim meet, a carnival, games, and lots of food.

New Jersey. Lower Alloways Creek Township has an Annual Crab and Craft Festival, a day in September full of food, fun, and entertainment. The biggest draw is the crab derby.

New York. Every year in July the Old Mill Yacht Club in Howard Beach, Long Island, holds a crab race. They offer blue claw crabs, corn, clams on the half shell, beer, wine, soda, dancing, and games.

Oregon. The Astoria Warrenton Crab and Seafood Festival is held in late April. It includes northwest cuisine, arts and crafts, a selection of Oregon and Washington wines, and a beer garden. A traditional crab dinner is served, with live music.

South Carolina. Little River (near Myrtle Beach) has a blue crab festival on the waterfront that includes arts and crafts, food, and entertainment.

Virginia. West Point's crab festival is the first weekend in October. The Crab Carnival includes eating, music, games, arts and crafts, antiques, and merchant booths.

Washington. The Dungeness Crab and Seafood Festival, held the second weekend of October in Port Angeles, has a "crab feed" with large kettles of fresh crab, fresh organic corn, and coleslaw. Local restaurants provide additional seafood and desserts. There is wine tasting, a beer garden, music, and a "Grab a Crab Derby" in which participants try to catch a crab from a large holding tank using crab snares and bait. Winners can purchase their catch and have the crab cleaned and cooked on the spot. Those who catch a tagged crab win a special prize. Visitors learn about the ecology and natural history of the Olympic Peninsula, and some of the proceeds support watershed education and other environmental issues.

changes during their lives, have fascinating behaviors, and interact in a variety of ways with other species with which they share their environment. Their populations are often being reduced by human activities such as overfishing, environmental pollution, climate change, and loss of habitat. It is hoped that readers of this book will have a greater understanding and appreciation of these wonderful animals and will develop an increased interest in their protection and conservation.

Bibliography

GENERAL BACKGROUND

Bliss, D.E. 1982. Shrimps, lobsters and crabs: Their fascinating life story. New Century Publishers, Piscataway, NJ.

Bliss, D.E., ed. 1983. The biology of crustacea. 10 vols. Academic Press, New York.

Burggren, W.W., and B.R. McMahon, eds. 1988. Biology of the land crabs. Cambridge University Press, Cambridge.

Fincham, A.A., and P.S. Rainbow, eds. 1988. Aspects of decapod crustacean biology. Zoological Society of London Symposia 59. Oxford University Press, Oxford.

Pechenik, J.A. 2000. Biology of the invertebrates. 4th ed. McGraw Hill, Boston.

I. INTRODUCING CRABS

Abele, L.G. 1974. Species diversity of decapod crustaceans in marine habitats. Ecology 55: 156–161.

Ju, S.-J., D.H. Secor, and H.R. Harvey. 1999. The use of extractable lipofuscin for age determination of the blue crab, *Callinectes sapidus*. Marine Ecology Progress Series 185: 171–179.

Plaisance L., M.J. Caley, R.E. Brainard, and N. Knowlton. 2011. The diversity of coral reefs: What are we missing? PLoS ONE 6(10): e25026. doi:10.1371/journal.pone.0025026.

2. HABITATS

Appel, M., and R.W. Elwood. 2009. Motivational trade-offs and the potential for pain experience in hermit crabs. Applied Animal Behaviour Science 119: 120–124.

Bell, G.W., D.B. Eggleston, and E.J. Noga. 2009. Molecular keys unlock the mysteries of variable survival responses of blue crabs to hypoxia. Oecologia 163: 57–68.

Decelle J., A.C. Andersen, and S. Hourdez. 2010. Morphological adaptations to chronic hypoxia in deep-sea decapod crustaceans from hydrothermal vents and cold seeps. Marine Biology 157: 1259–1269.

Elwood, R.W., and M. Appel. 2009. Pain experience in hermit crabs? Animal Behaviour 77: 1243–1246.

Frick, M.G., K.L. Williams, A.B. Bolten, K.A. Bjorndal, and H.R. Martins. 2004. Diet and fecundity of Columbus crabs, *Planes minutus,* associated with oceanic-stage loggerhead turtles, *Caretta caretta* and inanimate flotsam. Journal of Crustacean Biology 24: 350–355.

MacPherson, E., W. Jones, and M. Segonzac. 2005. A new squat lobster family of Galatheoidea (Crustacea, Decapoda, Anomura) from the hydrothermal vents of the Pacific-Antarctic Ridge. Zoosystema 27: 709–723.

Nordhaus, I., M. Wolff, and K. Diehle. 2006. Litter processing and population food intake of the mangrove crab *Ucides cordatus* in a high intertidal forest in northern Brazil. Estuarine, Coastal and Shelf Science 67:239–250.

Schuhmacher, H. 1977. A hermit crab, sessile on corals, exclusively feeds by feathered antennae. Oecologia 27: 371–374.

Silliman B.R., and M.D. Bertness. 2002. A trophic cascade regulates salt marsh primary production. Proceedings of the National Academy of Sciences 99: 10500–10505.

Somerton, D. 1981. Contribution to the life history of the deep-sea king crab, *Lithodes couesi,* in the Gulf of Alaska. Fishery Bulletin 79: 259–269.

Steimle, F.W., C.A. Zetlin, and S. Chang. 2001. Essential fish habitat source document: Red deepsea crab, *Chaceon (Geryon) quinquedens,* life history and habitat characteristics. NOAA Technical Memorandum NMFS-NE-163.

Stewart, H., S.J. Holbrook, R.J. Schmitt, and A.J. Brooks. 2006. Symbiotic crabs maintain coral health by clearing sediments. Coral Reefs 25: 609–615.

Trott, T., R. Vogt, and J. Atema. 1997. Chemoreception by the red-jointed fiddler crab *Uca minax* (Le Conte): Spectral tuning properties of the walking legs. Marine and Freshwater Behaviour and Physiology 30: 239–249.

3. FORM AND FUNCTION

Baldwin, J., and S. Johnson. 2009. Importance of color in mate choice of the blue crab, *Callinectes sapidus.* Journal of Experimental Biology 212: 3762–3768.

Bliss, D.E., ed. 1983. The biology of crustacea. Vol. 5, Internal anatomy and physiological regulation, ed. L.H. Mantel. Academic Press, New York.

Dunham, D.W. 1978. Effect of chela white on agonistic success in a diogenid hermit crab (*Calcinus laevimanus*). Marine Behavior and Physiology 5: 137–144.

Griffen, B.D., and H. Mosblack. 2011. Predicting diet and consumption rate differences between and within species using gut ecomorphology. Journal of Animal Ecology 80: 854–863.

Hemmi, J., J. Marshall, W. Pix, M. Vorobyev, and J. Zeil. 2006. The variable colours of the fiddler crab *Uca vomeris* and their relation to background and predation. Journal of Experimental Biology 209: 4140–4153.

Herreid, C., and S.M. Mooney. 1984. Color change in exercising crabs: Evidence for a hormone. Journal of Comparative Physiology B: Biochemical, Systemic and Environmental Physiology 154: 207–212.

Leschen, A.S., and S.J. Correia. 2010. Mortality in female horseshoe crabs (*Limulus polyphemus*) from biomedical bleeding and handling: Implications for fisheries management. Marine and Freshwater Behaviour and Physiology 43: 135–147.

Lovett, D.L., T. Colella, A.C. Cannon, D.H. Lee, A. Evangelisto, E.M. Muller, and D.W. Towle. 2006. Effect of salinity on osmoregulatory patch epithelia in gills of the blue crab *Callinectes sapidus.* Biological Bulletin 210: 132–139.

Palma, A., and R. Steneck. 2001. Does variable color in juvenile marine crabs reduce risk of visual predation? Ecology 82: 2961–2967.

Palmer, J.D. 2003. The living clock: The orchestrator of biological rhythms. Oxford University Press, New York.

Pardo, L., K. González, J.P. Fuentes, K. Paschke, and O.R. Chaparro. 2011. Survival and behavioral responses of juvenile crabs of *Cancer edwardsii* to severe hyposalinity events triggered by increased runoff at an estuarine nursery ground. Journal of Experimental Marine Biology and Ecology 404: 33–39.

Reddy, P.S., and M. Fingerman. 1995. Effect of cadmium chloride on physiological color changes of the fiddler crab, *Uca pugilator.* Ecotoxicology and Environmental Safety 31: 69–75.

Reid, D.G., and J.C Aldrich. 1989. Variations in response to environmental hypoxia of different colour forms of the shore crab, *Carcinus maenas.* Comparative Biochemistry and Physiology Part A: Physiology 92: 535–539.

Simpson S., A.N. Radford, E.J. Tickle, M.G. Meekan, and A.G. Jeffs. 2011. Adaptive avoidance of reef noise. PLoS One 6(2): e16625. doi:10.1371/journal.pone.001662.

Stensmyr, M., S. Erland, E. Hallberg, R. Wallén, P. Greenaway, and B.S. Hansson. 2005. Insect-like olfactory adaptations in the terrestrial giant robber crab. Current Biology 15: 116–121.

Sylbiger, N., and P. Munguia. 2007. Carapace color change in *Uca pugilator* as a response to temperature. Journal of Experimental Marine Biology and Ecology 355: 41–46.

4. REPRODUCTION AND LIFE CYCLE

Anderson, J., and C. Epifanio. 2009. Induction of metamorphosis in the Asian shore crab *Hemigrapsus sanguineus:* Characterization of the cue associated with biofilm from adult habitat. Journal of Experimental Marine Biology and Ecology 382: 34–39.

Bergey, L., and J.S. Weis. 2007. Molting as a mechanism of depuration of metals in the fiddler crab, *Uca pugnax.* Marine Environmental Research 64: 556–562.

Bliss, D.E., ed. 1983. The biology of crustacea. Vol. 2, Embryology, morphology, and genetics, ed. L.G. Abele. Academic Press, New York.

Christy, J. 1983. Female choice in the resource-defense mating system of the sand fiddler crab, *Uca pugilator.* Behavioral Ecology and Sociobiology 12: 169–180.

Christy, J. 2010. Pillar function in the fiddler crab *Uca beebei* (II): Competitive courtship signaling. Ethology 78: 113–128.

DeVries, M., and R. Forward. 1989. Rhythms in larval release of the sublittoral crab *Neopanope sayi* and the supralittoral crab *Sesarma cinereum* (Decapoda: Brachyura). Marine Biology 100: 241–248.

DeWilde, P.A. 1973. On the ecology of *Coenobita clypeatus* in Curaçao. Studies of the Fauna of Curaçao 44: 1–138.

Diesel, R. 1989. Parental care in an unusual environment: *Metapaulias depressus* (Decapods Grapsidae), a crab that lives in epiphytic bromeliads. Animal Behaviour 38: 561–575.

Ju, S.-J., D.H. Secor, and H.R. Harvey. 1999. The use of extractable lipofuscin for age determination of the blue crab, *Callinectes sapidus*. Marine Ecology Progress Series 185: 171–179.

Kim T.W., J.H. Christy, and J.C. Choe. 2007. A preference for a sexual signal keeps females safe. PLoS ONE 2(5): e422. doi:10.1371/journal.pone.0000422.

Kim, T.W., K. Sakamoto, Y. Henmi, and J.C. Choe. 2008. To court or not to court: Reproductive decisions by male fiddler crabs in response to fluctuating food availability. Behavioral Ecology and Sociobiology 62: 1139–1147.

Michener, J. 1974. Chesapeake. Random House, New York.

Morley, S.A., M. Belchier, J. Dickson, and T. Mulvey. 2006. Reproductive strategies of sub-Antarctic lithodid crabs vary with habitat depth. Polar Biology 29: 581–584.

Oppian. ca. 170 AD. Haleutika. Trans. A.W. Mair. Openlibrary.org. http://penelope. uchicago.edu/Thayer/E/Roman/Texts/Oppian/Halieutica/1*.html.

Stevens, B.G. 2003. Timing of aggregation and larval release by Tanner crabs, *Chionoecetes bairdi*, in relation to tidal current patterns. Fisheries Research 65:201–216.

Terossi, M., L.S. Torati, I. Miranda, M.A. Scelzo, and F.L. Mantelatto. 2010. Comparative reproductive biology of two southwestern Atlantic populations of the hermit crab *Pagurus exilis* (Crustacea: Anomura: Paguridae). Marine Biology 31: 584–591.

Thatje, S., and N.C. Mestre. 2010. Energetic changes throughout lecithotrophic larval development in the deep-sea lithodid crab *Paralomis spinosissima* from the Southern Ocean. Journal of Experimental Marine Biology and Ecology 386: 119–124.

Webb, J. 2009. Reproductive success of multiparous female Tanner crab (*Chionoecetes bairdi*) fertilizing eggs with or without recent access to males. Journal of Northwest Atlantic Fishery Science 41: 163–172.

Ziegler, T., and R. Forward 2006. Larval release behaviors of the striped hermit crab, *Clibanarius vittatus* (Bosc): Temporal pattern in hatching. Journal of Experimental Marine Biology and Ecology 335: 245–255.

5. BEHAVIOR

Abele, L., P.J. Campanella, and M. Salmon. 1986. Natural history and social organization of the semiterrestrial grapsid crab *Pachygrapsus transversus* (Gibbes). Journal of Experimental Marine Biology and Ecology 104: 153–170.

Backwell, P.I., J.H. Christy, S.R. Telford, M.D. Jennions, and N.I. Passmore. 2000. Dishonest signalling in a fiddler crab. Proceedings of the Royal Society B: Biological Sciences 267: 719–724.

Barshaw, D., and K. Able. 1990. Deep burial as a refuge for lady crabs, *Ovalipes ocellatus*: Comparisons with blue crabs. Marine Ecology Progress Series 66: 75–79.

Bauer, R.T. 1989. Decapod crustacean grooming: Functional morphology, adaptive value, and phylogenetic significance. In Functional morphology of feeding and grooming in crustacea, Crustacean Issues 6, ed. B. Felgenhauer, L. Watling, and A.B. Thistle, 49–73. Balkema Press, Rotterdam.

Briffa, M., and R.W. Elwood. 2000. The power of shell rapping influences rates of eviction in hermit crabs. Behavioral Ecology 11: 288–293.

Coen, L. 1988. Herbivory by Caribbean majid crabs: Feeding ecology and plant susceptibility. Journal of Experimental Marine Biology and Ecology 122: 257–276.

Cunningham, P., and R. Hughes. 1984. Learning of predatory skills by shorecrabs *Carcinus maenas* feeding on mussels and dogwhelks. Marine Ecology Progress Series 16: 21–26.

Detto, T., M. Jennions, and P. Backwell. 2010. When and why do territorial coalitions occur? Experimental evidence from a fiddler crab. American Naturalist 175: E119–E125.

Hazlett, B.A. 1966. Factors affecting the aggressive behavior of the hermit crab *Calcinus tibicen*. Zeitschrift für Tierpsychologie 6: 655–671.

Hoyoux, C.H., M. Zbinden, S. Samadi, F. Gaill, and P. Compere. 2009. Wood-based diet and gut microflora of a galatheid crab associated with Pacific deep-sea wood falls. Marine Biology 156: 2421–2439.

Hyatt, G.W. 1983. Qualitative and quantitative dimensions of crustacean aggression. In Studies in adaptation: The behavior of higher crustacea, ed. S. Rebach and D. Dunham, 113–139. John Wiley, New York.

MacDonald, J., R. Roudez, T. Glover, and J.S. Weis. 2007. The invasive green crab and Japanese shore crab: Behavioral interactions with a native crab species, the blue crab. Biological Invasions 9: 837–848.

Micheli, F. 1995. Behavioural plasticity in prey size selectivity of the blue crab *Callinectes sapidus* feeding on bivalve prey. Journal of Animal Ecology 64: 63–74.

Pereyra, P., M. Saraco, and H. Maldonado. 1999. Decreased response or alternative defensive strategies in escape: Two different types of long-term memory in the crab *Chasmagnathus*. Journal of Comparative Physiology A: Neuroethology, Sensory, Neural, and Behavioral Physiology 184: 301–310.

Ramey, P.A., E. Teichman, J. Oleksiak, and F. Balci. 2009. Spontaneous alternation in marine crabs: Invasive versus native species. Behavioral Processes 82: 51–55.

Rebach, S., and D. Dunham, eds. 1983. Studies in adaptation: The behavior of higher crustacea. John Wiley, New York.

Reichmuth, J.M., R. Roudez, T. Glover, and J.S. Weis. 2009. Differences in prey capture behavior in populations of blue crab (*Callinectes sapidus* Rathbun) from contaminated and clean estuaries in New Jersey. Estuaries and Coasts 32: 298–308.

Roudez, R.J., T. Glover, and J.S. Weis. 2008. Learning in an invasive and a native predatory crab. Biological Invasions 10: 1191–1196.

Stevens, B. W.E. Donaldson, and J.A. Haaga. 1992. First observations of podding behavior for the Pacific lyre crab, *Hyas lyratus*. Journal of Crustacean Biology 12: 193–195.

Wight, K., L. Francis, and D. Eldridge. 1990. Food aversion learning in the hermit crab *Pagurus granosimanus*. Biological Bulletin 178: 205–209.

Winn, H.E., and B.L. Olla, eds. 1972. Behavior of marine animals. Vol. 1, Invertebrates. Plenum Press, New York.

6. ECOLOGY

Bach, C., and B. Hazlett. 2009. Shell shape affects movement patterns and microhabitat distribution in the hermit crabs *Calcinus elegans, C. laevimanus,* and *C. lateens*. Journal of Experimental Marine Biology and Ecology 382: 27–33.

Blackmon, D.C., and D.B. Eggleston. 2001. Factors influencing planktonic, post-settlement dispersal of early juvenile blue crabs (*Callinectes sapidus* Rathbun). Journal of Experimental Marine Biology and Ecology 257: 183–203.

Bliss, D.E., ed. 1983. The biology of crustacea. Vol. 7, Behavior and ecology, ed. F.J. Vernberg and W.B. Vernberg. Academic Press, New York.

Boles, L.C., and K.J. Lohmann. 2003. True navigation and magnetic maps in spiny lobsters. Nature 421: 60–63.

Bortolus, A., P. Laterra, and O. Iribarne. 2004. Crab-mediated phenotypic changes in *Spartina densiflora* Brong. Estuarine, Coastal and Shelf Science 59: 97–107.

Boyko, C.B., and P.M. Mikkelsen. 2002. Anatomy and biology of *Mysella pedroana* (Mollusca: Bivalvia: Galeommatoidea), and its commensal relationship with *Blepharipoda occidentalis* (Crustacea: Anomura: Albuneidae). Zoologischer Anzeiger: A Journal of Comparative Zoology 241: 149–160.

Buckley, W., and J. Ebersole. 1994. Symbiotic organisms increase the vulnerability of a hermit crab to predation. Journal of Experimental Marine Biology and Ecology 182: 49–64.

Canepuccia, A., J. Alberti, P. Daleo, J. Pascual, J.L. Farina, and O. Iribarne. 2010. Ecosystem engineering by burrowing crabs increases cordgrass mortality caused by stem-boring insects. Marine Ecology Progress Series 404: 151–159.

Cannicci, S., R. Ruwa, and M. Vannini. 2010. Homing experiments in the tree-climbing crab *Sesarma leptosoma* (Decapoda, Grapsidae). Ethology 103: 935–944.

Carle, E. 1991. A house for hermit crab. Simon and Schuster, New York.

Damiani, C.C. 2003. Reproductive costs of the symbiotic hydroid *Hydractinia symbiolongicarpus* (Buss and Yund) to its host hermit crab *Pagurus longicarpus* (Say). Journal of Experimental Marine Biology and Ecology 288: 203–222.

Eggleston, D.B., and D.A. Armstrong. 1995. Pre- and post-settlement determinants of estuarine Dungeness crab recruitment. Ecological Monographs 65: 193–216.

Hultgren, K.M., and J.J. Stachowicz. 2009. Evolution of decoration in Majoid crabs: A comparative phylogenetic analysis of the role of body size and alternative defensive strategies. American Naturalist 173: 566–578.

Kim, T., T.K. Kim, and J.C. Choe. 2010. Compensation for homing errors by using courtship structures as visual landmarks. Behavioral Ecology 21: 836–842.

Layne, J.W., J.P. Barnes, and L.M. Duncan. 2003. Mechanisms of homing in the fiddler crab *Uca rapax*. 2. Information sources and frame of reference for a path integration system. Journal of Experimental Biology 206: 4425–4442.

McConnaughey, R.A., D.A. Armstrong, B.M. Hickey, and D.R. Gunderson. 1994. Interannual variability in coastal Washington Dungeness crab (*Cancer magister*) populations: Larval advection and the coastal landing strip. Fisheries Oceanography 3: 22–38.

Oppian. ca. 170 BC. Haleutika. Trans. A.W. Mair. Openlibrary.org. http://penelope.uchicago.edu/Thayer/E/Roman/Texts/Oppian/Halieutica/1*.html.

Pardo, L.M., C.S. Cardyn, and J. Garcés-Vargas. 2011. Spatial variation in the environmental control of crab larval settlement in a micro-tidal austral estuary. Helgoland Marine Research. doi:10.1007/s10152-011-0267-y.

Paulay, G., and J. Starmer. 2011. Evolution, insular restriction, and extinction of oceanic land crabs, exemplified by the loss of an endemic *Geograpsus* in the Hawaiian Islands. PLoS ONE 6(5): e19916. doi:10.1371/journal.pone.0019916.

Poltev, Y.N., and I.N. Mukhametov. 2009. Concerning the problem of carcinophilia of *Careproctus* species (Scorpaeniformes: Liparidae) in the North Kurils. Russian Journal of Marine Biology 35: 215–223.

Rotjan, R.D., J.R. Chabot, and S.M. Lewis. 2010. Social context of shell acquisition in *Coenobita clypeatus* hermit crabs. Behavioral Ecology 21: 639–646.

Shanks, A.L., and G.C. Roegner. 2007. Recruitment limitation in Dungeness crab populations is driven by variation in atmospheric forcing. Ecology 88: 1726–1737.

Shives, J.A., and S. Dunbar. 2010. Behavioral responses to burial in the hermit crab, *Pagurus samuelis:* Implications for the fossil record. Journal of Experimental Marine Biology and Ecology 388: 33–38.

Stachowitz, J.J., and M. Hay. 1999. Mutualism and coral persistence: The role of herbivore resistance to algal chemical defense. Ecology 80: 2085–2101.

Stachowitz, J.J., and M. Hay. 2000. Geographic variation in camouflage specialization by a decorator crab. American Naturalist 156: 59–71.

Stevens, B.G. 2003. Settlement, substratum preference, and survival of red king crab *Paralithodes camtschaticus* (Tilesius, 1815) glaucothoe on natural substrata in the laboratory. Journal of Experimental Marine Biology and Ecology 283: 63–78.

Steward, H.L., S.J. Holbrook, R.J. Schmitt, and A.J. Brooks. 2006. Symbiotic crabs maintain coral health by clearing sediments. Coral Reefs 25: 609–615.

Stoner, A. 2009. Habitat-mediated survival of newly settled red king crab in the presence of a predatory fish: Role of habitat complexity and heterogeneity. Journal of Experimental Marine Biology and Ecology 382: 54–60.

Tricarico, E., S. Bertocchi, S. Brusconi, L.A. Chessa, and F. Gherardi. 2009. Shell recruitment in the Mediterranean hermit crab *Clybanarius erythropus.* Journal of Experimental Marine Biology and Ecology 381: 42–46.

Walker, S.E. 1994. Biological remanie: Gastropod fossils used by the living terrestrial hermit crab, *Coenobita clypeatus*, on Bermuda. Palaios 9: 403–412.

Wells, R.J., R.S. Steneck, and A.T. Palma. 2010. Three-dimensional resource partitioning between American lobster (*Homarus americanus*) and rock crab (*Cancer irroratus*) in a subtidal kelp forest. Journal of Experimental Marine Biology and Ecology 384: 1–6.

7. CRAB PROBLEMS AND PROBLEM CRABS

Altieri, A., B. van Wesenbeeck, M. Bertness, and B. Silliman. 2010. Facilitation cascade explains positive relationship between native biodiversity and invasion success. Ecology 91: 1269–1275.

Becker, C., and M. Türkay. 2010. Taxonomy and morphology of European pea crabs (Crustacea: Brachyura: Pinnotheridae). Journal of Natural History 44: 1555–1575.

Blakeslee, A., C.L. Keogh, J.E. Byers, A.M. Kuris, K.D. Lafferty, and M.E. Torchin. 2009. Differential escape from parasites by two competing introduced crabs. Marine Ecology Progress Series 393: 83–96.

Britayev, T.A., A.V. Rzhavsky, L.V. Pavlova, and A.G. Dvoretskij. 2010. Studies on impact of the alien red king crab (*Paralithodes camtschaticus*) on the shallow water benthic communities of the Barents Sea. Journal of Applied Ichthyology 26 (Suppl. 2): 66–73.

Culbertson, J.B., I. Valiela, E.E. Peacock, C.M. Reddy, A. Carter, and R. Van der Kruik. 2007. Long-term biological effects of petroleum residues on fiddler crabs in salt marshes. Marine Pollution Bulletin 54: 955–962.

De la Haye, K., J.I. Spicer, S. Widdicombe, and M. Briffa. 2011. Reduced seawater pH disrupts information gathering, resource assessment and decision making in the hermit crab *Pagurus bernhardus*. Animal Behaviour 82: 495–501.

Edgell, T., and R. Rochette. 2009. Prey-induced changes to a predator's behaviour and morphology: Implications for shell-claw covariance in the northwest Atlantic. Journal of Experimental Marine Biology and Ecology 382: 1–7.

Gilardi, K.V.K., D. Carlson-Bremer, J.A. June, K. Antonelis, G. Broadhurst, and T. Cowan. 2010. Marine species mortality in derelict fishing nets in Puget Sound, WA, and the cost/benefits of derelict net removal. Marine Pollution Bulletin 60: 376–382.

Heinonen, K., and P. Auster. 2012. Prey selection in crustacean-eating fishes following the invasion of the Asian shore crab *Hemigrapsus sanguineus* in a marine temperate community. Journal of Experimental Marine Biology and Ecology 413: 177–183.

Holdredge, C., M.D. Bertness, and A.H. Altieri. 2009. Role of crab herbivory in die-off of New England salt marshes. Conservation Biology 23: 672–679.

Hollebone, A.L, and M.E. Hay. 2007. Population dynamics of the non-native crab *Petrolisthes armatus* invading the South Atlantic Bight at densities of thousands per m2. Marine Ecology Progress Series 336: 211–223.

Kropp, R. 1986. Feeding biology and mouthpart morphology of three species of coral gall crabs (Decapoda: Cryptochiridae). Journal of Crustacean Biology 6: 377–384.

Matheson, K., and P. Gagnon. 2012. Temperature mediates non-competitive foraging in indigenous rock (*Cancer irroratus* Say) and recently introduced green (*Carcinus maenas* L.) crabs from Newfoundland and Labrador. Journal of Experimental Marine Biology and Ecology 414–415: 6–18.

Mazumder, C., and N. Saintilan. 2010. Mangrove leaves are not an important source of dietary carbon and nitrogen for crabs in temperate Australian mangroves. Wetlands 30: 375–380.

McCall B.D., and S.C. Pennings. 2012. Disturbance and recovery of salt marsh Arthropod communities following BP Deepwater Horizon oil spill. PLoS ONE 7(3): e32735. doi:10.1371/journal.pone.0032735.

McDermott, J., J.D. Williams, and C.B. Boyko. 2010. The unwanted guests of hermits: A global review of the diversity and natural history of hermit crab parasites. Journal of Experimental Marine Biology and Ecology 394: 2–44.

Milner, R., T. Detto, M.D. Jennions, and P.R. Backwell. 2010. Hunting and predation in a fiddler crab. Journal of Ethology 28: 171–173.

Milner R., M.D. Jennions, and P.R. Backwell. 2010. Safe sex: Male-female coalitions and pre-copulatory mate-guarding in a fiddler crab. Biology Letters 6: 180–182.

Owen, J. 2003. Eat the invading alien crabs, urge UK scientists. National Geographic News. http://news.nationalgeographic.com/news/2003/11/1113_031113_mittencrabs.html.

Ries, J.B., A.L. Cohen, and D.C. McCorkle. 2009. Marine calcifiers exhibit mixed responses to CO2-induced ocean acidification. Geology 37: 1131–1134.

Rossong, M., P.A. Quijón, P.V. Snelgrove, T.J. Barrett, C.H. McKenzie, and A. Locke. 2012. Regional differences in foraging behaviour of invasive green crab (*Carcinus maenas*) populations in Atlantic Canada. Biological Invasions 14: 659–669.

Rossong, M., P.A. Quijon, P.J. Williams, and P.V. Snelgrove. 2011. Foraging and shelter behavior of juvenile American lobster (*Homarus americanus*): The influence of a non-indigenous crab. Journal of Experimental Marine Biology and Ecology 43: 75–80.

Schlacher, T.A., and S. Lucrezi. 2010. Compression of home ranges in ghost crabs on sandy beaches impacted by vehicle traffic. Marine Biology 157: 2467–2474.

Steinberg, M.K., and C.E. Epifanio. 2011. Three's a crowd: Space competition among three species of intertidal shore crabs in the genus *Hemigrapsus*. Journal of Experimental Marine Biology and Ecology 404: 57–62.

Trottier, O., D. Walker, and A.G. Jeffs. 2012. Impact of the parasitic pea crab *Pinnotheres novaezelandiae* on aquacultured New Zealand green-lipped mussels, *Perna canaliculus*. *Aquaculture, in press*. http://dx.doi.org/10.1016/j.aquaculture.2012.02.031.

8. CRAB FISHERIES

Blankenship, K. 2010. Maryland considers "catch share" program for blue crab fishery. Chesapeake Bay Journal 20: 6–7.

Blankenship, K. 2010. Watermen pull 10,500 derelict crab pots from Bay, rivers. Chesapeake Bay Journal 20: 7.

Bliss, D.E., ed. 1983. The biology of crustacea. Vol. 10, Economic aspects: Fisheries and culture, ed. A.J. Provenzano. Academic Press, New York.

Blue Ventures. 2010. Community festivals celebrate coastal conservation. Blue Ventures Research Update 31. http://blueventures.org/images/stories/bv/research/resupdates/Research_update_Autumn_2010_final_sml.pdf.

Cumberlidge, N., P.K.L. Ng, D.C.J. Yeo, C. Magalhães, M.R. Campos, F. Alvarez, T. Naruse, et al. 2009. Freshwater crabs and the biodiversity crisis: Importance, threats, status, and conservation challenges. Biological Conservation 142: 1665–1673.

Davis, G.E., D.S. Baughman, J.D. Chapman, D. MacArthur, and A.C. Pierce. 1978. Mortality associated with declawing stone crabs, *Menippe mercenaria*. South Florida Research Center Report T-522.

Diele, K., and V. Koch. 2010. Growth and mortality of the exploited mangrove crab *Ucides cordatus* (Ucididae) in N. Brazil. Journal of Experimental Marine Biology and Ecology 395: 171–180.

Friederich, S. 2010. "He's not just the crab guy." Daily World (Aberdeen, WA), November 28, C1.

Johnson, E., A.C. Young, A.H. Hines, M.A. Kramer, M. Bademan, M.R. Goodison, and R. Aguilar. 2011. Field comparison of survival and growth of hatchery-reared versus wild blue crabs, *Callinectes sapidus* Rathbun. Journal of Experimental Marine Biology and Ecology 402: 35–42.

Kramer, D., H. Herter, and A. Stoner. Handling of fresh crabs and crabmeat. Sea-Gram. Alaska Sea Grant Marine Advisory Program, Univ. of Alaska. doi:10.4027/hfcc.2009.

Parkes, L., E.T. Quinitio, and L. LeVay. 2011. Phenotypic differences between hatchery-reared and wild mud crabs, *Scylla serrata,* and the effects of conditioning. Aquaculture International 19: 361–380.

Safety in Dungeness fleet. 2011. Pacific Fishing, February.

Shanks, A.L., and G.C. Roegner. 2007. Recruitment-limitation in Dungeness crab populations is driven by temporal variation in atmospheric forcing. Ecology 88: 1726–1737.

Sheehan, E.V., R.A. Coleman, R.C. Thompson, and M.J. Attrill. 2010. Crab-tiling reduces the diversity of estuarine infauna. Marine Ecology Progress Series 411: 137–148.

Stevens, B.G., ed. 2006. Alaska crab stock enhancement and rehabilitation. Workshop Proceedings. Alaska Sea Grant College Program AK-SG-04. Univ. of Alaska. doi:10.4027/acser.2006.

Winger, P.D., and P. Walsh. 2011. Selectivity, efficiency, and underwater observations of modified trap designs for the snow crab (*Chionoecetes opilio*) fishery in Newfoundland and Labrador. Fisheries Research 109: 107–113.

Zheng, J., C.Y. Lee, and D. Watson. 2006. Molecular cloning of a putative receptor guanylyl cyclase from Y-organs of the blue crab, *Callinectes sapidus*. General and Comparative Endocrinology 146: 329–336.

Zohar, Y., A.H. Hines, O. Zmora, E.G. Johnson, R.N. Lipcius, R.D. Seitz, D.B. Eggleston, et al. 2008. The Chesapeake Bay blue crab (*Callinectes sapidus*): A multidisciplinary approach to responsible stock replenishment. Reviews in Fisheries Science 16: 24–34.

9. EATING CRABS

Stoner, A.W., C.S. Rose, J.E. Munk, C.F. Hammond, and M.W. Davis. 2008. An assessment of discard mortality for two Alaskan crab species, Tanner crab (*Chionoecetes bairdi*) and snow crab (*C. opilio*), based on reflex impairment. Fishery Bulletin 106: 337–347.

10. CRABS AND HUMANS

Bliss, D.E., ed. 1983. The biology of crustacea. 10 vols. Academic Press, New York.

McLaughlin, P.A., and S. Gilchrist. 1993. Women's contributions to carcinology. In History of carcinology, Crustacean Issues 8, ed. F. Truesdale, 165–206. A.A. Balkema, Rotterdam.

Wolff, T. 2000. Fiddler crabs through customs. Ecdysiast 19 (2): 9.

Index

Page numbers followed by *f* and *t* indicate figures and tables respectively; numbers preceded by *pl.* indicate color plates.

Abele, Lawrence, 32, 100
Able, Ken, 92
acoustic signals, 54, 66, 96–97
Adamsia palliata, 118
African freshwater crabs, 41–42
aggression, 97–99
aging of crabs, 84
Alaska King Crab Research, Rehabilitation and Biology Program (AKCRRAB), 159*f*, 179
Alaskan crab migration study, 113
Alaskan fisheries, 155, 157, 158–60, 170–71
Alaskan spider crabs, 92
Aldrich, J.C., 60
Alexandrium, 193
algae, 125, 193–94
algal blooms, 141
allergies, 194–95
allometric growth, 83
Altieri, Andrew, 149
Alvin, 3, 38, 204
amebocytes, 47
American lobsters, 9, 37, 123, 163
amphipods, 123
anatomy, 5, 6*f*, 7*f*, 8*f*, 44–45
Anderson, Julie, 77
androgenic hormone, 62
anemones. *See* sea anemones

anomurans (Anomura)
    anatomy, 7*f*, 8*f*, 45
    described, 5, 6–10
    evolution, 10, 12–13
    families of, 19*t*
    reproduction, 67
Anoplolepis gracilipes, 136
antennae, 5, 44–45
antennal glands, 50
antennules, 5, 44
Appel, Mirjam, 55
appendages, 5
aquaculture, 177–81
aquaria, 196–97, *pl.*26
aquatic vegetation habitats, 29–31
Aratus pisonii, 66, 101
Aratus spp. *See* mangrove crabs
Armases cinereum, 24, 70
Armstrong, David, 107
arrow crabs, 101, 101*f*
arrow goby, 127
art, crabs in, 197, *pl.*26
arthropods (Arthropoda), 4, 18, 80
Asian shore crabs, 77, 78*f*, 148–50
Astacidea, 9
astaxanthin, 188
Astoria Warrenton Crab and Seafood Festival, 213
astrology, 209

Astropyga radiata, 121
Atema, Jelle, 55
Atergatis floridus, 193
Atlantic rock crabs, 14*t*, 60, 123, 152, 158, *pl.*2
Attack of the Crab Monsters (film), 145, *pl.*28
Auster, Peter, 149
autonomous underwater vehicles (AUV), 205
autotomy, 92–93
avian predators, 11–12, 135

Bach, Catherine, 110
Backwell, Patricia, 94
bacterial diseases, 129–30
Baltimore crab cakes, 190–91
Bang, Frederik, 47
barnacles, 123, 124*f,* 134
Barshaw, Diana, 92
beach habitats, 26–28
beach nourishment, 136
Becker, Carola, 144
Beebe, William, 203
behavior
　aggression, 97–99
　communication, 96–97
　feeding, 85–92
　grooming, 102–3
　learning, 103–4
　predator avoidance, 92–95
　swimming, 96
　territoriality, 99–102
　walking, 95
Bell, Geoffrey, 47
benthic juvenile transition, 107–8
Bergey, Lauren, 81
Bering Sea and Aleutian Islands (BSAI), 36–37
Bertness, Mark, 24, 152
biogenic substrates, 107
biological rhythms, 49
biomagnification, 138
biomedical use of horseshoe crab blood, 47
biomedicine research, 56
bioturbation, 26, 127
bird predators, 11–12, 135

Birgus latro. See coconut crabs
bitter crab disease, 130–31
bivalve mollusks, 89, 122–23, 143–44
black gill disease, 131
Blakeslee, April, 149
Blepharipoda occidentalis, 122
Bliss, Dorothy, 204
blue crabs, 5, 14*t*, 203, *pl.*3
　aquaculture, 178–79
　behavior, 29, 96, 97–98
　climate change and, 142
　color, 59, 62
　diseases, 129
　ecology, 106
　feeding, 88, 89–90
　fisheries for, 154–55, 156, 169–70, 173–74, 177
　habitat, 24, 29, 31, 37, 40
　hibernation, 112
　human consumption of, 154–55, 187–88
　hypoxia response of, 47–48
　as invasive species, 152
　larval development, 76–77, 107–8
　learning in, 104
　life cycle, 76–77, 80, 84, 105
　migrations, 112, 113
　molting, 80–81, *pl.*21
　osmoregulation in, 50
　recreational crabbing for, 198–99
　reproduction, 63–64, 66–67, 69
blue king crabs, 19*t*
　aquaculture, 179
　fisheries for, 158, 159*f,* 166, 172
　habitat, 37
　larval development, 75
blue land crab, 42
blue swimmer crabs, 14*t*, 156, 161, 176
Boles, Larry C., 115
bopyrids, 132
Bortolus, Alejandro, 126
box crabs, 14*t*, 119
boxer crabs, 118–19, 210, *pl.*20
brachyurans (Brachyura)
　anatomy, 5–6, 6*f,* 7*f,* 44–45
　evolution, 13
　families of, 14–15*t*
　mating, 66

as pets, 208–10
and sea anemones, 118–19
BRDs (bycatch reduction devices), 167
Briffa, Mark, 98
Brockmann, Jane, 11
bromeliad crabs, 41, 74, 75*f*
brown crabs, 156, 158
brown rock crabs, 157
BSAI (Bering Sea and Aleutian Islands),
    36–37
Buckhaven, Simon, 187
Buckley, William, 120
burrowing crabs, environmental effects of,
    26, 126, 127
burrows, 28–29, 65, 65*f*
bycatch, 166, 168–69
bycatch reduction devices (BRDs), 167
Bythograea thermydron, 19*t*, 38–39

Calappa sp., 14*t*, *pl.*4
Calappidae, 14*t*, 89, 119
calcification, 142–43
Calcinus elegans, 208
Calcinus spp., 19*t*
calico crabs. *See* lady crabs
Calliactis polypus, 117–18, *pl.*19
Callinectes sapidus. See blue crabs
cancer, 18
Cancer antennarius, 157
Cancer anthonyi. See Metacarcinus anthonyi
Cancer borealis, 56, 158
Cancer edwardsii, 51–52, 106
Cancer irroratus. See Atlantic rock crabs
Cancer magister. See Metacarcinus magister
Cancer pagurus, 156, 158
Cancer productus, 60, 157
Cancer spp., 14*t*, 112, 156–58
Cancridae (cancer crabs), 14*t*. *See also* rock
    crabs
Canepuccia, Alejandro, 126
cannibalism, 88, 90, 177
Cannicci, Stefano, 116
canning process, 186
carapace, 5, 6*f*
carbamate pesticides, 138
carcinology, 18, 199–205
Carcinonemertes carcinophilia, 134
Carcinus maenas. See green crabs

Carcinus spp., 18
Cardisoma guanhumi, 42
Cardisoma spp., 15*t*, 42, 43*f*, 51
Careproctus, 127, 134
Caribbean hermit crabs, 73–74, 205, *pl.*8
Caribbean spiny lobsters, 37, 115, 163, 164
Carle, Eric, 110
carrier crabs, 121, 122*f*
castration, parasitic, 132
catadromous crabs, 113
catch limits, 169–70
catch share programs, 170
cave-dwelling crabs, 41
ceca, 45, 51
Census of Marine Life, 2
central nervous system, 56–57
cephalothorax, 44
Chaceon fenneri. See golden crabs
Chaceon quinquedens. See deep-sea red crabs
Charybdis hellerii, 150
Charybdis spp., 156
Chasmagnathus sp., 103
chelae, 5, 44
chelipeds, 5, 44
chemical contaminants, 137–40, 192
chemoreception, 54, 55, 85
chemosynthesis, 38, 39
Chesapeake (Michener), 80
Chesapeake Bay, 155, 168, 173–74
children's literature, crabs in, 110
chimney, 65
China
    crab exports to, 157
    crab symbolism in, 210
    mitten crab culture in, 179–80
Chinese mitten crabs, 41*f*
    aquaculture, 179–80
    in freshwater habitats, 40
    human consumption of, 183
    as invasive species, 147–48
    migrations, 113
Chionoecetes bairdi. See tanner crabs
Chionoecetes opilio. See snow crabs
chitin, 4, 78–79, 189, 195
chitosan, 189
chlorinated hydrocarbons, 138
Christmas Island, 114–15, 136
Christy, John, 65, 66, 199–200

chromatophores, 57, 58, 58*f*
circadian rhythms, 49
circulatory system, 46
Cittarium pica, 111
clams, as diet, 89
Clastotoechus, 121
claws, 44, 83
Clevelandia ios, 127
Clibanarius erythropus, 109
Clibanarius spp., 19*t*
Clibanarius vittatus, 70–71
climate change, 107, 142–43, 172
cloak anemone, 118
cnidarians, 117–20
coconut crabs, 19*t*, *pl.*1
    evolution, 12–13
    feeding, 88, 91
    fisheries for, 176
    gill chamber adaptations in, 48
    habitats, 42–43
    life cycle, 78
    reproduction, 67
    toxin accumulation in, 194
Coen, Loren, 87
Coenobita brevimanus, 205, 206
Coenobita cavipes, 205
Coenobita clypeatus, 73–74, 109, 111, 205,
    206
Coenobita compressus, 205
Coenobita perlatus, 61, 205, 206
Coenobita rugosus, 205, 206
Coenobita spp., 19*t*, 42, 208*f*, *pl.*8
Coenobita violascens, 206
Coenobitidae, 19*t*, 42, 208*f*, *pl.*8. *See also*
    land hermit crabs
cold seeps habitat, 39–40
color and color change in crabs, 35, 57–61,
    80–81
Columbus crabs. *See* Sargassum crabs
commensal relationships, 122, 134
commercial fisheries, 156–63
common names, 5
common reed, 137
communication, 53–54, 64–66, 96–97
compound eyes, 52–53, 53*f*
contaminants, molting and, 81
copepods, 134
copulation, 64
coral gall crabs, 15*t*, 22, 119–20, 144, 146

coral reef habitats, 32–33
coral reefs, crab species on, 3–4
corals, symbiosis with, 119–20
cordgrass, 24, 137, 149, 152
courtship behaviors, 67
crabbing gear, 164–67, 165*f*
crab bisque, 191
crab cakes, 185–86, 188, 190–91
crab characteristics, 1–2
crab dishes, 190–91
crab festivals, 213–14
crab fisheries. *See* fisheries
crab jambalaya, 191
crabmeat
    dishes using, 190–91
    food safety issues, 191–95
    imitation product, 188–90
    nutritional value of, 182
    preparation of, 186–91
    processing of, 183–86, 185*f*
crab-picking houses, 184–85, 185*f*
crab pots, 164–67, 165*f*, 199
Crab Rationalization Program, 160, 172
crabs, classification of, 5–10, 14–15*t*, 19*t*
crab scrape, 154–55, 168
crab shells, products from, 189
crab species, discovery of new, 2–4
Crab Street Journal, 207
crab tiling, 168
crab traps, 198
crab watching, 196–98
Crane, Jocelyn, 203–4
crayfish, 5, 9
crested reef crabs, 193
crustaceans (Crustacea)
    overview, 4–5
    parasitic, 131–32
    symbiotic, 123
Crustastun, 187
Cryptochiridae (coral gall crabs), 15*t*, 22,
    119–20, 144, 146
Cryptolithodes sitchensis, 93, *pl.*12
Culbertson, Jennifer, 139
Cunningham, P., 103
Cycliophora, 117

dactyls, 54, 55
Damiani, Christine, 120
Dardanus spp., 117–18, *pl.*19

Davis, Gary, 161
DCTF (Dungeness Crab Task Force),
    175–76
Deadliest Catch, 160, 171
dead zones, 141
Deas, William, 190
decapods (Decapoda), 4–5
decorator crabs, 102–3, 124–25, 125*f*
deep-sea cold seeps. *See* cold seeps habitat
deep-sea habitat, 34–36
deep-sea red crabs, *pl.*13
    feeding, 90–91
    fisheries for, 90, 158
    habitat, 35, 36
    oil pollution, 140
Deepwater Horizon, 139–40
de Fur, Peter, 202
de la Haye, Kate, 143
Demania spp., 193
demon crabs, 193
deposit feeders, 86
derelict crab pots, 166–67
Detto, Tanya, 99
development. *See* life cycle
DeVries, M. C., 70
DeWilde, P. A., 73
Dictyota menstrualis, 125
Diele, Karen, 163
Diesel, Rudolph, 74
diet, and crab coloration, 61. *See also*
    feeding
digestion/digestive system, 45–46
Diogenidae (left-handed hermit crabs), 19*t*,
    83, 110
diseases, 129–31
Dissodactylus mellitae, 121–22
domoic acid, 194
Dorippe frascone, 121, 122*f*
Dotilla, 27
Dotillidae, 27
downwelling, 174
dream interpretation, 209
dredges, 168
droving, 87
Dungeness Crab and Seafood Festival, 214
Dungeness crabs, 14*t*, 30*f*
    feeding, 90
    fisheries for, 155, 156–57, 174–76
    habitat, 29–30

human consumption of, 186
larval development, 74, 106, 107
recreational crabbing for, 199
reproduction, 64, 69
toxin accumulation in, 193
Dungeness Crab Task Force (DCTF),
    175–76
Dyspanopeus sayi, 70

Ebersole, John, 120
ecdysis. *See* molting
ecdysones, 64
ecdysteroids, 82
echinoderms, 121–22
Echinometra spp., 121
ecology
    environmental effects of crabs, 127–28
    hermit crabs and snail shells, 108–11
    hibernation, 111–12
    invertebrate interactions, 117–23
    migrations, 112–15
    navigation and orientation, 116–17
    planktonic to benthic transition, 105–8
    plant interactions, 124–26
    vertebrate interactions, 126–27
Edgell, Timothy, 89
eel grass, 29, 107
EFH (essential fish habitat), 36–37
egg development, 70
egg hatching, 70–71
egg laying, 69
Eggleston, David, 107
elegant hermit crab, 208
Elwood, Robert, 55, 98
Emerita spp. *See* mole crabs
Emerita talpoida, 9*f*, 19*t*
endocrine disruptors, 140
endotoxin assay, 47
entoniscids, 132
environmental effects of crabs, 127–28
Epifanio, Charles, 77, 150, 201
Eriocheir sinensis. *See* Chinese mitten crabs
essential fish habitat (EFH), 36–37
estuarine fronts, 106
estuarine habitats, 23
estuarine oxygen levels, 47–48
European clawed lobsters, 163
European spider crabs, 161
Eurypanopeus sp., 24

Eustrombus gigas, 110
eutrophication, 141
evolution of crabs, 10, 12–13
exoskeleton, 4, 78–79
externa, 132, 133*f*
exuvium, 78
eyes, 44, 52–53, 53*f*
eyestalk, and molting hormones, 82–83

facilitation cascade, 149
false crabs, 8, 8*f*, 10. *See also* anomurans
    (Anomura)
fecundity, 69
feeding, 85–92
fiddler crabs, 15*t*, 25*f*, *pl.*18
    behavior, 85, 92, 94*f*, 96–97, 99–100
    color in, 57, 59–60
    ecology, 106
    feeding, 86, 87–88
    habitat, 23, 24, 28
    life span, 84
    mating, 64–66, 65*f*
    navigation and orientation, 116
    oil pollution and, 139
    as pets, 209–10
films, crabs in, 145, 211
filter feeders, 88
fisheries
    aquaculture, 177–81
    commercial crabbing, 156–63
    gear for, 164–69, 165*f*
    history, 154–55
    for horseshoe crab, 11–12
    for lobster, 163–64
    overfishing, 171–77
    regulations and management, 36–37,
        169–71
Fisheries Management Councils, 169
Fisherman's Wharf, 155, 197, *pl.*25
Fishery Management Plan (FMP), 171
fish habitat, essential, 36–37
fish interactions, 126–27, 134
flatworms, parasitic, 133–34, 194
Florida stone crabs, 160–61
flukes, 133, 194
FMP (Fishery Management Plan), 171
food allergies, 194–95
food safety, 191–95

foregut, 45
Forward, Richard, 70
fossils of crab ancestors, 10
freshwater crabs, 74, 77, 135
freshwater habitats, 40–42, 135
Frick, Michael, 33
frozen crabmeat, 192

Gagnon, Patrick, 147
galatheid crabs (Galatheidae, squat lob-
    sters), 19*t*, *pl.*9
    deep-sea species, 38, 39, 40, 91, 120
    described, 10
    evolution, 12–13
    new species discovery, 2
    trawling for, 168
Galen, 18
ganglion, 56–57
gastrulation, 70
gazami crabs. *See* horse crabs
gecarcinids (Gecarcinidae). *See* land crabs
Gecarcinus lateralis, 15*t*, 42, 91, 113, *pl.*6
Gecarcinus spp., 51, 73, 81
Gecarcoidea natalis, 114–15, *pl.*23
Geograpsus severnsi, 128
Geothelphusa dehaani, 59
Geryon fenneri. See Chaceon fenneri
Geryon quinquedens. See Chaceon
    quinquedens
ghost crabs, 15*t*, 27*f*
    burrows of, 28–29
    feeding, 87
    habitat, 23, 27, 28–29
    habitat loss and, 136
    hibernation, 112
    mating, 66
    walking behavior, 95
ghost fishing, 166
giant mud crabs, 176. See also *Scylla
    serrata*
Gilardi, Kirsten, 141
gill bailer, 46
gill barnacles, 123, 134
gill chambers, 34–35, 46, 107
gill nets, 141
gills, 45, 46, 50, 51
glaucothoe stage, 75, 76
glider vehicles, 205

global warming, 142–43
Globonautes macropus, 41–42
golden crabs, 35–36, 40, 166, *pl.*14
golden king crabs, 19*t*
  aquaculture, 179
  fisheries for, 158, 166
  habitat, 34, 37
  larval release and development, 71, 74
  snailfish association, 127, 134
Golowasch, Jorge, 201
Gontmakher, Arkadi, 172–73
graceful decorator crabs, 124, 125*f*
grapsids (Grapsidae), 14*t*, 23, 66, 87, 96.
    See also marsh crabs; shore crabs
Grapsus grapsus, *pl.*5
gray crab disease, 129
Greek crab knowledge, 83
Greek mythology, 210
Greek poetry, hermit crabs in, 111
green crabs, 14*t*, 16*f*
  aggression in, 98
  color, 60, *pl.*17
  feeding, 89, 90
  fisheries for, 168
  habitat, 24, 29
  as invasive species, 146–47
  learning in, 103–4
  migrations, 112
green egg crabs, 193
green glands, 50–51
green porcelain crabs, 100, 150
Griffin, Blaine, 45
grooming, 102–3
guard crabs, 33, 119, *pl.*11
Gulf of Mexico, 37, 39, 139–40
gulfweed crabs. *See* Sargassum crabs
gut (digestive system), 45–46

Habitat Areas of Particular Concern
    (HAPC), 36
habitats
  aquatic vegetation, 29 31
  burrows, 28–29
  cold seeps, 39–40
  coral reefs, 32–33
  deep sea, 34–36
  estuarine, 23
  for fish, 36–37

freshwater, 40–42
hydrothermal vents, 38–39
land, 42–43
for lobster, 37
loss of, 135–36
mangrove forests, 24–26, 31
open ocean, 33–34
oyster reefs, 31
rock pools and rocky areas, 31
salt marsh, 23–24
sandy beach, 26–28
sea mounts, 40
settling larvae preferences in, 107–8
hairy crabs. *See* Chinese mitten crabs
Halieutica (Oppian), 83
Hall, Sally, 13
Hapalocarcinus marsupialis, 15*t*
Hapalocarcinus spp. *See* coral gall crabs
HAPC (Habitat Areas of Particular
    Concern), 36
Harvey, Rodger, 84
hatchery-reared crabs, 178–79
Hawaiian Islands, 128
Hay, Mark, 120, 150
Hazlett, Brian, 98, 110
hearing, 53–54
heart, 46
Heinonen, Kari, 149
Helice tientsinensis, 137
helmet crabs, 64
Heloecius cordiformis, 26, 65
Hematodinium perezi, 130–31
Hemigrapsus nudus, 150
Hemigrapsus oregonensis, 101, 150
Hemigrapsus sanguineus, 77, 78*f*, 148–50
Hemmi, Jan, 59
hemocyanin, 46, 48
hemolymph, 50
hepatopancreas, 45
herbivores, 86–87
Hermit Crab Association, 207–8
hermit crabs, 19*t*, 20*f. See also* land hermit
    crabs; marine hermit crabs
  anatomy, 6, 7*f*, 8
  behavior, 93, 95, 97, 98
  evolution, 10, 12–13
  feeding, 88, 91
  habitats, 23, 24, 29, 32, 42

hermit crabs *(continued)*
  larval development, 76
  learning in, 103
  in literature and mythology, 110, 111
  pain sensation in, 55
  as pets, 205–10
  reproduction, 67
  and snail shells, 108–11
  symbiotic relationships, 117–18, 120,
    *pl.*19, *pl.*24
Herrnkind, William, 115
Hexapanopeus sp., 16*f*
hibernation, 111–12
hindgut, 45
Hippidae. *See* mole crabs
Hippocrates, 18
Hippoglossus stenolepis, 126
Holdredge, Christine, 152
Hollebone, Amanda, 150
Homarus americanus, 9, 37, 123, 163
Homarus gammarus, 163
Hopkins, Penny, 202–3
hormones, 62, 64, 82
horse crabs, 156, 162, 179
horsehair worms, 132
horseshoe crabs, 11–12, 12*f*, 47
House for Hermit Crab, A (Carle), 110
Hoyoux, Caroline, 92
Hughes, R., 103
Hultgren, Kristen, 125
Hyas araneus, 15*f*
Hydractinia, 120, *pl.*24
hydroids, 120, *pl.*24
hydrothermal vent crabs, 19*t*, 38–39, 48
hydrothermal vents, 1, 38–39, 48
hyperparasites, 132, 133
hypoxia, 29, 47–48

Imocaris fossil, 10
individual transferable quotas, 170
Indo-Pacific swimming crabs, 156
industrial chemical pollution, 140
insecticide pollution, 138–39
intermolt, 79
invasive species, 136–37, 146–53
invertebrate interactions, 117–23
Ischyrocerus commensalis, 123
isopods, 132
ivory bush coral, 120

Japanese blue crabs. *See* horse crabs
Japanese freshwater crabs, 59
Japanese spider crabs, 14*t*, 17–18, 21*f*, 22,
    84, 125, 197
jellyfish, 119
jewel crabs, 193
jimmies, 155
jimmy potting, 169
Johnson, Eric, 179
Jonah crabs, 56, 158
Ju, Se-Jong, 84
jubilee, 141
Just So Stories (Kipling), 82,
    210

kelp crabs, 58–59, *pl.*15
Kim, Taewon, 116
kinesthetic memory, 116
king crabs, 19*t*. *See also* blue king crabs;
    golden king crabs; red king crabs; scar-
    let king crabs
  anatomy, 8
  aquaculture, 179
  evolution, 10, 12–13
  feeding, 88
  fisheries for, 154–55, 158–60, 159*f*, 166,
    172
  habitat, 34, 36–37
  human consumption of, 188
  as invasive species, 151–52
  new species discovery, 2–3
  predator avoidance behavior, 92
  reproduction, 67
Kipling, Rudyard, 82, 210
Kiwa hirsuta, 1, 21*f*, 22, 39
Kiwa puravida, 39–40
Koch, Volker, 163
Kodiak Crab Festival, 213
Kona crab, 162
Kropp, Roy, 144, 146

lady crabs, 14*t*, 29, 90, 92
LAL (Limulus amebocyte lysate), 47
land crabs (gecarcinids), 15*t*, *pl.*6
  environmental effects of, 127–28
  feeding, 91
  fisheries for, 162*f*, 163, 176
  gill chamber adaptations in, 48
  habitat, 42, 43*f*

in mangroves, 26. *See also* mangrove
crabs
migrations, 113–15
molting, 81
reproduction, 66, 73, 78
senses, 54
water balance in, 51
land habitats, 42–43
Land Hermit Crab Owners Society, 207
land hermit crabs, 19*t*, 208*f*, *pl.*8. *See also
under* Coenobitidae; *Coenobita*
behavior, 29, 101–2
environmental effects of, 127–28
evolution, 13
feeding, 88, 91
gill chamber adaptations in, 48
grooming/behavior, 102
habitat, 42
migrations, 112, 113–14
as pets, 205–8, 208*f*
reproduction, 73–74
sense of smell in, 54
and snail shells, 108, 109, 111
Land of the Lost (film), 145
langouste, 163
large-clawed spider crabs, 35
larval development, 71–77, 72*f*, 76*f*,
105–7
larval release, 70–71, 73–74
Layne, John, 116
learning, 103–4
lecithotrophic development, 75
left-handed hermit crabs, 19*t*, 110
legs. *See* limbs
lemon-yellow clawed fiddler crab, 99–100,
*pl.*22
Libinia dubia, 125
Libinia spp., 106
life cycle
aging crabs, 84
embryonic development, 70
growth and molting, 78–83
larval development, 71–77, 72*f*, 76*f*,
105–7
settlement, metamorphosis, and early
crab stages, 77–78, 106–8
limb regeneration, 94–95, 94*f*
limbs, anatomy of, 44
Limulus amebocyte lysate (LAL), 47

Limulus polyphemus, 11–12, 12*f*, 47
line crabbing, 167
lipofuscin, 84
Lissocarcinus orbicularis, 122
literature, crabs in, 80, 82, 110
Lithodes aequispinus. *See* golden king
crabs
Lithodes couesi, 19*t*, 34, 71
Lithodidae. *See* king crabs
Little Mermaid, The, 211, *pl.*27
live crabs, sale of, 182–83
Livona pica. See *Cittarium pica*
lobsters
anatomy, 5, 6, 9, 95
classification of, 4, 5, 6
fisheries for, 163–64
habitats, 37
human consumption of, 163
largest recorded, 9
migrations, 115
shell disease, 129–30, 130*f*
Symbion pandora and, 117
lobster shells, products from, 189
Lohmann, Kenneth J., 115
long-eyed swimming crabs, 162
longnose spider crabs, 125
Lopholithodes mandtii, 124*f*
Lophozozymus pictor, 192–93
Lovett, Donald, 51
lung fluke, 194
Lybia tessellata, 118–19, *pl.*20

MacDonald, James, 97
Macrocheira kaempferi. *See* Japanese spider
crabs
Macrophthalmus sp., 24, 25*f*
Macroregonia macrocheira, 3, 35
Magnuson–Stevens Fisheries Conservation
and Management Act, 36
Maine lobster fisheries, 163
Maja squinado, 67, 161
Majidae. *See* spider crabs
Malaysian myths, 210
mandibles, 5, 45, 86
mangrove crabs, 30*f*. See also *Scylla
serrata*
aquaculture, 177–78
behavior, 101
feeding, 87, 91

mangrove crabs *(continued)*
   fisheries for, 156, 161–62, 162*f*, 163, 176
   habitat, 26, 31
   navigation and orientation, 116–17
   plant usage by, 125–26
   reproduction, 66
mangrove forest habitat, 24–26, 31
Mantel, Linda, 202
marine debris, 141–42
marine hermit crabs, 19*t*, 20*f*, 24, 76, 208.
   See also under Diogenidae; Paguridae;
   Pagurus
Marine Stewardship Council, 174–75
Marshall Island electric blue hermit crabs,
   208
marsh crabs, 14*t*, 17*f*, 24, 152. *See also*
   grapsids
mate attraction, 63–66, 65*f*
Matheson, Kyle, 147
mating, 66–69, *pl.*17
maxillae, 5, 45, 86
maxillipeds, 5, 45, 86, 102
McCall, Brittany, 140
McConnaughey, Robert, 106
McDermott, John, 132
McLaughlin, Patsy, 200
mechanoreceptors, 55–56
megalopa larva, 76, 76*f*, 106–7
melanophores. *See* chromatophores
Menippe mercenaria. See stone crabs
Mestre, Nélia C., 75
metabolic rate, 48–49
Metacarcinus anthonyi, 157
Metacarcinus edwardsii. See *Cancer edwardsii*
Metacarcinus magister. See Dungeness
   crabs
metallothioneins, 137–38
metal pollution, 137–38
metamorphosis, 75–76, 77, 105–6
Metapaulius depressus. See bromeliad crabs
Micheli, Fiorenza, 104
Michener, James, 80
Microphallus bassodactylus, 133
midgut, 45
midgut gland, 45
migrations, 112–15
Milner, Richard, 87, 99

Mithraculus forceps, 120
Mithrax spp., 87
mitten crabs. *See* Chinese mitten crabs
mole crabs, 9*f*, 19*t*
   behavior, 29, 93, 96
   described, 8, 10
   feeding, 88
   habitat, 26, 29
   interspecies associations, 122
   migrations, 112
   reproduction, 68
   toxin accumulation in, 194
mollusks, 89, 122–23, 143–44
molting, 78–83, 178, *pl.*21
molting hormones, 64
Monaco Aquarium, 197, *pl.*26
Morley, S. A., 69
mosaic reef crabs, 192–93
Mossblack, Hallie, 45
mottled shore crabs, 100
mouthparts, 45, 86
movies, crabs in, 145, 211
mud crabs, 16*f*, 24, 31, 70, 90, 152, 193.
   See also *Scylla serrata*
mud-flat crabs, 103
Munidopsis andamanica, 91–92
mussels, 89, 143–44
Myctyris longicarpus. See soldier crabs
Mykles, Don, 200
Mysella pedroana, 122
Mysterious Island (Verne), 145
myths, 210

names, scientific and common, 4–5
National Fisheries Institute, 176
National Marine Fisheries Service (NMFS),
   36, 169
navigation, 115, 116–17
Nematomorpha, 132
nemertean worms, 134
Neoliomera pubescens, 3
Neolithodes diomedeae, 70
Neopanope sayi, 70
Neopetrolisthes maculosus, 19*t*
Neopetrolisthes spp., 32, 118, *pl.*10
Nephrops norvegicus, 9, 117
Nereis fucata, 121
neuromodulation, 56

neuroscience research, 56
neurosecretion, 82–83
NMFS (National Marine Fisheries Service), 36, 169
Nordhaus, Inga, 26
North Pacific Fishery Management Council, 171
Norway lobsters, 9, 117
nutritional value of crabmeat, 182

ocean acidification, 107, 142–43
Octolasmis muelleri, 123, 134
octopuses, 135
Oculina arbuscula, 120
Ocypode quadrata, 27
Ocypode spp. *See* ghost crabs
ocypodids (Ocypodidae), 15*t*, 23, 66, 87.
     See also fiddler crabs; ghost crabs
oil pollution, 139–40
olfaction, 54
omega-3 fatty acids, 182
ommatidia, 52
omnivores, 90–91
open ocean habitat, 33–34
Oppian, 83, 111
Oregonia gracilis, 124, 125*f*
Oregon shore crabs, 101
organophosphates, 138
orientation, 115, 116–17
Ormes, Carol, 206–7
osmoconformers, 50
osmoregulation, 50 52
osmoregulators, 50
osmoregulatory patches, 51
Ovalipes ocellatus. See lady crabs
ovaries, 62
overfishing, 171–77
oviducts, 62
ovigerous female, 69
oxygen levels, 47–48
oxygen minimum zones, 34, 48
oyster reef habitats, 31

P (urine), 51
Pachygrapsus spp., 64
Pachygrapsus transversus, 100
Pacific halibut, 126
Pacific hermit crabs, 205

Paguridae (right-handed marine hermit crabs), 19*t*, 20*f*, 24, 76, 83, 208
Paguristes cadenati, 208
Paguritta sp., 32
Pagurus bernhardus, 98
Pagurus dalli, 19*t*, *pl.*24
Pagurus exilis, 67
Pagurus longicarpus, 19*t*, 20*f*
Pagurus prideaux, 118
pain sensation, 55
Palawan, 3
Palma, Alvaro, 60
Palmer, John, 49
Panopeus herbstii, 31
Panopeus sp., 24
Panulirus argus, 37, 115, 164
Panulirus spp., 115
Paragonimus spp., 194
Paralithodes brevipes, 177
Paralithodes camtschaticus. See red king crabs
Paralithodes platypus. See blue king crabs
Paralomis spinosissima, 70, 75
Paralomis stevensi, 3
paralytic shellfish poisoning (PSP), 193
Paramoeba parasites, 129
Parasesarma leptosoma, 116–17
parasites, 131–34, 133*f*, 149, 194
parasitic castration, 132
parasitic crabs, 143–46
Parathelphusidae, 40–41
Pardo, Luis, 51–52, 106
Parkes, Lee, 178
Paromola cuvieri, 123
pasteurization, 184
Pau Amma, 82
Paulay, Gustav, 128
PCBs (polychlorinated biphenyls), 140
pea crabs, 15*t*, 22, 96, 143–44, *pl.*7
peelers, 155, 186, 188
Pennings, Steven, 140
pepper spot disease, 133
Percnon gibbesi, 151
Pereyra, Patricia, 103
pericardial sacs, 81
periwinkle snails, 24
Perry, Harriet, 140
Persselin, Sara, 20*f*
pesticide pollution, 138–39

pet crabs, 205–10, 208*f*
Petrochirus diogenes, 110
Petrolisthes armatus, 100, 150
pheromones, 63–64, 97
Phragmites australis, 137
phytoplankton, 70
pigments, 57
pillar, 65
Pinnotheres maculatus, 144
Pinnotheres ostreum, 144
Pinnotheres pisum, 15*t*, 143, *pl.*7
Pinnotheres sinensis, 144
Pinnotheres spp., 15*t*
Pinnotheridae. *See* pea crabs
Planes minutus. See Sargassum crabs
plankton, 70
planktonic larvae, 71–73, 105–7
planktotrophic larvae, 74–75
plant interactions, 124–26
Platypodia granulosa, 193
pleopods, 5, 69
Podophthalmus vigil, 162
pods of juvenile crabs, 92, 93*f*
pollution, 137–43, 192
polychaete worms, 121
polychlorinated biphenyls (PCBs), 140
polyculture, 177
pom-pom crabs. *See* boxer crabs
popular culture, crabs in, 197, 210
porcelain anemone crabs, 19*t*, 32, 118,
    *pl.*10
porcelain crabs, 19*t. See also* porcelain
    anemone crabs
    anatomy, 8
    feeding, 10, 88
    as invasive species, 150
    symbiosis with urchins, 121
    territoriality/behavior, 100
Porcellanidae. *See* porcelain crabs
portunids (Portunidae). *See* swimming
    crabs
Portunus pelagicus. See blue swimmer crabs
Portunus sayi, 33
Portunus trituberculatus, 156, 162, 179
postmolt, 79
predator avoidance, 92–95, 126
predators, 134–35
predatory crabs, 88–90
premolt, 79

prepubertal molt, 83
protist, 133
Pseudocarcinus gigas, 22
Pseudonitzschia, 194
PSP (paralytic shellfish poisoning), 193
Puget Sound king crabs, 124*f*
Pugettia producta, 58–59, 124, *pl.*15

queen conch, 110
queen crabs, 156

Rainbow, Philip, 148
Ramey, Patricia, 104
Ranina ranina, 162
Rathbun, Mary Jane, 203
recreational crabbing, 198–99
recruitment, 77, 105–7
red coloration in deepwater crustaceans,
    35
red crabs. *See also names of specific crabs*
    habitat, 10, 35
    migrations, 114–15, *pl.*23
red deep-sea crabs, 35, 36, 90–91, 140,
    158, *pl.*13
red frog crabs, 162
red king crabs, 19*t*, 20*f*
    aquaculture, 179
    coloration of larvae, 60
    fisheries for, 156, 158, 159–60, 166,
        170–71, 172
    habitat, 34, 36–37
    as invasive species, 151
    larval development, 107
    migrations, 113
    predator avoidance behavior, 92, 93*f*,
        126
    reproduction, 67–68, 68*f*
    symbiotic or commensal relationships,
        121, 123
red knots, 11
red mangrove, 25
red-ridged clinging crabs, 120
red rock crabs, 60, 157
reef crabs, 32, 192–93
regeneration of limbs, 94–95, 94*f*
Reichmuth, Jessica, 89, 97
Reid, D. G., 60
Rembrandt, 197
remotely operated vehicles (ROVs), 204–5

reproduction
  attraction of mate, 63–66, 65*f*
  egg laying, development, and hatching,
    69–71
  mating and sperm storage, 66–69, 68*f*
  seasonality, 62
reproductive system anatomy, 62–63
respiration, 46–48
rhabdom, 52
Rhett, R. Goodwyn, 190
Rhithropanopeus harrisii, 152
rhizocephalan parasites, 131–32, 133*f*
Rhizophora, 25
Ries, Justin B., 143
ring net, 198
Rochette, Remy, 89
rock crabs, 14*t*, 112, 156–58, *pl.*2. *See also under* Cancridae; *Cancer*
rock lobsters, 163
rock pools and rocky area habitats, 31
Roegner, G. Curtis, 174
Rossong, Melanie, 147
Rotjan, Randi, 109
Roudez, Ross, 103
ROVs (remotely operated vehicles),
    204–5
Russian king crab fisheries, 172–73

Sacculina, 131–32, 133*f*
Sally Lightfoot crabs, 14*t*, 151, *pl.*5
salt balance, 50–52
saltmarsh cordgrass. *See* cordgrass
salt marsh habitats, 23–24, 127, 135–36
sand bubbler crabs, 27
sand crabs. *See* mole crabs
sand dollars, 121–22
sand fiddler crabs, 25*f*, 65–66
sandy beach habitat, 26–28
Sargassum crabs, 14*t*, 33–34, 59, *pl.*16
SAV (submerged aquatic vegetation),
    29–31
saxitoxin, 193
scaphognathites, 46, 48
scarlet hermit crabs, 208
scarlet king crabs, 19*t*, 34, 71
scavengers, 87–88
scientific names, 4–5
scoop nets, 198
Scopimera, 27

scuba diving, 197, 204
Scylla serrata, 26, 153, 156, 161–62, 176,
    177–78
sea anemones, 91, 100, 117–19, *pl.*19
sea cucumbers, 122
sea level rise, 142
sea mounts, 40
sea urchins, 100, 121
Secor, David, 84
semaphore crabs, 26, 65
seminal receptacles, 63
semiterrestrial crabs, 85, 96, 112
senses, 52–56
sensilla, 54
sentinel crabs, 24, 25*f*
Sesarma cinereum, 70
Sesarma reticulatum, 14*t*, 17*f*, 24, 152
setae, 86
settlement, 77, 106–7
sexing of crabs, 7*f*, 62
sex reversal, 68
shame-faced crabs, 14*t*, 119, *pl.*4
Shanks, Alan, 106, 174
she-crabs, 155
She-Crab Soup, 190
shell disease, 129–30, 130*f*, 131
shellfish poisoning, 193–94
Sherman's Lagoon, 211–12, 212*f*
shipment of live crabs, 182–83
shorebirds, 11–12, 135
shore crabs, 64, 77, 78*f*, 100, 101, 148–50.
    See also grapsids
shrimp, 4, 5, 95, 180–81
Sibuet, Myriam, 2
Silliman, Brian, 24
Simpson, Stephen, 54
Skinner, Dorothy, 204
sleep, 49
Sleer, Jeff, 159*f*
slipper lobsters, 163
Slow Crab Festival, 213
smell, sense of, 54
Smith Island Crab Meat Cooperative,
    185
smooth cordgrass. *See* cordgrass
snailfish, 127, 134
snails, periwinkle, 24
snail shells, 89, 108–11
snorkeling, 197, 204

snow crabs, 14*t*
  essential fish habitat for, 37
  fisheries for, 156, 160
  larval development, 74
  mating, 66
  migration study, 113
Snyders, Franz, 197
soft-shelled crabs, 154–55, 169, 178, 188, 191, 192
soldier crabs, 27, 28*f*
Somerton, David, 34–35
sooks, 155
sound communication, 53–54, 66, 96–97
spanner crabs, 162
Spartina alterniflora. See cordgrass
Spartina densiflora, 126
spawning, 67, 69
sperm, 63, 66–68
spermatophores, 63
sperm limitation, 176–77
spider crabs, 14*t*, 15*f*
  behavior, 87, 92, 102–3
  ecology, 106
  fisheries for, 156, 161
  new species discovered, 3
  spermatophore storage, 67
  symbiotic relationships, 120–21
spiny king crabs, 177
spiny lobsters, 9, 37, 115, 163, 164
spiny (mole) sand crabs, 122
spoilage prevention, 191–92
sponge, 68*f*, 69
SpongeBob Square Pants, 211
sponges, symbiosis with, 120–21
spring transition, 106, 174
squat lobsters. *See* galatheid crabs
Stachowicz, John, 120, 125
Starmer, John, 128
Stehlik, Linda, 200
Steinberg, Mia, 150
Steneck, Robert, 60
Stenorhynchus seticornis, 101, 101*f*
Stensmyr, Markus, 54
Stevens, Bradley, 3, 20*f*, 71, 107
Stewart, Hannah, 33, 119
stomach, 45
stomatogastric ganglion (STG), 56
stone crabs, 14*t*, 17*f*, 31, 37, 89, 160–61

Stoner, Alan, 126, 183
strawberry hermit crabs, 61. See also *Coenobita perlatus*
stridulation, 96, 97
striped hermit crabs, 70–71
striped urchin crabs, 121
submerged aquatic vegetation (SAV), 29–31
submersibles, 204–5
substrate preferences for larval settlement, 107–8
surimi, 188–90, 195
Sustainable Fisheries Act, 36
swamp ghost crabs, 162*f*, 163
swash zone, 26
swimmer crabs, 122
swimming, 96
swimming crabs (Portunidae), 14*t*
  adaptations for swimming, 96
  aquaculture of, 177–79
  fisheries for, 156, 161–62
  invasiveness, 150, 153
Symbion pandora, 117
symbiosis, 33
symbolism, 210

tanner crabs, 14*t*, 157*f*
  essential fish habitat for, 37
  fisheries for, 156, 160, 173
  larvae release, 71
  spermatophore storage, 67
Tasmanian king crabs, 22
taste, sense of, 55
telemetry, 205
Telmessus cheiragonus, 64
telson, 5
temperature, and metabolic rate, 48–49
Terossi, Marianna, 67
terrestrial crabs. *See* land crabs
territoriality, 99–102
testes, 63
Tethys, 205
Thalassia, 29
Thatje, Sven, 13, 75, 151
thoracic ganglion, 57
thorax, 44
tidal influences, and settlement, 106–7
Toomey, Jim, 211
Toste, Ray, 175